I0762227

same sun
same moon

same sun
same moon

MICHAEL KENNA

PICO IYER

PRESTEL

Munich · London · New York

Brother from Another Planet

You might never guess from the still, elegant, even prayerful images you will meet in this book that the man who made them is a merry pillar of fun who listens to Everton soccer matches in his darkroom and is known for his karaoke renditions of old Japanese love songs. Nor, perhaps, that the other writer of texts here is a sports-mad, ping pong-playing, Paddington Bear-loving devotee of Kit-Kats. But that's the beauty of art: it gives voice to a private, even secret self, hidden deep within, which sometimes even we can't see or remember ourselves.

The great pandemic of 2019, for all the doors it terribly slammed shut, opened windows, too. In the silence of lockdown, I unexpectedly received a two-sentence message from Michael Kenna, whom I'd never met, asking, with great courtesy, if I might one day write some text to go together with his work. I instantly said yes and overnight we began exchanging long, zesty, fully paragraphed letters, sometimes every day. The vigorous marathon-running man of northern England and the diminutive, bookish guy from the south turned out to be twins of a kind.

We'd been born in Britain only three years apart, and we'd studied our respective arts around Oxford in the mid-1970s. We both moved to the West Coast of the United States in the late 1970s, and we both started working in Japan, our secret home, in 1987. More deeply, Michael had spent seven years in a Catholic seminary even as I was now spending much of my time in a Benedictine hermitage. The editor who had assigned Michael to offer photographs for long articles I'd written on Koyasan and Nara could never have known that we both loved France, spent much of our time around Buddhas, and were like-minded connoisseurs of Lawson convenience stores.

She certainly could never have guessed that Michael purchased my book about falling in love with an Asian beauty and her two small children the very day he began to fall in love with an Asian beauty of his own, and her two small children. He'd purchased it just next to the Gateway of India, in the hotel where my wife and I had culminated our honeymoon.

One summer day my wife Hiroko and I were walking down the street in Paris and there, walking towards us, were Michael and his wife Mamta. Three months later, we found ourselves dining together in Nara. Four months after that, as the snow fell all around us, I walked down a narrow lanterned lane in Kyoto—and there were Mamta and Michael. By springtime we were dining together in Seattle.

Michael and I are no longer young, but we delight in the fact that life is never without new discoveries. They say you make few new friends after the age of thirty; but in this case, after the age of sixty, we each made a stalwart friend who feels, against all odds, like a long-lost brother.

We do hope you might enjoy this unexpected fraternal conspiracy. Michael chose sixty-five images from his inexhaustible archive, and invited me to write down anything each one of them inspired. Then he wrote down essays of his own. Neither of us had any sense of what the other was writing. Sometimes, of course, our words fly off in very different directions; sometimes they mysteriously converge. But in either case, the hearts beneath them, and their silences, seem to be heading along a strikingly similar path.

Pico Iyer
Christmas Day, 2023
Kyoto

Flight Paths

Michael spends much of his life in movement; I sometimes find myself in three continents in a week—for my job, but also in an attempt to rescue myself from provincialism. For more than half a century we've been whizzing past one another in midair, wondering in recent years whether we might intersect in that crowded terminal at Haneda or in an airport lounge in San Francisco.

Yet what Michael has been seeking out for many of these years is something that anchors us all; what he works so hard to share—through long sessions in the darkroom, after long, long exposures—is an image that returns us to some sanctuary within. Some lost place or hidden self, some forgotten truth perhaps that lies beneath the tumult of our days.

I, too. A reader marvels at my travels—Bhutan, Antarctica, Yemen—and I remind her (or him) that for every two weeks of movement I spend two months at my desk, going nowhere. She or he is witnessing only the froth on the waves of a very still ocean.

So maybe this is how we live beyond appearances: sitting where we are, finding something quiet and steady that guides us through all our movements.

It's by sitting so still, after all, that the Buddha moves us so deeply.

PI

Cloud of Unknowing

I was brought up Roman Catholic and studied for seven years in my early desire to become a priest. My beloved Indian wife, Mamta, is Hindu, and we were married in a Buddhist ceremony in Thailand. We both love to visit and pray in Shinto shrines and Buddhist temples in Japan, and have stopped into Muslim mosques, Jewish synagogues, and random Christian churches whenever and wherever we happily come across them. My cherished mother-in-law, Mithilesh, conducts Hindu prayer ceremonies every day in our home, and we have a collection from around the world of religious statuary, icons, and paintings, set up as an altar in our living room. One could easily be forgiven for concluding that I am a little confused about my religious persuasions, which would be an accurate assessment of my growing Cloud of Unknowing. At seventy-two, and getting towards the end of my journey, it is has become increasingly clear to me what I suspected closer to the beginning, that as I continue to search for meaning and answers in life, the more confusing it all becomes.

There are so many wise Buddhist sayings. A personal favorite is: "To insist on a spiritual practice that served you in the past is to carry the raft on your back after you have left the river." I envy those who are sure of their way, confident in a particular path, religion, or faith. Early on, I had an absolute belief that God exists. Now, I find myself in the agnostic camp, content and enthusiastic to attend ceremonies and rituals in any and all places of adoration, whether religious or secular. I regard the world as a vast shrine, temple, synagogue, mosque, church, or sacred site. When I photograph, whatever the subject matter, I try to do so with the same courtesy, respect, reverence, kindness, consideration, and humility expected in such places. This is also how I like to pray, and to live my life. Paul Tillich reminds us that "Doubt is not the opposite of faith," which is a philosophy that I can truly get behind.

MK

Amidha Buddha, Kotoku-in, Kamakura, Honshu, Japan, 2007

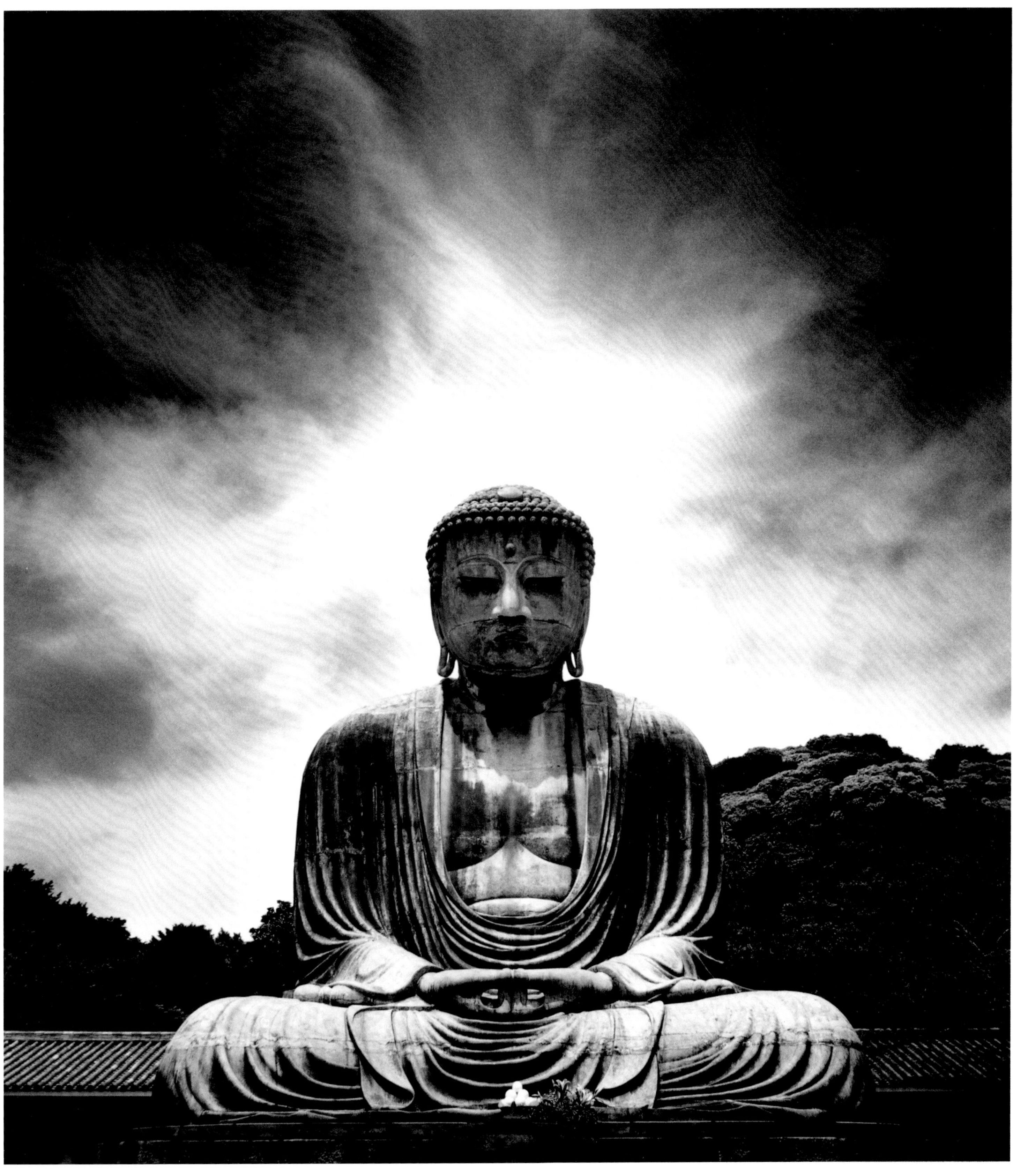

The Streets of Paris

The human element in France bewitches: it's hard to resist the allure of Paris, not just for its buildings, but for the straight-backed statues and models of chic striding between them. A scarf carelessly thrown across one shoulder; a face that seems barely made-up, but is made for blushing and sparkle; a confidence that treats a crowded sidewalk as a catwalk. Even a banker in a well-cut suit Segwaying home can outshine the structures around him.

But when I traveled around France for four weeks as a student, descending into bottom-end guest houses and the cheapest cafés in town while pretending to gather information for the young person's Bible of the day, *Let's Go: France*, most of what I saw—in Provence and Champagne and the Dordogne—were scenes like this: a landscape so orderly, it could only be in France.

In Japan my neighbors plant trees to set off explosions of color every April and November; in France they set them up to make an honor guard of sorts, as thin and tall as the figures in uniform I see every Bastille Day thronging the streets of Paris.

A seditious idea begins to form: maybe it was scenes like these that taught Henri Cartier-Bresson his geometry, as much as he who taught us the same everywhere he went?

PI

Rumi's Concise Guide to Photography

One of the great French masters of photography, Eugène Atget, spent his life photographing in and around Paris. In 1921, he made a now famous study of conical trees in Saint-Cloud. I photographed these same trees, albeit from a different angle, in 1987, 1988, 1996, 1999, and 2019. Each time, the trees appeared slightly or greatly different, dependent, I suppose, on the individual whims of the designated pruners. I think they were at their most splendidly extravagant in this 1999 study. I wonder, where else but in France would one find such whimsically decorated topiary?

One of the many lessons I learned from Atget's work has become a fundamental principle of my life—nothing is ever the same. He often returned to identical locations over and over to find fresh inspiration and new subject matter, and now I do the same. Atget's influence set me off on a decades-long journey to explore gardens designed by the seventeenth-century landscape architect André Le Nôtre, which included Saint-Cloud, as well as Versailles, Vaux-le-Vicomte, Sceaux, and a host of others. Which led to questions I often ask myself: How does a photographer decide what to photograph? Where does style come from? With all the subject matter available, how on earth do we make personal choices? Is it through nature or nurture, or both? I gravitate to the pertinent and concise words of the poet Rumi: "Let yourself be silently drawn by the strange pull of what you really love. It will not lead you astray." I seriously doubt he had cameras in mind when he gave this sage advice, but he was certainly onto something very special!

MK

Atget's Trees, Study 4, Saint-Cloud, France, 1999

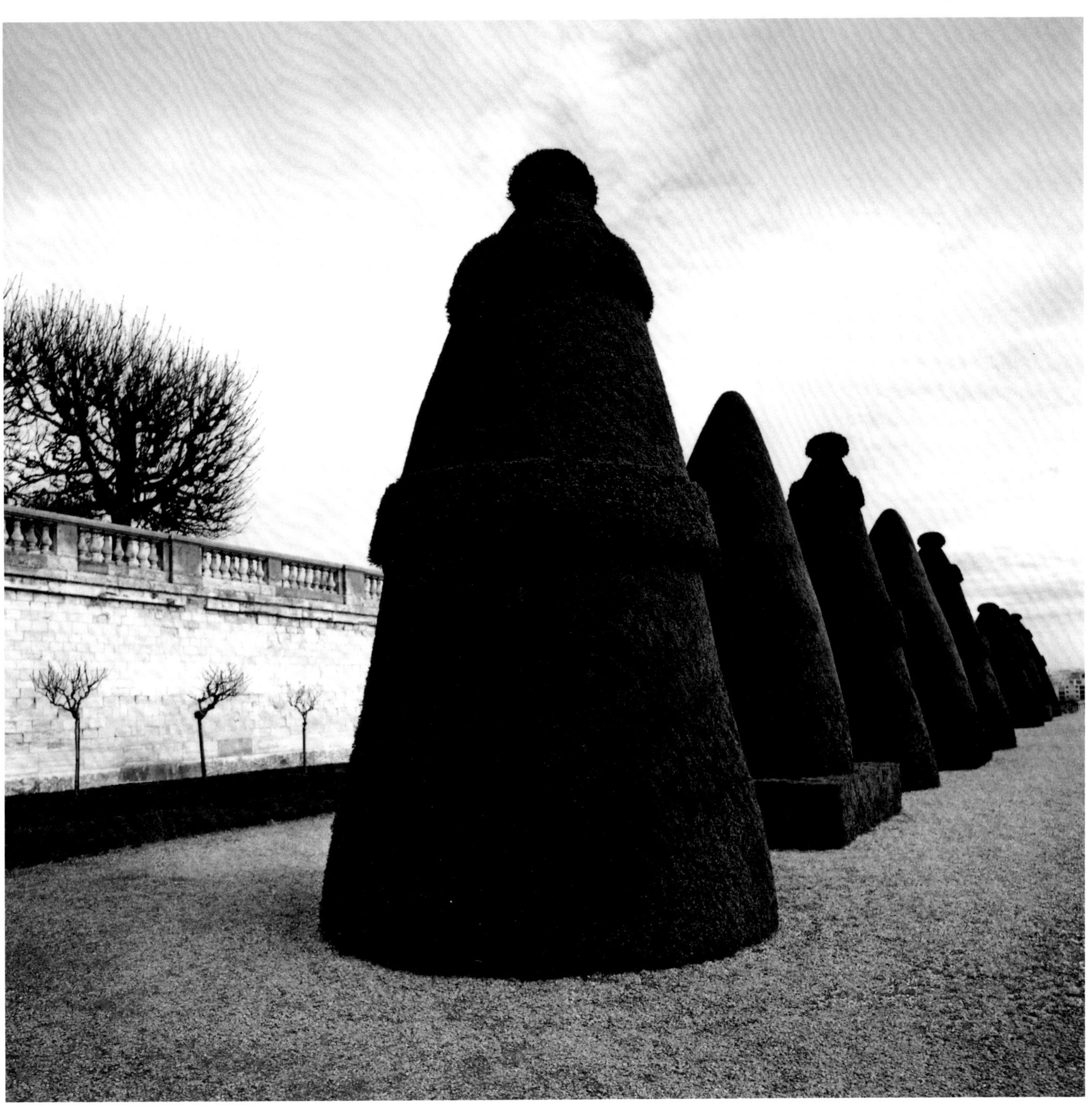

The Rules of Attraction

What most attracts us is what has yet to be revealed; nothing is so exciting as what may yet come to be. We may joyfully inhabit the present, but we often live with the prospect that the future may disclose something even more delectable.

The first thing I learned, on arriving in Japan, is that a haiku goes inside one as no 700-page novel ever can. Why? It leaves almost everything to the imagination. It invites us to complete it. A suggestion opens more doors than a statement ever can, as a whisper draws us in as no shout will ever do.

Maybe that's why a Kenna photograph and Japan go together as naturally as pen and ink. They offer the viewer acres of space in which to roam. They invite us into a conversation rather than a lecture.

That was the second lesson I learned on arrival in Japan: the nape of a neck may be more enticing than any full-body nude. It's the inch of skin that can be glimpsed above a formal kimono that moves and draws one in as no thong ever could. The American architect who designed my mother's mountain-top home in California gave her "Zen windows" in one corridor, on the wise Japanese assumption that seeing only a little of the ocean in the distance would fill her up more deeply than the whole, postcard-worthy canvas.

So of course Ayako, even when unclothed, has to stand behind these doors, an outlined shimmer. Of course she has to conceal as much as she reveals. Her image is designed to be the beginning of the story, not the end.

PI

In Praise of Ruth Bernhard

From so many points of view, including visual, the human body is a mysterious miracle. Representing the nude as an artistic genre has a long, rich history in the arts of painting, drawing, sculpture, printmaking, and photography. For over a decade, I had the honor to print beautiful classical studies of the female body, works of the photographer Ruth Bernhard. By her example and osmosis, I was her constant and grateful student. A huge bonus was our many conversations together, which often went on late into the night. After over fifty years of photographing, I still regard myself as a student. After my time with Ruth, I knew that photographing her favorite subject matter would always be a challenge.

In 2018, Nazraeli Press published *Rafu*, a book that contained forty-two of my photographs of female Japanese nudes. The depicted women were friends of friends and their associates: actresses, dancers, office workers, photographers, and yoga practitioners. I photographed them as I photograph the landscape, with absolute respect and admiration, in a series of impromptu dialogues between model and photographer, using whatever available ambient light and props we found in the various locations.

Ayako was my first model, and I take this opportunity to thank her for working with somebody who had absolutely no idea what he was doing. When I first saw these flowing tonalities and abstract shapes veiled behind the geometrical lines and rectangles of the shoji screen, it felt as though it was meant to be, as if a kind offering had somehow been arranged by Ruth. My responsibility was simply to acknowledge the gift, express my thanks and gratitude, and press the camera shutter release cable.

MK

Ayako, Study 3, Japan, 2010

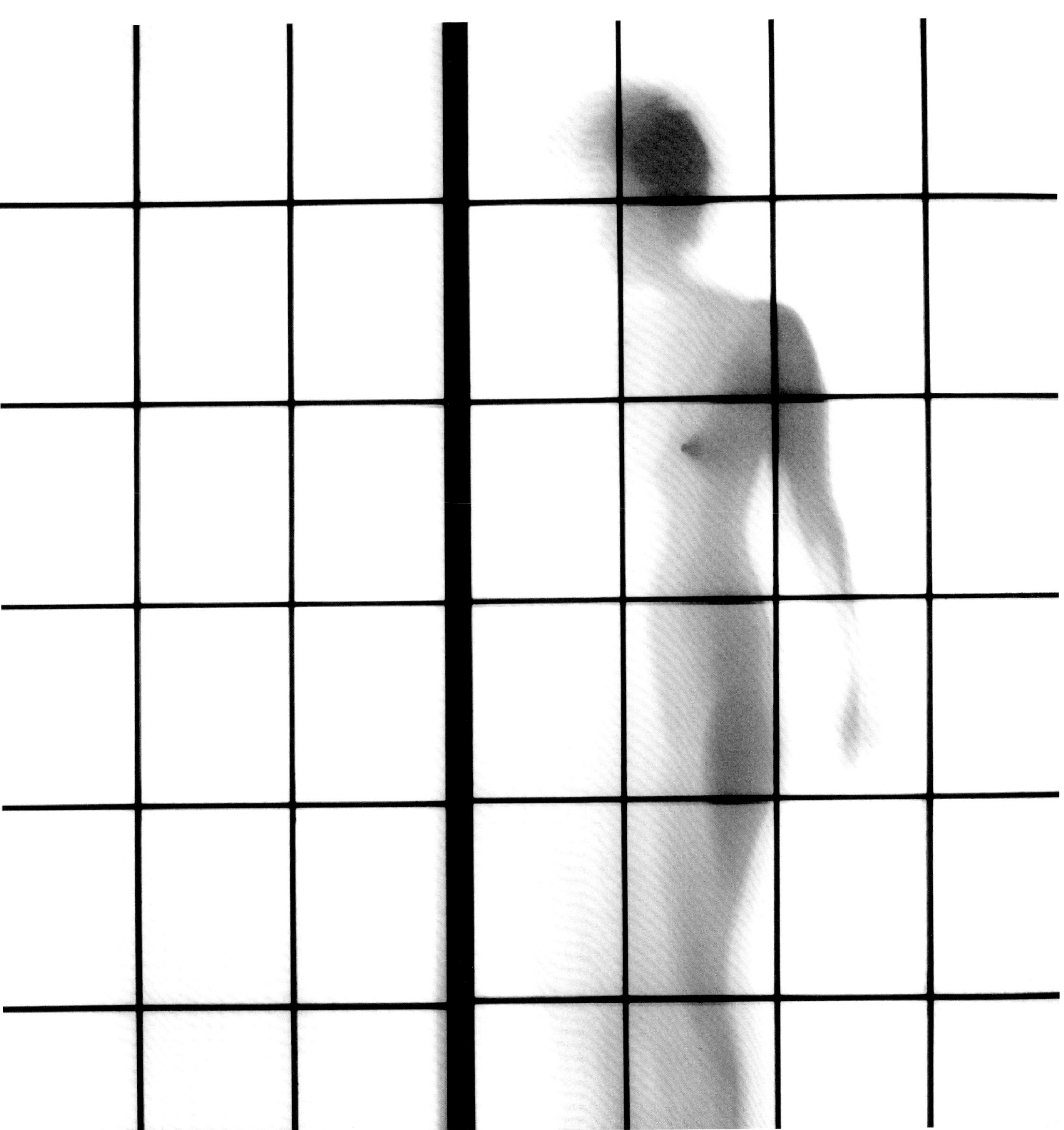

The Fog

Weeks after my mother stepped off the boat from Bombay, to go to college in England, a fog descended on the capital so enveloping that as many as eight thousand people lost their lives. A generation later, when Michael and I were at school—not long before this photograph was made—miners' strikes left the whole country fumbling in the dark, without electricity for four days every week, reading by candlelight. Charles Dickens made a whole poetry of murk, as in the celebrated passage in *Bleak House*: “Fog everywhere. Fog up the river, where it flows among green aits and meadows; fog down the river ... Fog on the Essex marches, Fog on the Kentish heights.”

It's surely no coincidence that London fog has even given rise to the name of a raincoat. “London was a sooty spectre,” in Dickens's memorable words, “divided in purpose between being visible and invisible, and so being wholly neither.”

So too was the whole nation in the days when Michael and I were edging through the pea souper of adolescence. Empire was gone, and we had no idea of what replaced it. Big Ben was tolling, but we couldn't always tell whether it was announcing dawn or dusk. Politicians inside Westminster kept debating, but it wasn't easy to make out if they were saying yes or no. Everything was lost in that most classic of English states, a muddle.

Is it any surprise that both Michael and I dreamed of, and then sought out, the wide-open horizons of California? Sunshine wasn't always on offer in Fog City, but to live in the realm of hopeful dreams at least offered a future tense.

PI

Bed Bugs and Big Ben

Moving to London in September 1973, I was excited and anxious. Having been raised in a small industrial town, I spent seven years in a boarding school before a year at the Banbury Art School. I wasn't a city kid! Yet now I was going to the London College of Printing (LCP) for a three-year course. Some months earlier, a morning interview in the photography department there had gone well, and I had been accepted on the spot. With my teenage brain, I didn't even consider going to the scheduled second interview in the graphics department.

Finding accommodation was a challenge, and I ended up at King George's House, the Young Men's Christian Association (YMCA) premises on Stockwell Road, two tube stops from the LCP. For a year, I lived in a small room with a bed, closet, sink, desk, and chair. I made my first experimental night photographs out of the window. My friends there included the resident bedbugs. I would try to catch them, as evidence, so that the room would be fumigated. But they never disappeared completely and I still have souvenir scars.

During this time, newspapers reported that the Provisional Irish Republican Army (IRA) were placing bombs around London, particularly in transport hubs and government buildings. There were constant warnings for the public to be vigilant. Yet I remember freely walking into a government building with a friend, and somehow, via many back staircases, finding our way to the roof, where I made this photograph. The setting sun, Big Ben, and the twin towers of Westminster Abbey were all perfectly positioned in typical London hazy light.

MK

 Big Ben and Westminster Abbey, London, England, 1975

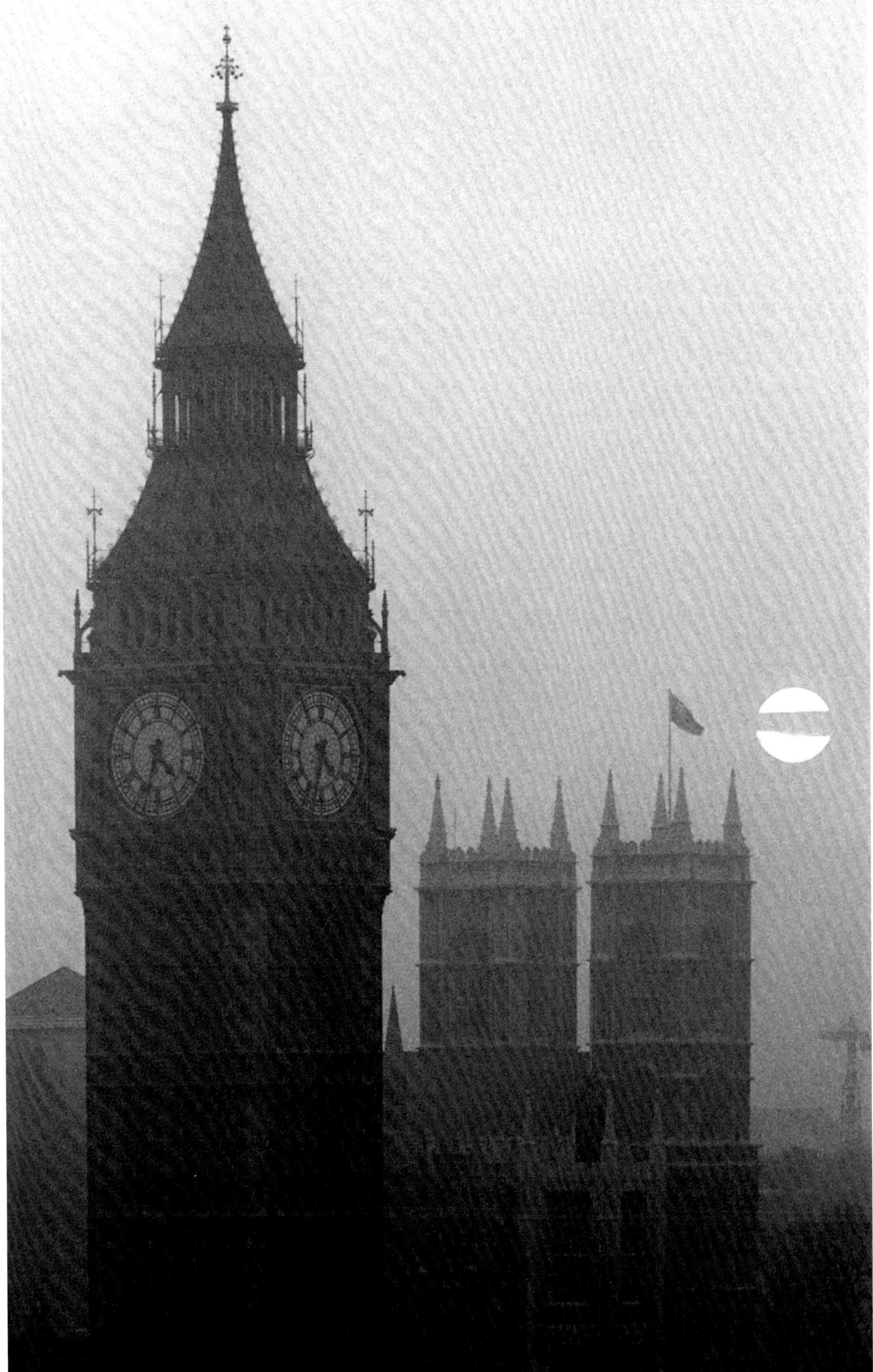

The Ascent

This is a homage of sorts, to a photographer who was essential to Michael. But what I love about it is the discordance, the harsh contrasts, the sense that this is several images in one, joined in an unlikely collage. It's so artfully put together that it's hard to believe that it has been taken from life.

I love the fact the "snicket"—not a word I've heard before—belongs to Bill Brandt. I love the way it asks whether the alleyway is the center of this picture or the house. I savor the way its darkness makes the house seem even more illuminated, but ghostly, too, at a time and in a place where everything seems to be in shadow.

I like the fact that the image shows an ascent, perhaps towards whatever lies in that house of light. It could be a pub, it could be a moonlit B and B, but I prefer to take this as an image of Bill Brandt's ghost.

Maybe this should have been the cover for the book I wrote as tribute to my own shadowy master, a grainy figure from the age of black and white who exploded all black-and-white simplicities and gave me the larger world, Graham Greene.

He lived in the shadows of the back alleyway, but always with his gaze fixed upon the house.

PI

Snicket in Time

You will not find the word "snicket" in most dictionaries. It is a Yorkshire term for a steep, ascending cobblestone walkway, which in this case leads to a bridge over railway lines. The wool and cotton mill workers lived in rows of tenement houses on one side of the rail lines; their mills were located on the other side. For every shift, day or night, the workers climbed up and down this snicket. Bill Brandt's famous photograph of this scene was made in the 1930s when the "Satanic" mills were still in operation and numerous chimneys belched dark clouds of smoke over town and landscape.

I made my homage to Brandt's snicket during what I considered to be a pilgrimage to the North of England in the 1980s, when I searched for places he had photographed. The mills had long been abandoned and most were derelict. The chimneys were disused or had been knocked down. I was happy and honored to climb up onto Brandt's giant shoulders to view this unusual perspective as if through his eyes. Somebody once said, "I can copy because I love him so much." Somebody very smart.

Bill Brandt's powerful and imaginative photographs have been a constant source of inspiration and sustenance for my own work since I stumbled on the *Land* exhibition, at the Victoria and Albert Museum, that he curated in 1976. An aspect of Brandt's vision that continues to affect me so deeply is the way he distilled a complex world into essential elements to evoke mystery and atmosphere. Brandt often worked at night, in harsh lighting conditions. He left large areas of undetailed black shadow areas in his prints, places for our eyes to rest and imagine what is hidden. Brandt, at least for me, is the Caravaggio of photography, the ultimate master of black-and-white chiaroscuro. His philosophy, to photograph as if seeing a subject for the very first time, with absolute curiosity and astonishment, inspires me to try to do the same.

MK

 Bill Brandt's Snicket, Halifax, West Yorkshire, England, 1986

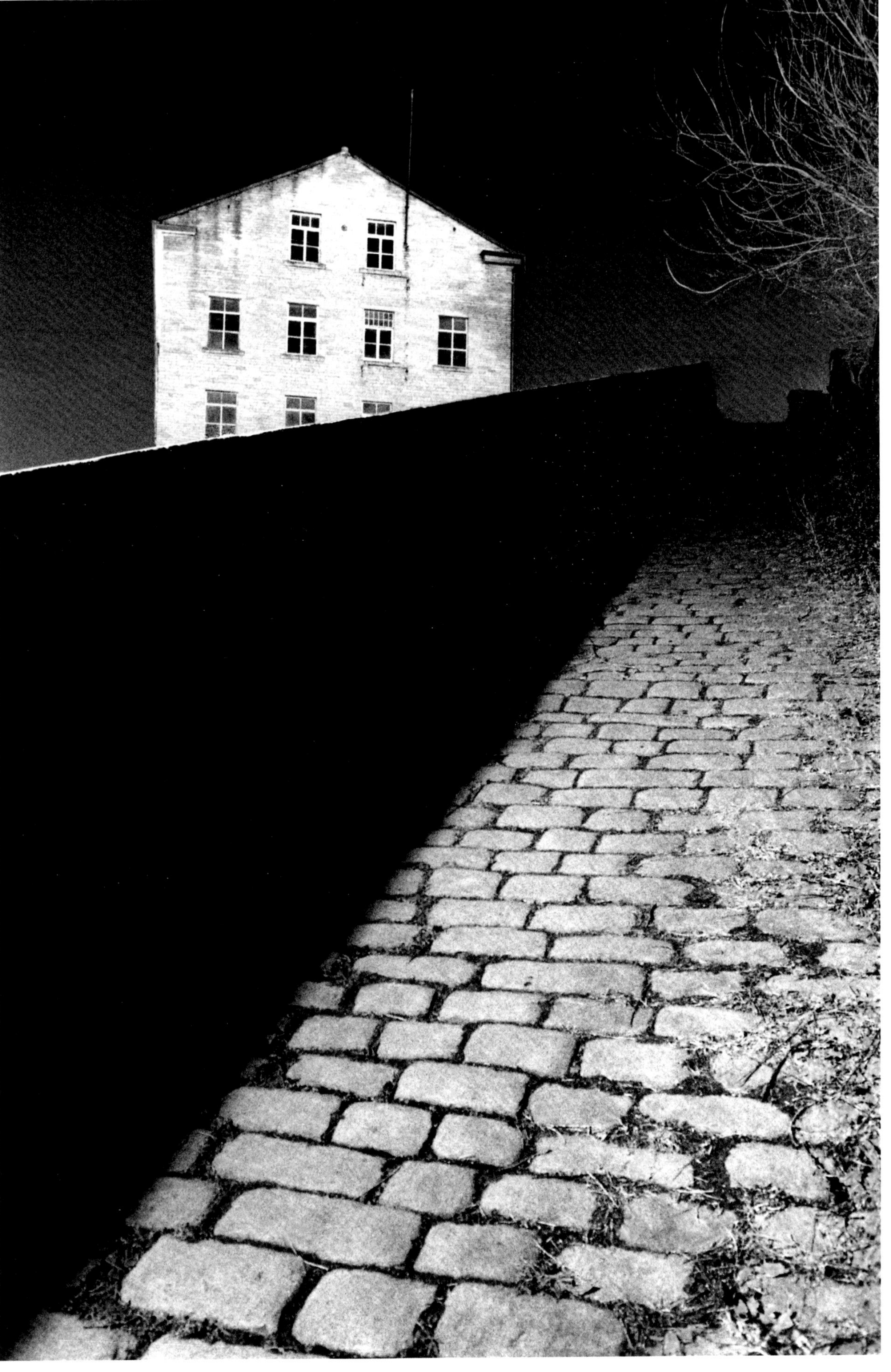

Our Long Season in the Emptiness

I look at the date on this image, and I'm pulled back to the memorable year in which I first met Michael. In January of 2020, my wife and I went down to Buenos Aires for two days in the elegant Argentine capital. Then we flew down to Tierra del Fuego and stepped onto a ship to sail across Drake Passage for the heart-stopping silences of the Antarctic Peninsula.

For a week we drifted among icebergs, emerald and aquamarine, five stories high. Among leopard seals and orca whales, albatrosses winging overhead and penguins waddling busily along their paths as we stepped into a Hokkaido of our own.

At journey's end, we got off the ship, and fifty passengers got on from China, where reports of a virus were emerging.

We flew back to California, and then Japan, and in February I flew from Osaka to San Diego for a day, enjoying a cheerful afternoon in the sun and an evening onstage before flying back.

Three weeks later, most of the world looked like this: a long, enforced isolation in which we felt lonely as this tree.

When would it end? Who would come to save us? Why could we see nothing else?

Months later, I received an email from a photographer I'd long admired, and something began growing in the icy wasteland of a pandemic.

PI

Keep Friends Close and Locations Closer

It is good to have friends, make new friends, and share friends. Although I'm no longer sure about the sharing part, based on a recent experience. In 2004, I met a large poplar that sat in the middle of a farmer's field near Biei, Hokkaido. Standing about thirty meters tall, with a diameter of almost two meters, it had been named the Philosopher's Tree, based on its resemblance to a philosopher lost in thought, with its head tilting to one side. It was a striking, glorious tree, abruptly cut down in February 2016. The farmer who owned the field cited the age of the tree (poplars grow quickly but have a short lifespan), and also the many trespassing tourists and photographers who would trample through his planted crops during the growing seasons to photograph, despite signs asking them not to. A sad end to a glorious presence.

The tree was a friend, and I photographed it many times, without considering issues of anonymity. I cannot take all the blame for the tree's demise, for it was known before I made it even more well known. Yet, I still feel some guilt that I contributed to its untimely departure by inadvertently helping to make it a tourist attraction. There have been other trees that have been felled after I have photographed them. Again, I cannot presume to have unduly influenced their ends, but perhaps I did, and nowadays I am not so liberal in openly sharing the locations of my tree friends. Increased popularity is decidedly not beneficial to their health.

I have visited this beautiful Blackstone Hill tree several times. It is a solitary, stately being, living alone, high up on hillside. I am delighted to share the photograph, and am equally happy to follow my guide's sage advice to allow this lovely tree to live a long, quiet, and anonymous life.

MK

 Blackstone Hill Tree, Hokkaido, Japan, 2020

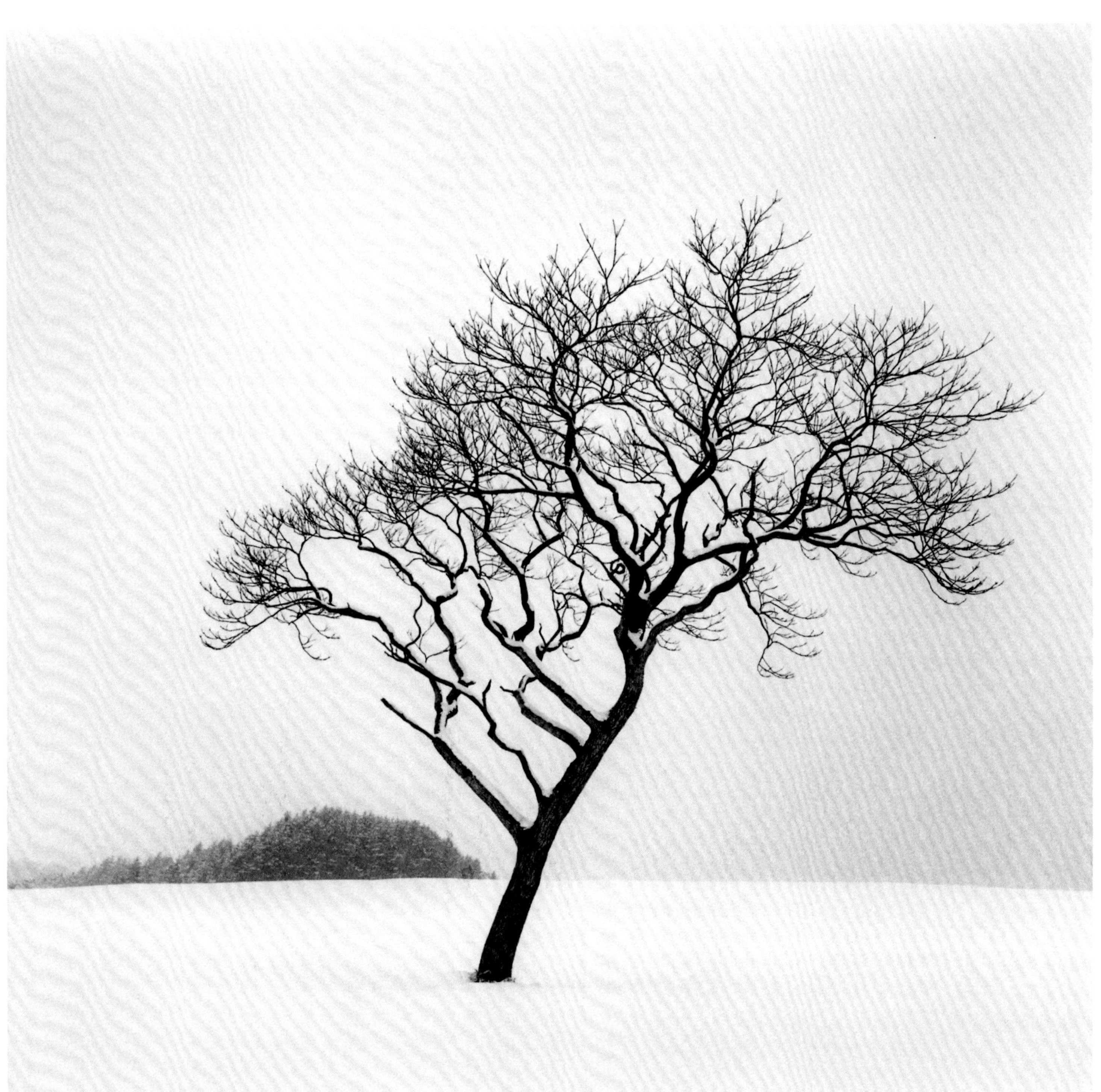

High Above the Clouds

I'm told that this is a castle, but to me it's somehow a monastery, a hidden sanctuary, a fortress where I've been taking shelter above the clouds for thirty-four years now, half my lifetime.

As soon as I saw this image, from Italy, I recognized it as secretly (and under an alias) the Benedictine hermitage on the coast of California where I've made my home over more than a hundred retreats. Quite often, the hillside below the monastery is swathed in heavy fog, and mists so thick they seem cognate with the "mysterious," even the "mystic." Clouds race up the slopes, remaking the landscape every moment. Then, out of nowhere, the skies clear once more and I'm surrounded by a radiance—blue sky and the outstretched blue sea far below—that seems to slip into forever.

Such places are always hidden from view, as if to represent the deepest parts of us that come out only in private, and seclusion. They're even harder to spot in a world ever more in a rush and eager to be close to the center of things. But this photograph reminds me that they're always there, if only we have the patience, the stillness to open our eyes to them. It also makes me think of Mr. Kenna, alone in his darkroom or wandering through Mont-Saint-Michel all night, seeking out the buried treasure that lies within what a nun rightly called *The Inner Castle*.

PI

All About Mauro

Viewing this tower on the grounds of Castello di Felina, one easily imagines Rapunzel-like fairy tales. Indeed, one of the great benefits of seeing things for the first time, or as if for the first time, is that we have a clean slate to allow our imaginations to create whatever stories we wish. Nestled into a hillside, with mist floating around, this tower kindles thoughts of my friend and erstwhile guide Mauro Lorenzini. With bright blue eyes, an always ready smile, and typical exuberant Italian charm, Mauro speaks not a word of English, and my Italian is restricted to bare necessities such as: good morning, thank you, good evening, and goodbye. However, within a few days we greeted each other with "dov'è la nebbia?" and a wink. Where is the fog?

Caffè corretto is an espresso "corrected" with a shot of grappa, and is a popular after-meal drink in Italy. Mauro and I would usually start the day with one, then perhaps have another for elevenses. In my photography practice I have learned to be lean and mean when I can. I try to maximize the potential of any location by photographing for as long as possible at any and all times during the day and/or night. Mauro was an even greater practitioner of the sacred Italian tradition of the *pranzo*, the long lunch. Much as I pleaded to grab a quick sandwich, Mauro insisted that we linger in some village restaurant to savor course after delicious course of home-cooked food, accompanied by carafes of local Lambrusco wine, before finishing with a *caffè corretto* or two.

I like to photograph in early morning mist and fog, when detailed subject matter transforms into two-dimensional planes of graphic tonalities. The hint of what is unseen can be a powerful force of suggestion and invitation. The issue with those post-*pranzo* photo sessions was that I was never quite sure if the fog was in front of the lens, or in my head. *Dov'è la nebbia? Tra gli alberi, intorno alla torre.* In the trees, around the tower. Grazie mille, Mauro.

MK

 Castello di Felina, Emilia Romagna, Italy, 2008

Our Fleeting, Flight Rulers

In the last week of March every year, just before my wife counts off another birthday, we have to set aside every afternoon, canceling other plans, for a series of walks around our suburb in the eighth-century capital of Nara. We take a bus to the hypermarket and then follow a narrow canal into what quickly becomes countryside.

On one side of us are the vegetable patches of locals, an old woman or two, or a little girl, working in the fields. On the other are children's haiku and drawings pinned to every tree, exulting in the blossoms that blaze for a few days and then are gone before you know it. Ducks set sail beside the banks of the water and dogs scurry beside their demurely bicycling masters along the narrow path.

We keep walking, farther and farther from the road, through what seems a perfect image of Japan: contained cheerfulness. The pretty, delicate explosions of early spring, made quiet and collective by the ordering of trees.

They're on the other side of the main road, too, in the new religion's fancy shrine; they're scattered across our modern neighborhood. All Japan joins hands in sanctioned exuberance for the uncertain days when they surround us, and then they're gone again, for fifty weeks or more.

As we walked along the bowing avenue of our rulers in 2002, who knows but we might have passed a cheerful photographer, striding past us in the other direction, none of us guessing that one day, twenty years on, we'd all be walking side by side?

PI

He Vants to Be Alone

Throughout Japan, cherry blossoms, also known as *sakura*, are venerated as reminders and symbols of the transience, vulnerability, and blissful glory of life. Festivals are planned and national meteorological advisories are broadcast to predict and document the sweeping pink wave starting on the southern island of Okinawa in late February and moving up to northern Hokkaido by early May.

In 2002, I was fortunate to be in Nara, at the perfect blossom time. After a long day of exploring, and with the light fading, I came across these lush trees along the banks of a small canal as I walked back to my hotel. I had no tripod, and to keep the camera steady I jammed it up against a roadside fence. I could hardly see anything in the viewfinder, yet it resulted in this lovely, sweeping, out-of-focus, foreground shape. I quite forgot about this photograph until the negatives were processed and contact sheets made. The subsequent discovery was delightfully unexpected and a wonderful surprise.

Looking back, I could easily imagine Pico and his wife Hiroko enjoying these or other cherry blossoms at exactly the same time, somewhere close by, for this is their neighborhood. I made this photograph four years before Pico and I first corresponded. In the same year he published an article titled "I Vant to Be Alone," which starts, "Being alone is of all the states of grace the one most frequently discredited, or at least distrusted." I wish that I had read the article at the time. It would have given me great comfort to know that a fellow loner and family man was also out there in the world, plying his solitary trade with elegance, grace, and equanimity, and that our paths would surprisingly cross in so many ways and in so many places.

MK

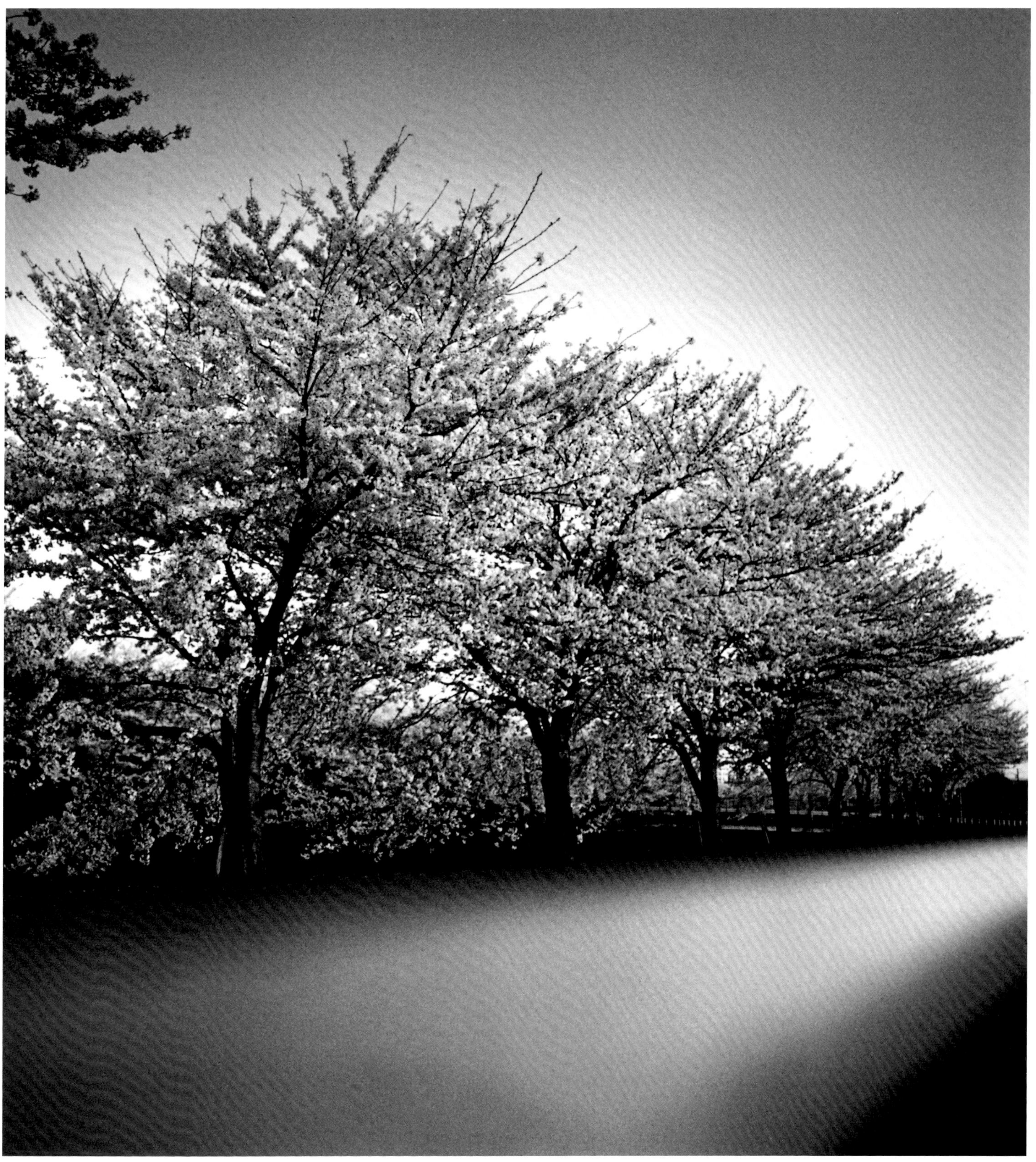

What Remains

It all comes down to this, in the end: nothing fancy, nothing wordy or complex or surprising. Here in Japan, there's often only one thing in a room—a scroll—which means you have to find everything you need within that scroll.

The world, you come to see, is not what's around you so much as what you make of it. Basho came upon the beautiful island of Matsushima and his most eloquent tribute was to let all words fall away and just sigh the name itself, as we may do when we're in love.

A tree in the snow: the tree changes, slowly, the snow may come and go. Next year it may look not so different, which is one reason a Kenna from 1973 might well be a Kenna from tomorrow.

The man behind the lens changes, too, and in some ways not at all. As I am the kid who got on the bus in Tijuana fifty years ago, though on the surface his aging grandfather. So many of the questions of youth are dissolved, and what remains are certainties outside—and far beyond—my monkey mind.

The end of life may look like the beginning, except at the beginning of life we can't see that a tree in a snow is enough.

PI

Asahikawa to the Rescue

The morning had been difficult. My guide, Tsuyoshi, and I had walked in snowshoes for an hour, up a steep hill. It was predawn and freezing cold. We had almost reached our goal—a specific glorious tree that sat on a high horizon. My normal modus operandi is to first make pictures from a distance with my Hasselblad cameras, before moving closer. This is practical as it avoids disturbing the foreground with footprints. On reaching what I considered to be the best spot for a fine perspective on the tree, I stamped down the snow and planted the tripod. Framing and focusing, I measured the light with my handheld exposure meter, breathed in, and pressed the cable release to trigger the camera shutter. A healthy exposure sounded. Winding the film on, I bracketed half a stop and attempted another. This time, only silence. My lens shutter had jammed, or froze.

In my experience, old mechanical cameras sometimes misbehave in subzero conditions, but I was not worried. Being a "professional," I carried two camera bodies with me. After swapping them out, I went through the same process, but was again greeted by an ominous silence. In my fifty years of photographing, I had never before had two cameras go on strike at the same time. After much fumbling, cajoling, pleading, cursing, and trying every which way to remedy the situation, I gave up and hiked back down to the car.

Tsuyoshi phoned all around Hokkaido before finding a ninety-year-old camera repair person, miles away in Asahikawa. He was able to temporarily fix one, but not the other, and expressed concern that none of the photographs I had made that morning, before the camera jammed, would come out. Imagine my delight and relief, many months later, after the film was processed, to find one well-exposed image. Good fortune is one of the most valuable pieces of equipment a photographer can be blessed with.

MK

Cikisani Kamuy, Study 1, Sorachi, Hokkaido, Japan, 2023

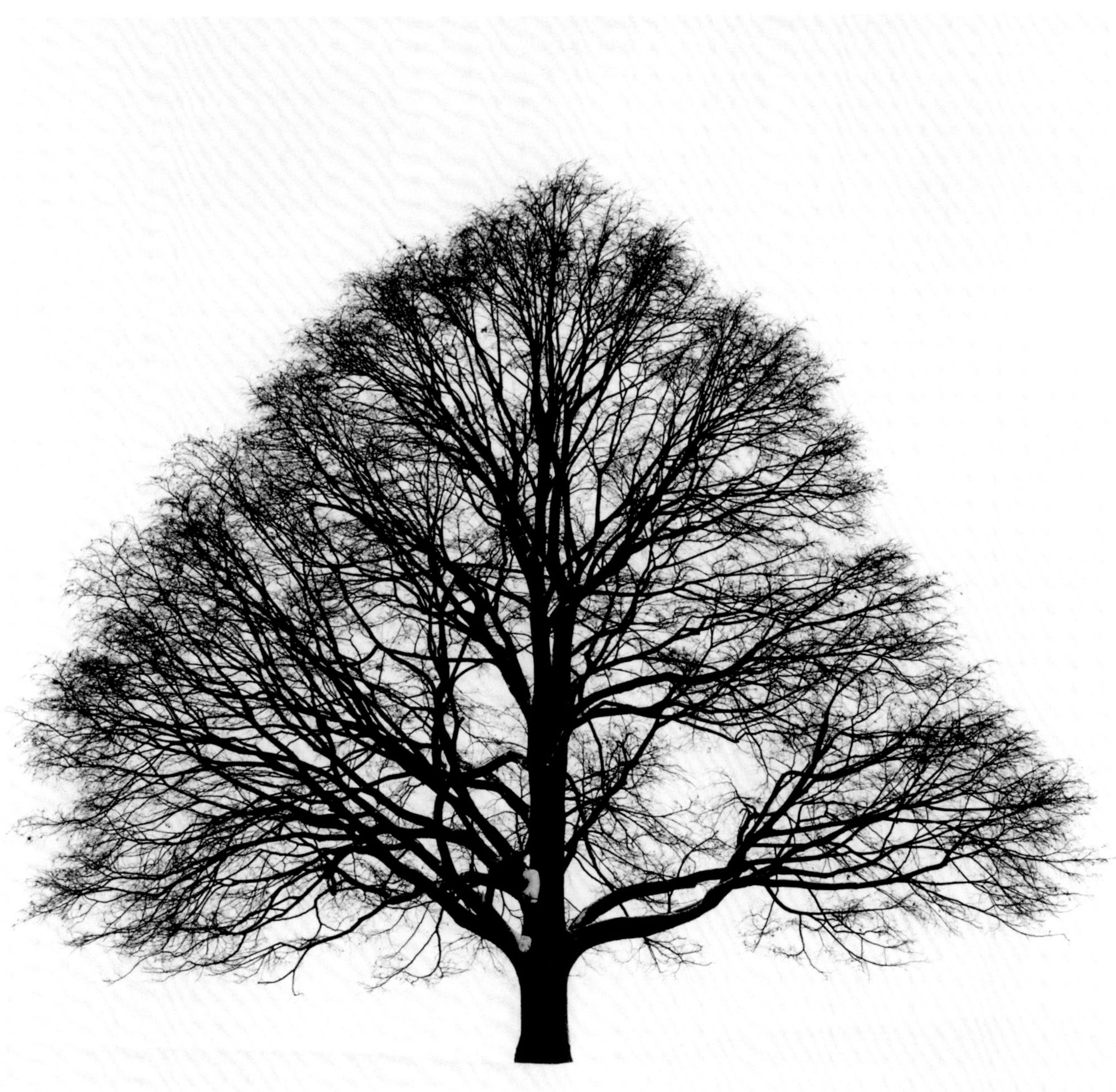

Where the Spirit Moves

In my secret home this week—a monastery—I read that the operations of what is sometimes called "the Holy Spirit" are often likened to the wind. We make our plans, we gather our savings, we plant our seeds, and then the wind blows through, reminding us all that it has no interest in our hopes, that it speaks for everything that we can never control or define, that something determines our lives much more deeply than anything we plot ourselves.

So it's the breeze in this photograph that moves me most, and brings humanity—change, possibility, sweetness—to what might otherwise be a rather stern and static image.

Or maybe I hold onto that vision of caprice because otherwise the confessional awakens far too somber thoughts. How much any of us might whisper inside that dark box, and how little any of our whispers might protect us from making the same mistake again!

Whenever I see Michael's images of chapels, I think of the boarding schools we shared, in the same land, at the same time, and how much they made us what we are. We could never have known that what is translated as "the Holy Ghost" could, a religious scholar told me two weeks ago, be rendered, simply, as "mother."

The force that moves those otherwise penitent and kneeling figures in the dark.

PI

Bless Me Father

Confession is one of seven sacraments in the Roman Catholic religion. As a boy, every week I entered a dark wooden box in my local church to confess my sins to a priest. He sat behind a metal grill on one side of the box, and I knelt on the other. After reciting from memory "Bless me, Father, for I have sinned. It has been one week since my last confession," I listed whatever naughty things I could remember or invent. After receiving a penance from the priest, usually a series of Hail Marys and/or Our Fathers, forgiveness or absolution was granted. It was always a relief, although I don't know if it was because I was forgiven, or that I didn't need to repeat the ritual for another week.

This confessional box is part of a series of seventy-six studies made between 2007 and 2016 in and around Reggio Emilia. On rainy days, when it was too wet to photograph outside, I ventured inside the many regional churches. In almost every one, I found wooden confessional boxes, all unique and quite different from each other. I set out to make a photographic collection. Most of the churches were dark, and the process involved long exposures of twenty to thirty minutes with my camera on a tripod. What a wonderful excuse to spend countless hours in empty churches.

I like to think that if words, thoughts, and emotions could be made visual, these confessionals would reveal a host of experiences and secrets, confessed and discarded in exchange for a priest's absolution. Confessionals are not for everybody, of course. I well remember my young nephew's comment when he came to see my London exhibition: "Uncle Michael, why are you showing all these pictures of wardrobes?" I imagine C.S. Lewis would approve.

MK

Confessional, Study 50, Chiesa di Santa Maria Assunta, Reggio Emilia, Italy, 2015

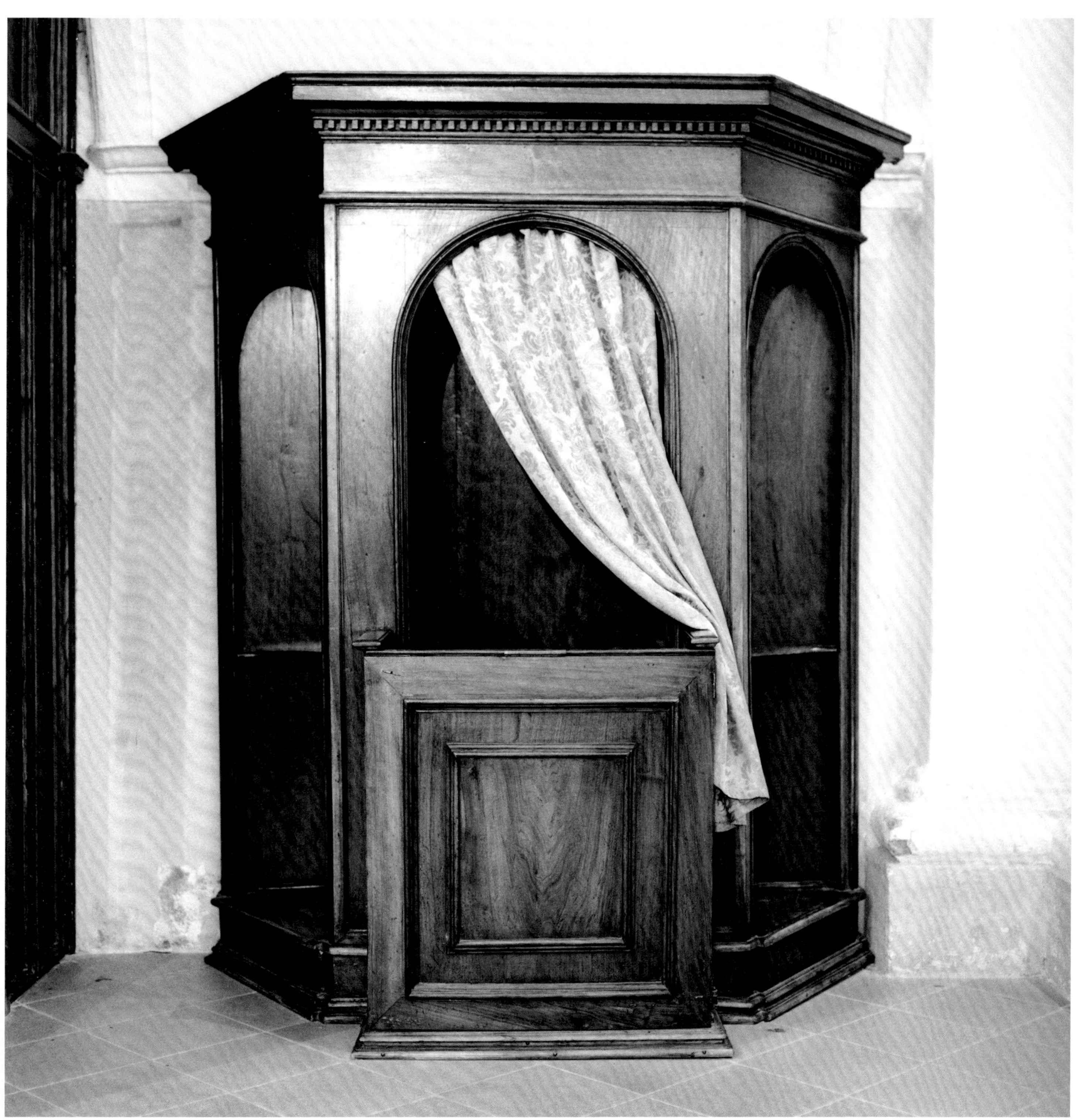

Revenge of the Nerds

The India where my parents grew up was thick with religions; around them in Bombay were serious practitioners of Sikhism, Jainism, Christianity, Judaism, Islam, Hinduism, and, most of all—the ritual that brought all of them together—cricket. The sport the Brits introduced to them became a pastime, a slow and genteel passion and, in time, a sacrament.

In those days it wasn't obvious that India would soon be defeating Britain in the sport the British imported to India. Or that the captain of the English team might soon bear an Indian name. But in the Dragon School on Bardwell Road, Oxford, we had no thought of ironies or the Empire striking back. Cricket went with long summer days, a sense of delight, freedom at last from the mud and slog of rugger.

White-flannelled opening batsmen walked in tandem to the crease; there were breaks for tea each day and murmurous claps for heroics and mishaps; soft-voiced announcers on the BBC purred of googlies and silly midwickets.

In our world, success was measured by one thing only: sporting achievement. Not sportsmanship, but simply the attempt to run faster, jump higher, hit harder: heroics on the fresh-lawned greensward. I could manage none of that and so was relegated to a scorer's hut, much like this pavilion, to tally every thwack and notate every tremor over a game that lasted from mid-morning till dusk.

By day's end, I had scored more runs than anyone else, but not in any way that counted.

PI

Back Entry Chronicles

Irate homeowners and guard dogs can be excellent incentives to good cricket practice. The "entry" (as it was called) behind each row of tenement houses in Widnes where I lived was composed of flat pieces of oblong stones, about twelve inches wide, running down the center, with cobblestone areas on either side. Close to the back of our house stood a lamp, placed in the middle of one of the entryways' end, next to a wall. It was a perfect cricket wicket where I spent many solitary hours, when I was nine and ten, practicing my fast bowling.

Given the conditions, accuracy was imperative. The ball was hard and unforgiving. If it hit the cobblestones and not the center flat area, it would likely fly over somebody's wall, entailing a climb over their gate to retrieve it. Hence the homeowners and dogs reference. An errant ball could result in a broken window, as happened on at least one occasion. My dad, a builder by trade, replaced and reinstalled our neighbors' glass a few times, which greatly impacted my small supply of pocket money.

Aged eleven, during my first year at boarding school, the first sweet whiff of freshly cut spring grass signaled the beginning of a new cricket season—the time to put my bowling to the test. In the first game, I bagged seven wickets. A few weeks later, I broke a fellow classmate's front tooth. I felt terrible, and still do. The Prefect of Discipline was decidedly unamused. I got a right bollocking (as they say in that part of the world). The prerogative of my current age is that I can forget the many times I was hit for fours and sixes. History is usually written by victors. It can also be written by those with fading and sentimental memories.

MK

 Cricket Pavilion, Saltaire, Yorkshire, England, 1984

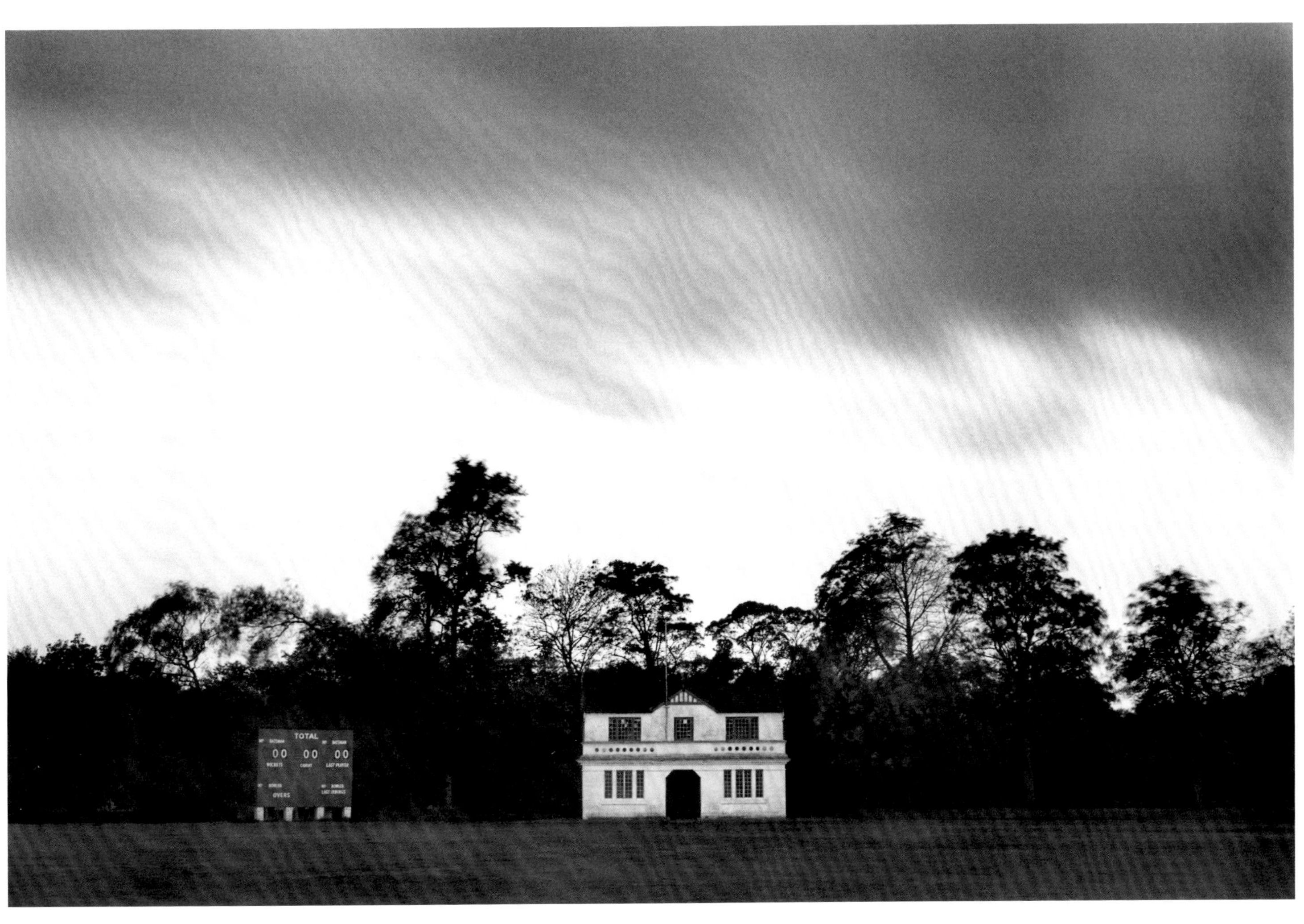
TOTAL
00 00 00
OVERS

The World as It Is

Why do we travel? To be confronted by our planet head-on, in all its stark reality. To be silenced, lifted, upended by the power of what humans have wrought and what Nature is doing and continues to do constantly. To encounter immensities that shake us out of words.

But never out of images. I was stunned—and powerfully spooked—the first time I met the great stone faces of the Bayon in Angkor, not quite smiling and never really reassuring. I could feel the ghosts from a genocide only twenty years before, imagine the cries of children behind the trees or hiding behind temples. Monks and nuns filled the holy places, but nothing could erase the simple fact of all that had been done here, all that had been suffered.

To climb Angkor Wat at dawn, I was told, was to witness the possibility of renewal, the reemergence of the light. I clambered in and around three hundred other foreigners crowding the steps as the sun came up. Only to witness the souvenir in every iPhone.

Here is the scene I should have been looking for: none of us foreigners in sight and no postcard vendors, promised epiphanies, or Photoshopped pasts on offer.

Just the world as it is, irreducible, undesperate, home to so much light and dark, indifferent to our ideas of it.

PI

Alone in the Crowd

My Beijing representative Lu Xiao along with a mutual friend and collector Howard Cao were planning a trip to Angkor Wat. Did I want to come along? Of course I did! In all the beautiful images I had seen of this glorious twelfth-century Hindu-Buddhist temple, originally dedicated to the Hindu deity Vishnu, it was remote, hidden deep in a jungle, empty, calm, and peaceful. The reality turned out to be slightly different.

Traveling for countless hours, from Seattle to Beijing to Siem Reap, and after an almost sleepless night, we rose hours before dawn to take a prearranged rickshaw to the temple. Dodging in and out of long caravans of coaches, full of tourists, we edged our way forwards before getting stuck in a traffic jam with bicyclists and pedestrians weaving and squeezing their way through. Opting to walk, we joined in a slowly moving, jostling, ruck of people, many with torches, everybody anxious to enter the temple complex as soon as possible to claim the best vantage points for sunrise photographs. I was one of thousands of tourists.

As a photographer, I am trained and practiced to concentrate, to keep the main thing the main thing, to mentally extricate myself from complicated surroundings when necessary in order to focus on the scene in front of me, which was truly magical. A glow of red dawn light spread over the dark silhouette of this sacred site. I heard spontaneous whispers of appreciation as the sky brightened and details of the temple emerged from the shadows. It was a captivating show, full of anticipation. For whatever reasons people had chosen to be in that place, at that time, we were now together, witnessing, humbled and awed by the sheer beauty and majesty of nature collaborating with ancient human efforts to honor their gods. It was a precious moment. I felt alone in the crowd, but far from lonely, and I photographed. The resulting image is how I always imagined a remote, secluded, and empty Angkor Wat would be.

MK

Daybreak Reflection, Angkor Wat, Cambodia, 2018

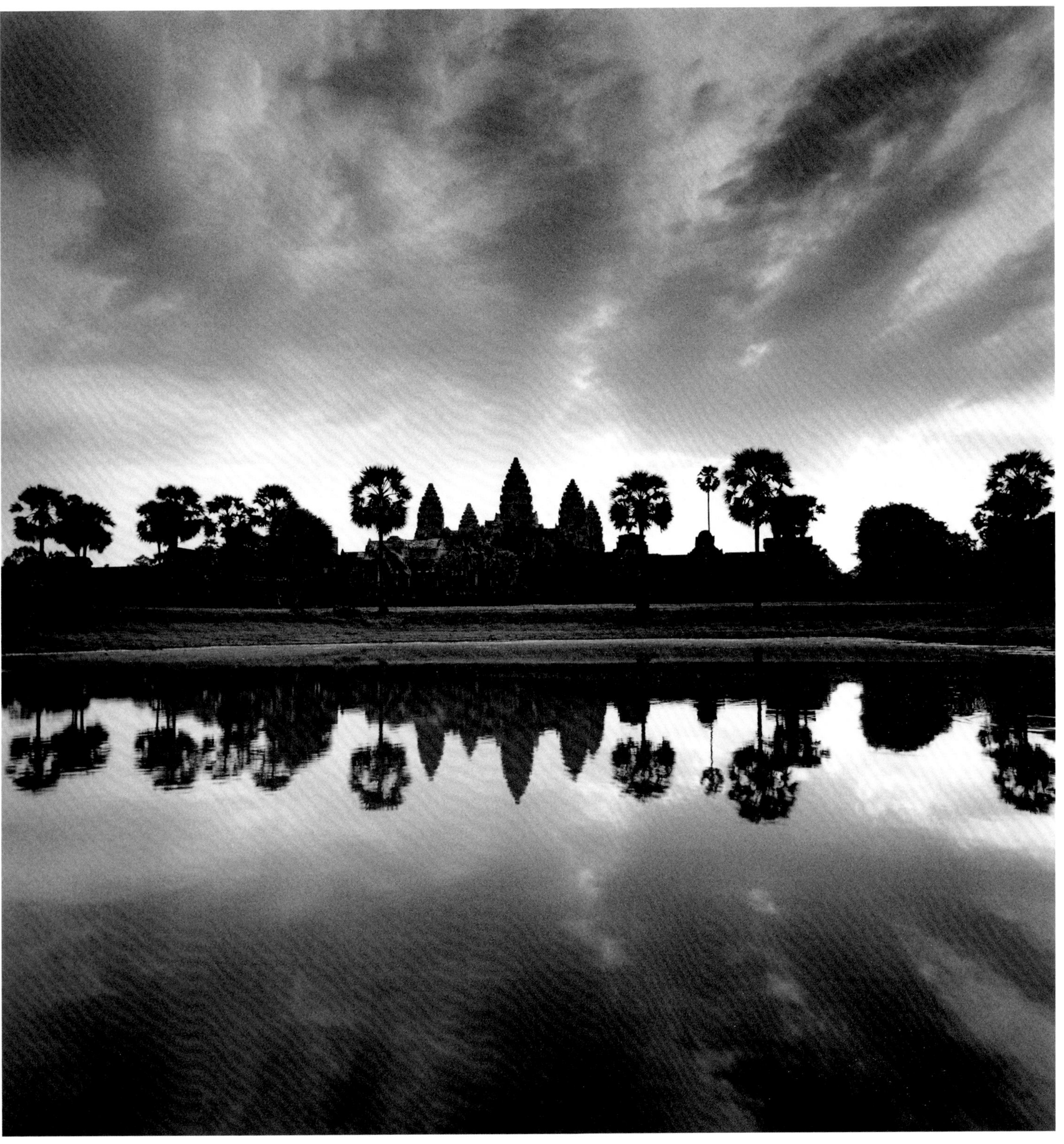

Stairways to Heaven

The year I turned sixty-five, I realized there are always fresh ways of breaking ground. Yes, I'd go to Zanzibar this year, two years after sailing around the breathtaking silences of Antarctica. Yes, I could keep writing new books as if my life depended on it. But the years were pushing me to define adventure more imaginatively.

Maybe I'd act in a movie and see the movies I'd always loved in a different light? Maybe I would drive into the New Mexico desert and engage in an intimate, intense psychological workshop of the kind I'd always recoiled from? Maybe I could fashion a work made up of silences? Or talk by Zoom, this new bridge across the oceans, to a fourteen-year-old student about what she could do in her life that I could never imagine?

Maybe it was time for setting ladders, not against a wall, but into the sky, like stairways to heaven? Maybe I was old enough at last to see them as grown-up sequels to Quixote's windmills?

Maybe I could even write riffs to images sent to me across the sea in the hope that, every now and then, 1+1 might come to 3?

I wonder what magic Michael had in mind when he made this photograph and I come up with excitements of my own.

PI

Walking Under Ladders

I am a big fan of the board game Snakes and Ladders. Competitive, without being personal, no strategies are involved and it comes down to luck, good and bad, on any given day. I have a thoroughly enjoyable time ascending ladders and sliding down snakes. At any stage, the journey ahead is unpredictable, and it is not possible to estimate when the game will end—perhaps in a few minutes or much longer. The unexpected expectedly happens. I suppose this game taught me early on that sometimes it is OK to let go, to patiently and good humoredly meet destiny face-on, win or lose, sooner or later.

The ladders in this tree, installed around 2009 by the French artist François Méchain on the grounds of Château de Chaumont-sur-Loire, were inspired by Italo Calvino's wonderful book *The Baron in the Trees*. The artist is suggesting that we should climb these ladders to achieve different and higher perspectives both of the landscape and of life, away from the stresses of our everyday existence, up there in the branches of a tree. I enthusiastically second his proposal.

In the Chinese zodiac, I was born in a year of the snake. In Western astrology, my birth date makes me a Scorpio. Whereas it is difficult for me to feel great affinity towards either snakes or scorpions, many a ladder has appeared in my photographs. I do not follow the superstitious directive not to walk under them. The reasons cited include a belief that a ladder represents the Holy Trinity. Walking underneath would be a desecration, a sin against the Holy Spirit, never to be forgiven. A second reason refers to ancient Egyptian beliefs regarding pyramids and their power and spells. A third compares a leaning ladder with steps leading to the gallows. Sometimes, I hope and trust, ladders are really just ladders.

MK

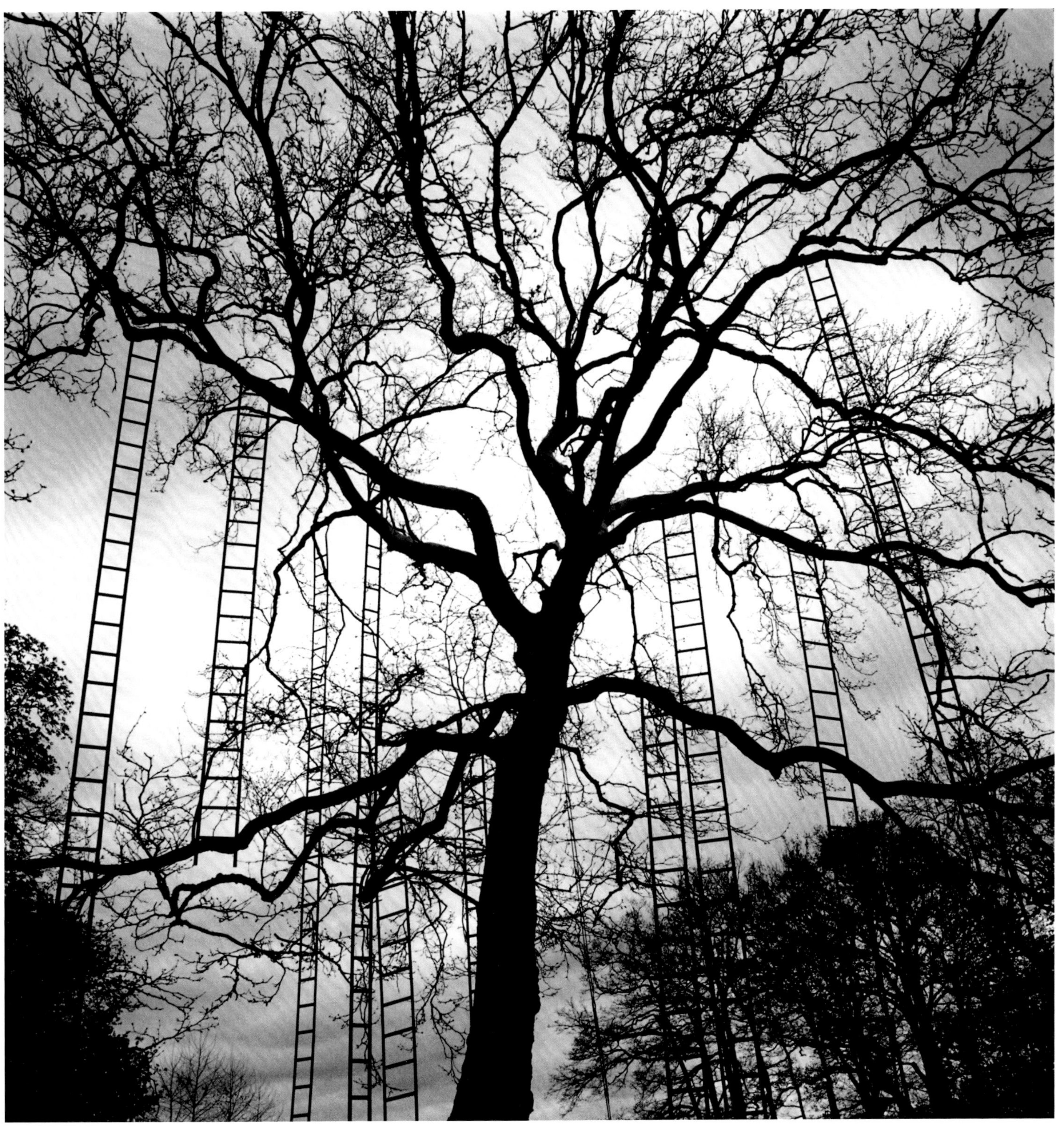

My Shadow Self

I took a bus from my two-room flat to the local train station. I boarded an express train for the cavernous terminal where many lines meet in central Osaka. I walked along thronged passageways, through corridors, up escalators, made my way to another private railway line, and stood in line for an even slower train.

For ninety minutes, we passed through countryside that grew ever quieter. Then we came to a deserted small platform under a sign, "Gokurakubashi," or "The Bridge of Heaven." A handful of us stepped out and walked towards a cable car.

At the top of our clanking ascent was an empty mountain road. At the end of the country bus's passage was a town made up of 117 esoteric Buddhist temples, set amidst centuries-old trees, and 250,000 graves.

After nightfall, I walked all the way through the darkened realm where all lives lead. At one point I glimpsed a tanuki, the legendary badger-dog that haunts many a Japanese folktale. At the end of the path, where the founder of the mountain, Kobo Daishi, is believed to be meditating still, nearly 1,200 years after his arrival, I saw a lone petitioner in the dark, hands joined in prayer.

If only I had known where to look as I came back out, perhaps I'd have seen another figure, or just a camera, deputed by my uncommon editor Hanya to gather images for the article I was writing. A silent conspirator, walking the same path at dead of night, unseen, my constant and yet-unmet shadow.

PI

Things That Go Bump in the Night

I had the great fortune to meet Pico Iyer in the Koyasan Okunoin at 9:45 p.m., on October 8, 2006, albeit not in person, but by email. That is the date stamp on the first email from Pico I have saved in my jungle of a computer. He had been commissioned by Condé Nast to write about this sacred and ancient Buddhist sanctuary. I had been asked to make photographs for the same article. As would become a familiar pattern, we missed each other on the mountaintop by just a few weeks (Pico cited an ongoing engagement with the Dalai Lama). But our communications began, and happily continue to this day, and in this book.

The Okunoin was founded in 835 AD and is over a mile in length, surrounded by conifer trees. It is reputed to be the largest cemetery in Japan, with more than two hundred thousand graves and memorial monuments. It contains the mausoleum of Kobo Daishi, aka Kūkai, the founder of the Shingon school of esoteric Buddhism. Each day he is brought fresh food and other offerings by his faithful followers. Pilgrims from all over the world come to visit, and especially those who have just completed the eighty-eight-temple pilgrimage in Shikoku.

Being in the Okunoin, especially alone at night, is a special and singular experience. If ever there was a place where spirits run free and ghostly magic happens, it is there. This could be just in my imagination, for I did not feel frightened, threatened, or in danger, to the point that I was able to lie on a bench, in the middle of the night, and sleep for some hours, while my camera, with its shutter open, exposed this photograph. However, I suspect my chosen bed would not be so comfortable for the many Japanese people I have met and talked with who sincerely believe that a Buddhist cemetery does not house dead bodies, but provides space for living, waiting, spirits.

MK

Entrance Path, Okunoin, Koyasan, Japan, 2006

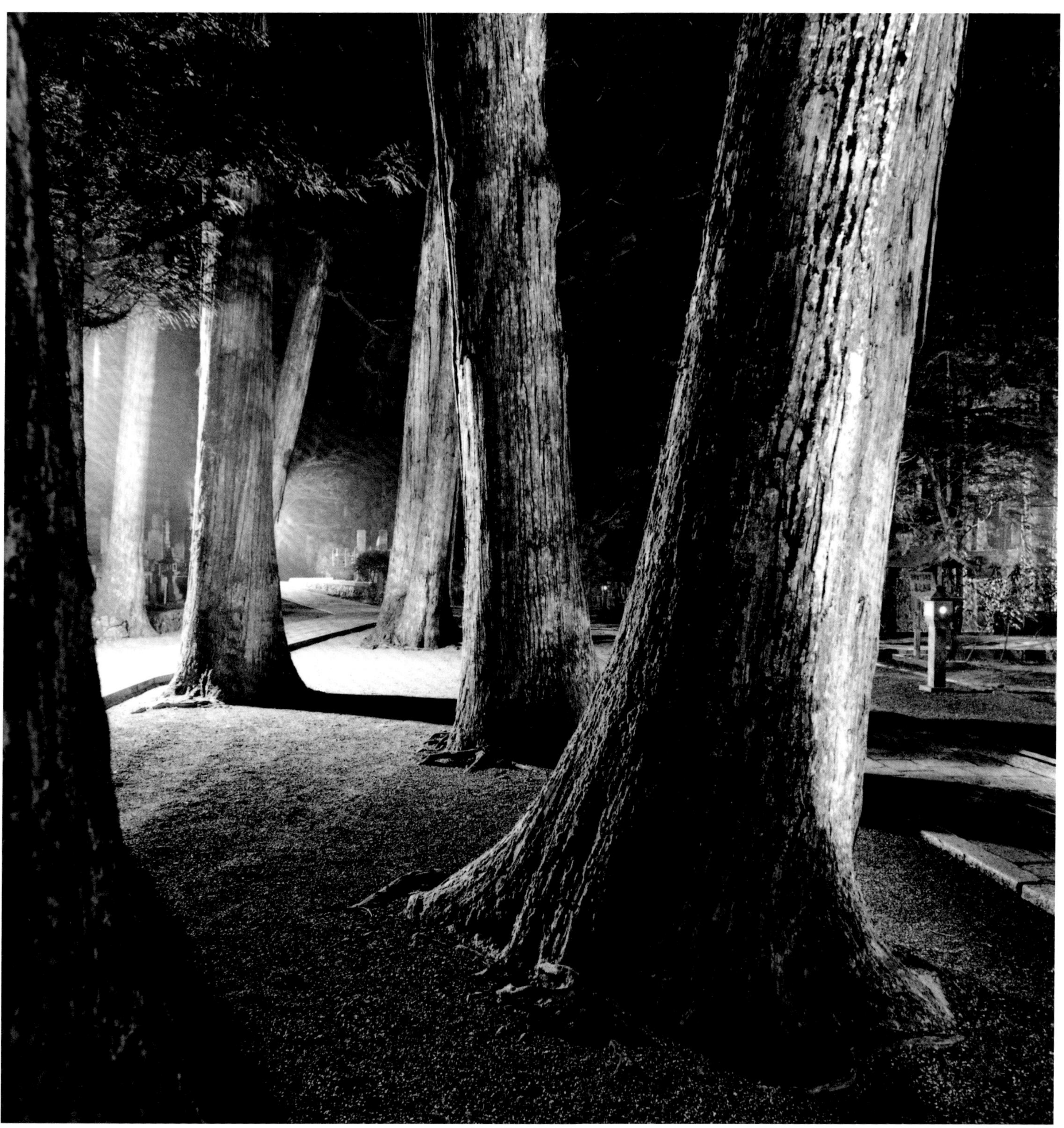

The Black Door

Cities, like most of us, put on a bright and cheerful face as soon as visitors are on the way; they make their living, as a rule, through being festive and affirmative, a home to fun. Arriving in Prague for the first time recently, I could hardly move for the Korean honeymoon couples streaming side by side across the Charles Bridge, the large groups of Indian men cracking open Pilsners in the cafes and delighting in the air of license all around. After dark, all of Old Town turned into an open-all-night al fresco nightclub crowded with girls in flimsy tops and boys carrying cans in their hands as they reeled, singing, over cobblestones.

But this is the city of Kafka. It's overbrooded by a huge castle that looks over everything, chill sentinel; it's thick with narrow, winding streets that can make you feel you're in a maze from which there's no escape. For long months in winter, Prague is dark, and cold, and feels as if it's haunted: famous for its golems and ghosts and, perhaps worse, for those neighbors whose nose is always in every other neighbor's business.

A summertime tourist like myself revels in the pretty picturesque surfaces and the switched-on gaiety of a place throwing its door open to the world with a bright "Hello!" An artist steals out by himself and catches the place when no one's looking.

PI

Past and Present

My first visit to Prague was in 1982 when I drove from Vienna with my wife at the time, Kathryn. It seemed like an exciting adventure; now I think it was sheer madness. This was back in the days when the frontier between East and West was filled with mines, machine guns, barbed wire, great suspicion, and much hostility; and we were in a bright red BMW—hardly inconspicuous. The internet tells me the journey today would take three and a half hours. It probably took longer then, with regular police stops en route to check papers and passports, and dog teams sniffing over the car. Somehow we made it, with no hotel reservations, a very bad plan. I remember driving around the famous Wenceslas Square, the wrong way, searching for a place to stay. I could blame it on the naïveté of the young, but I was already twenty-nine.

Waking early after a restless night in a decrepit hotel under construction, with smelly bathrooms down the hall, I ventured out into the streets. Prague was dark, Kafkaesque, lit only with occasional orange lamps, smothered in thick smog. Through an empty city, I found my way to the Charles Bridge, deserted but for two young military men with machine guns, marching up and down. Intimidated but undaunted (another gift of youth), I photographed, even lying face down on the cobblestones for the vantage point of a ghostly row of black statues. I walked and photographed for some hours along the Vltava before heading back for dry bread and ersatz coffee, and the long drive back to Vienna.

I have revisited Prague many times since, and was there during the Velvet Revolution in 1989, even detained between rows of armed military police during the days and nights of demonstrations. Prague is now happily free from such oppressive occupation, swarming with tourists and vendors. Light has entered the city; shops and cafés abound. And I still look for hidden, shadowy spots, unpopulated corners, suggestive entrances that lead my imagination back into the past I witnessed, with its dark stories, fading traces, and distant memories.

MK

Entrance, Prague, Czechoslovakia, 1990

Lines of Power

As I've grown older, I've come to see the world as a never-ending contest between what the heavens give to us humans and what we humans do with the heavens. We're so good at linking continents, at inspecting distant stars, at building machines that are brighter than we could ever be; yet wildfires and typhoons and earthquakes and floods keep reminding us who's really in charge.

This image comes to represent for me life as I see it now: the trees look so mighty and enduring when we small humans walk among them; they're our elders, even our guardians. They bore witness to our grandparents' grandparents; they will preside—we hope—over our grandchildren's grandchildren.

But here, on a larger canvas, they look as frail as we are.

The clouds move through the skies, portending danger and disruption. All we can do is await the heavens' next capricious move.

This image dates from the end of the last millennium, when many of us worried that Y2K might bring the end of the world. We couldn't see then that far stronger forces are at work than anything man-made, and they're surging through the heavens as we chatter.

PI

It's Not Always What's in Front of You

"When you have finished photographing what is in front of you, turn around, and look at what is behind you, for it is sometimes more interesting," wisely counsels the distinguished photographer Ansel Adams. I had stopped to park, and observed the fourteen trees sitting on the hilltop with such a marvelous sky as backdrop. At the time I was experimenting with a 35mm Leica camera and was able to make a series of quick handheld snaps. The clouds in this photograph are ominous, menacing, and threaten a storm, which seemed appropriate to me. In a bit of a hurry, I turned around to walk to the main subject of the day, the reason I had driven to this specific location: the Nazi concentration camp of Mauthausen in Austria.

Between 1988 and 2000 I photographed all the Nazi camps I could find in Europe, and eventually donated two sets of prints, with their respective negatives and usage rights, to the erstwhile Patrimoine photographique, now known as the Médiathèque de Patrimoine et de la Photographie (MPP). Later I would donate another set of prints, the remaining 6,000 negatives, and all the work prints to the Musée de la Resistance. Both organizations are in France. Other donations of these prints have been made in Japan and the United States.

Looking back, photographing in concentration camps for twelve years, albeit difficult and emotionally stressful, was personally formative and significant. I sometimes think we choose projects, and at other times they choose us. Accepting this subject, I photographed it in a way that was personally true and honest, and then gave it all away. As I left Mauthausen on that late afternoon, the trees were still on the horizon, the sky had cleared, the threatened storm had passed. It was good to know that tomorrow would be another day.

MK

Fourteen Trees, Marbach, Austria, 1999

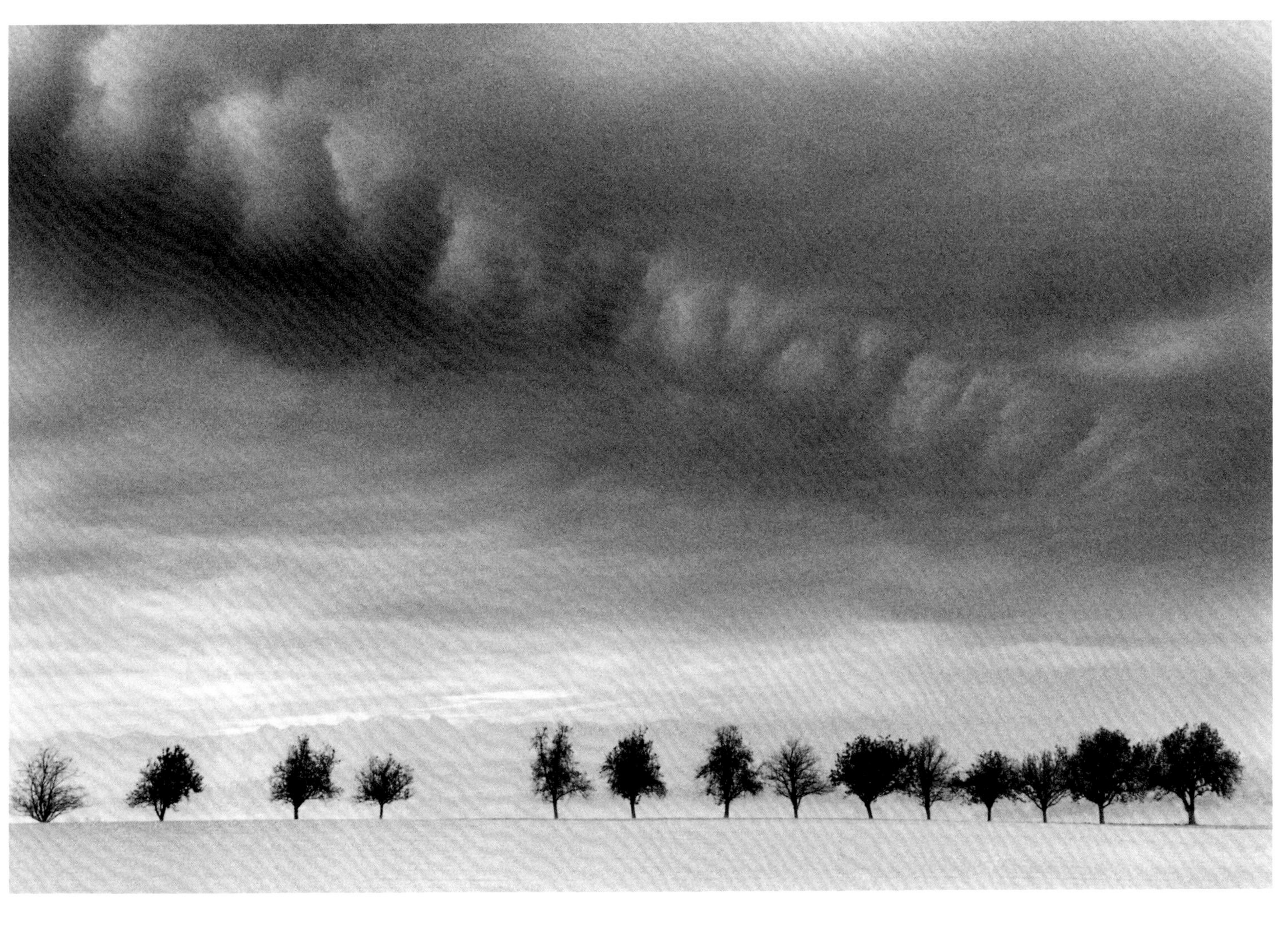

Forgotten Beauty

Every city has a reputation and sometimes, all too often, the reputation outlasts the reality. Paris will always be the City of Light, even on rainy days that continue through months of endless winter. Kyoto is the city of temples, even though many of its Buddhist sites are obscured now by selfie sticks and the fourteen-story skyscraper known as the Kyoto Hotel. Thailand sells itself as the Land of Smiles, though none of us knows what those smiles betoken.

Detroit, sadly, is the City of Darkness. Of urban blight and poverty, of an evacuated downtown. Of industries that now come to seem outdated. Of racial tensions and extreme cold. Of sporting teams that never win the championship. The name itself evokes something metallic, rebarbative, tough.

Then why do all the people I meet who come from Detroit love it so? Why does so much of our richest music emerge from there—and those shiny tail-finned cars that were the glory of America when America was the hope of the world? Why do I often hear of elegant suburbs and why did so many of us thrill to *Searching for Sugar Man*, the story of an enigmatic singer profoundly rooted in Detroit?

The inspiring novelist Richard Powers reminds us that the transformation of consciousness we need is unlikely to come from governments or corporations, let alone tech bros, because they're all too captive to their own interests. But an artist, ideally, speaks for and from the interests of us all. Look at this photograph and weep for all the ways you might have overlooked—or not looked correctly at—Detroit.

PI

Hunting Magic

One of the many joys of being a photographer is the splendid excuse of expending vast amounts of time wandering around the world, observing, appreciating, evaluating, thinking, choosing, hunting, and witnessing miracles and mysteries. While photographing the Rouge steelworks in Dearborn, Michigan, between 1992 and 1995, very much as a homage to the painter and photographer Charles Sheeler, I occasionally visited Belle Isle. Known locally as a colorful and popular summer picnic area for Detroit residents, it was empty and frozen on the early February morning when I happened on this intriguing and spectacular ice sculpture. Somebody had consciously or unconsciously left a water tap running in a period of subzero temperatures. My good fortune!

I first circled, looking at and evaluating possible perspectives. The sky was dark gray and brooding, but from time to time a few light rays crept through and exquisitely illuminated the curious oddity. Finding what I thought was the most interesting point of view, I lay on the ground waiting, and saw through my viewfinder what appeared to be a towering iceberg, surrealistic in the confines of this urban park. The small tree on the right helped to make it seem even more massive than it was. I only managed a few exposures in the brief moments of sunlight before the clouds closed in, my fingers froze, and wet snow began to seep into the camera and fog up the lens.

I returned to Belle Isle a number of later times hoping that somebody would again create a magical sculpture. With all due respect to the distinguished fountain, I never witnessed such a spectacle again. Which is a shame, for we could all use more magic in our lives.

MK

 Frozen Fountain, Belle Isle, Detroit, Michigan, USA, 1994

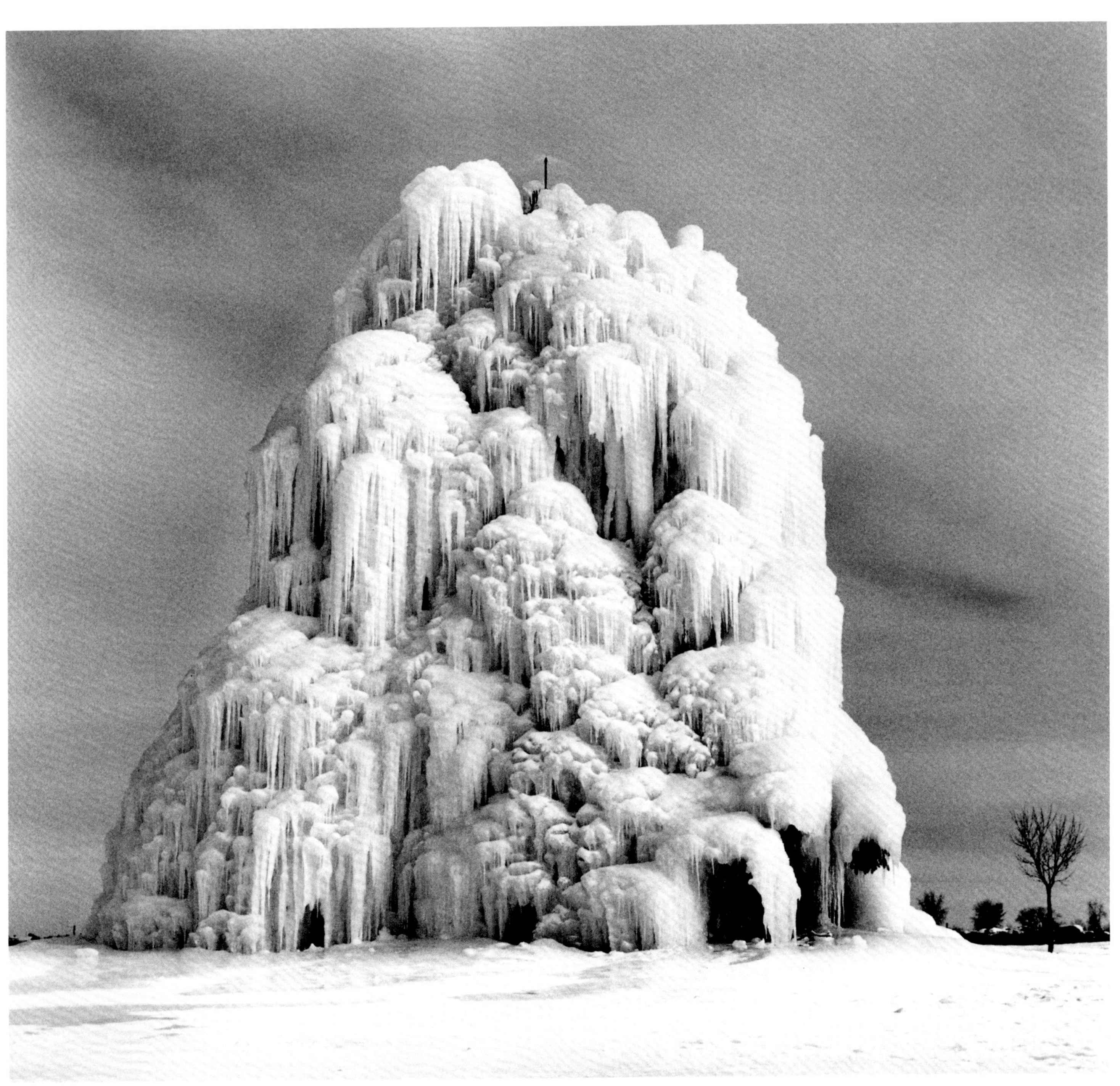

Baubles or Bubbles?

What can I possibly make of this? The beauty of such work is that the viewer completes it, making it up in effect in his or her own viewfinder. Every reader to some extent writes the book he or she reads, and the most emancipating art leaves space enough for the viewer to respond in any way, so that it becomes not statement but conspiracy. I could tell you these are beads of sweat writ large, that they are pieces of a necklace to be hung around a sweetheart's neck, that they're baubles that speak of a Christmas tree on the way.

What Michael is doing in such work is freeing us from the ordinary. As from external markers. Taking us to some quiet place we can't define. Black-and-white is already turning life into parable, a representation of something beyond the moment. Abstraction is an invitation to go directly to emotion.

Michael tells me now that this is an image from a kindergarten in San Francisco in 1997, and I think of the marbles that were my prize possession—sometimes my most constant friends—in the boarding school that was my equivalent of Michael's seminary. But let me not confine anyone with particulars: the best thing to be said about this is that it could be what you like—or even love. Tell me what you see in it and I'll tell you who you are.

PI

Monique's Kindergarten

Playing marbles requires scant resources and little money. These glass orbs were everywhere in my northern England working-class childhood, and they probably still are. It is a common game available to many, as a circle can be scratched or chalked onto the ground practically anywhere, and then the excitement begins. The rules are straightforward: whatever marbles you knock out of the circle with another marble that you flick or roll—you keep!

Being invited, in 1993, to photograph in the kindergarten classroom of the San Francisco Waldorf School was both a wonderful opportunity and a great challenge. My daughter, Olivia, had proudly informed her class teacher, Monique Grund, that her dad was a photographer—hence the invite. When the project first came up, Monique had certain expectations. She presumed, quite appropriately, that I would photograph the children at play, or so she told me later. Whereas my intentions were entirely different. I wanted to photograph the memories and traces in the classroom, what was left behind after the children had left.

I used a 4×5-inch bellows camera for this project in an attempt to slow down and concentrate on objects as if I was seeing them through a child's eyes. With this large camera, and being 6 foot 2 inches myself, I felt for the most part like the proverbial bull in a china shop. Over a period of four years I repeatedly observed and photographed whatever I could find: peacock feathers, beeswax dogs, tiny brooms, paintbrushes, flowers, Christmas decorations, Easter baskets, summer dresses, and these marbles. They bring back memories of my own, younger years, and they simultaneously evoke for me a universe of childhood innocence and possibilities.

MK

Games in the Sun, San Francisco, California, USA, 1997

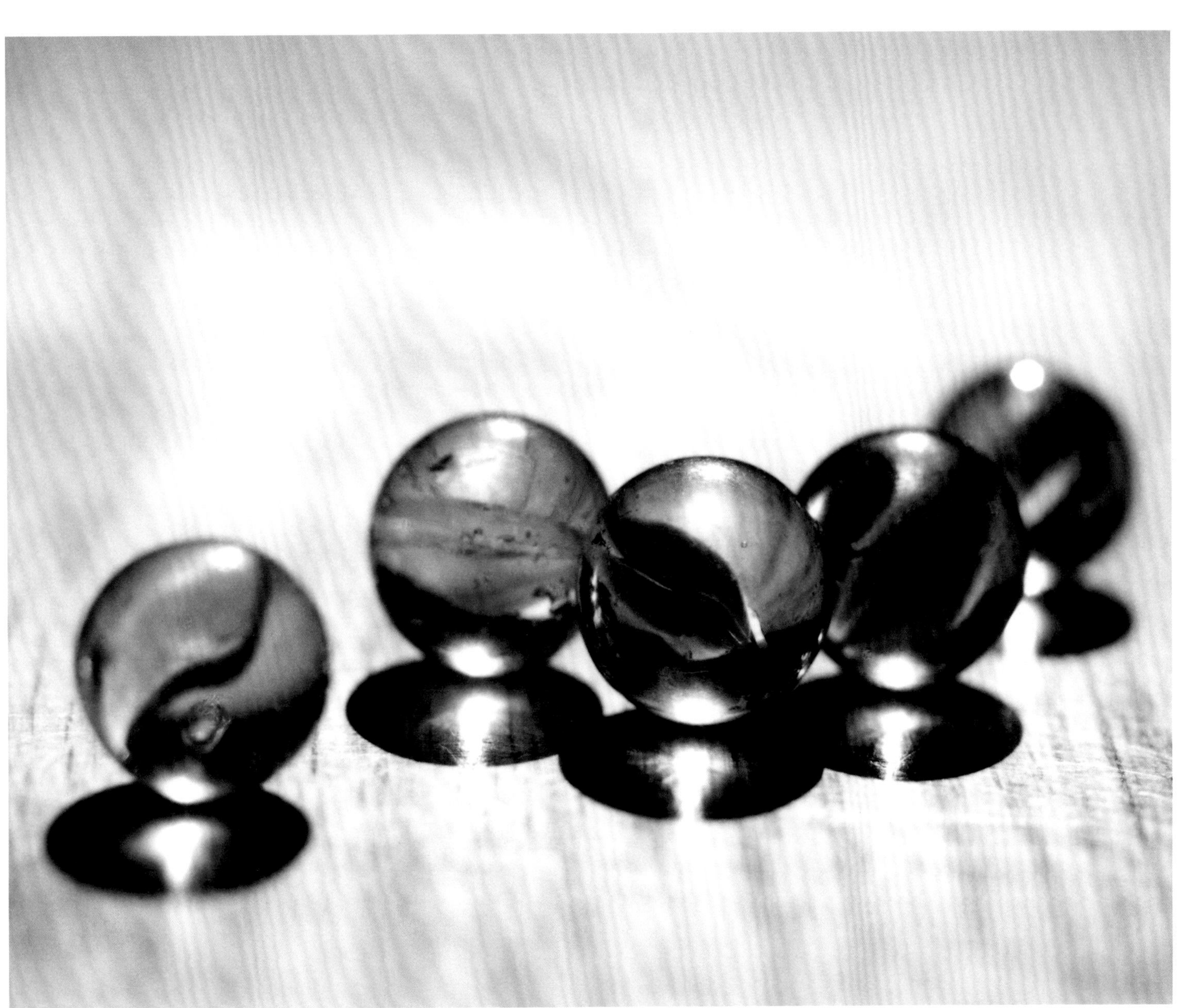

The Gateway to New Life

The Gateway of India is a gateway to a kind of life for me. I learned to walk, I'm told, at my grandparents' flat just down the road from this monument to Empire, on my first trip to India from the Britain where I'd been born. I see my parents, one after the other, sailing away from nearby, a few years after the British departed, carrying their rich knowledge of Shakespeare and the Bible and 1066 and all that to the suburb of Bombay known as Oxford.

I think of my wife and myself, staying just in front of the archway, on the last day of our honeymoon: her first trip to the India she'd been dreaming of since she was a little girl in Kyoto. Both of us stepping, with excited trepidation, through the entranceway, into a new kind of life.

And I think of my mother, raised not many minutes away from the great arch—and the Taj Hotel and so many other monuments to the complex relationship between empires—cherishing it from the far side of the world as the emblem of the very special land, and the mingling of cultures, she was so grateful to grow up with. Again and again, before she died, she told me that the Gateway was one of seven places across the planet where she wanted me to scatter her ashes.

I made that trip not long ago, and the grand portal began to seem the gateway, as in so many Michael photographs, to a truly other world.

PI

Living the Dream

May 25, 2006. Little did I know that my life was about to be turned upside down and inside out. Dazed and jet-lagged after a twenty-three-hour flight from Seattle to Mumbai, the advertising campaign crew I was working with had its first meeting with pre-dinner drinks in the Taj Hotel bar. The account handler from New York mentioned that the client had just arrived from London. "A real piece of work" was her rather strange description. Mamta Mani breezed into my life as if she had always been there. We sat next to each other at the bar, reading a menu listing exotic drinks—all outside my limited experience. When Mamta politely asked me which to order, it was as if I had been posed a differential algebraic equation problem. Attempting to cover my ignorance, I suggested she try one of each—after all, her company was paying for them!

A sad coincidence would soon be noted about this first meeting of client, creative director, and photographer—we were each in mourning, having all lost our respective fathers in the previous month. I began to quietly regard this newly formed working trio as the "Dead Dads Society."

Another coincidence would be noted some years later. It was on this same day that I was introduced to the writings of Pico Iyer, having earlier in the day purchased his publication *The Lady and the Monk* at the hotel gift shop. I have now read this book more times than any other. Its deeply resonant and beautiful descriptions of Kyoto in the autumn of 1987 recall my own explorations in this same city at the very same time. And it is an irresistible love story.

Over the following few days, Mamta persuaded the hotel staff to remove screens from her bedroom window that overlooked the Gateway of India. From this perspective, my assistant Zac Frackleton and I made several long exposures of up to an hour each. The thousands of people milling around, the moving water, boats, and clouds, and all the loud sounds, softened together, became quiet, almost dreamlike, exposed and accumulated on film. Five years after meeting Mamta, I became her husband.

MK

Gateway of India, Mumbai, India, 2006

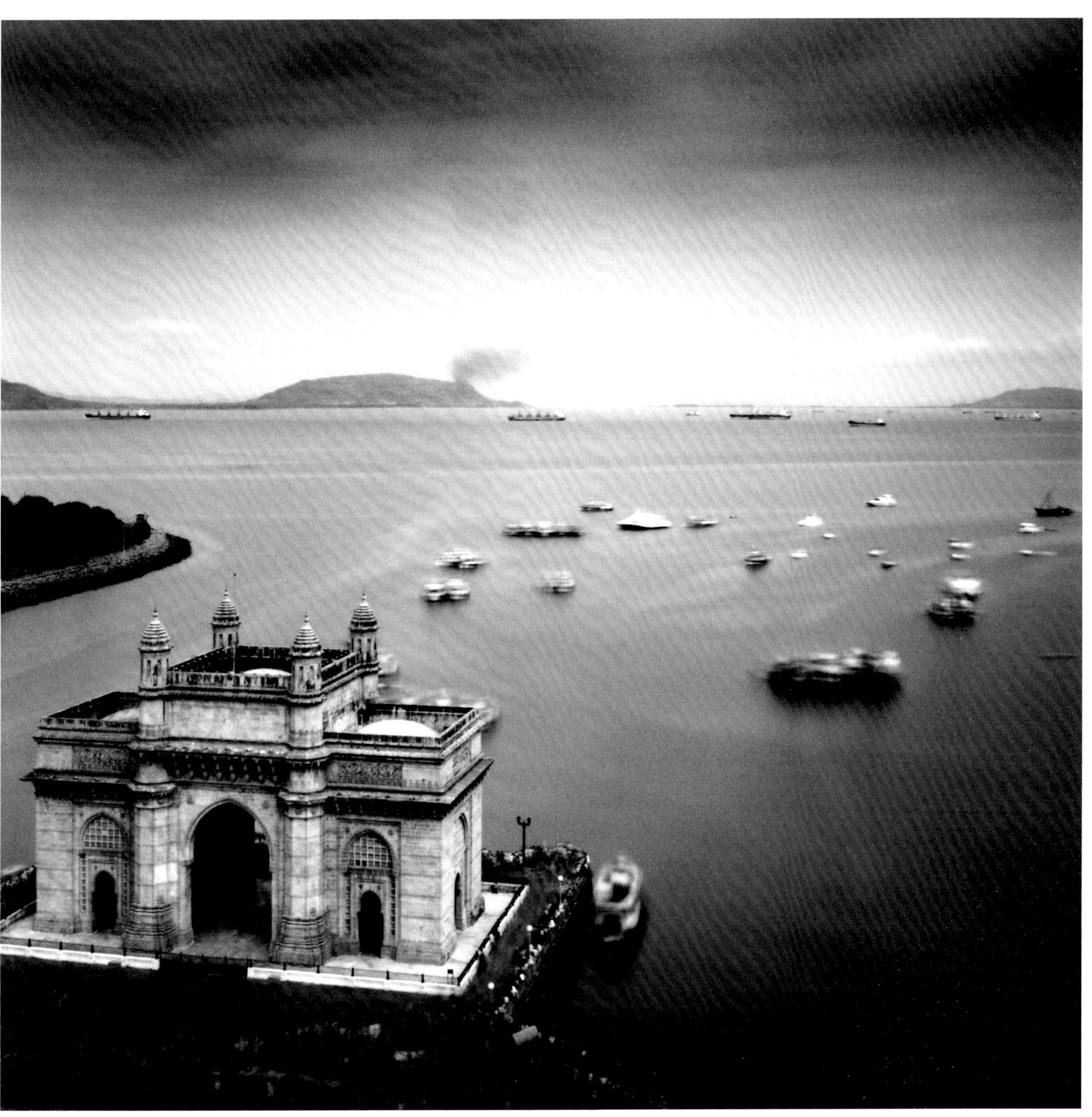

Upstairs, Downstairs

A grimy room in the Hotel d'Inghilterra: I might, even in Rome, have been seeking out a mistranslated version of home. Long afternoons in sunlit hill towns that had closed down for the afternoon—or was it the summer?—so everyone could sit outside their houses and follow the World Cup. A clamorous evening that stretched till dawn as Paolo Rossi claimed a hat trick and the Azzurri won the World Cup and all of Rome spilled out into the streets for a through-the-night carnival of honking horns and drunken shouts.

I was in Italy at almost the same time as Michael—of course—and yet the ghostly shimmer of his Venice, the haunting beauty that he brought back, could not have been farther from my glamourless footsteps. Having escaped graduate school for a summer to write parts of guidebooks to England and France, I had returned for a second summer of work in which I was entrusted with the most choice locations: the Côte d'Azur, the Ionian islands, Corsica, the Mani.

In the middle of that enchanted interlude I spent a month in Italy. But my $5-a-day budget allowed no space for gondolas or lagoons, let alone the gossamer beauty of a Michael Kenna portrait. As poets and photographers drifted down back canals to the plash of oars and through passageways hymned by Casanova and Vivaldi, I quarreled with a school friend over how many pizzas we could buy for ten lire, and wondered how an all-night celebration might save me another night in a run-down hotel.

Every land has a thousand faces, and all we can see is the one that reflects back our exalted—or impoverished—circumstances.

PI

Echoes, Memories, Reflections

When I think of Venice, various adjectives spring to mind: dreamy, sparkling, mysterious, extraordinary, romantic, unreal. Venice has been described as a city of mirrors and mirages, serene and tranquil, La Serenissima. Perhaps no words can ever do justice to this singular treasure, and, for that matter, no photograph, although innumerable writers and photographers have made attempts.

Just last year, as I was looking back through my negative archives during the preparation of a recent book project, I came across a negative, made almost forty-five years ago, that I had never printed, for it was a complete accident. Two or three exposures had recorded on one frame by mistake, and the negative was therefore overexposed. It was not possible to see an image on the contact sheet—which seems to be an oft-repeated pattern of mine. However, an alluring facet of the traditional silver gelatin photography process is that hidden treasures are often overlooked, perhaps to be discovered and printed much later. Such was the case here.

I must admit to having no recollection of making this photograph, and I therefore take no credit. Who knows, maybe somebody borrowed my camera. The whimsical nature of the picture, the surrealistic aspect of three suns in the sky, the shimmering and ethereal quality of the Basilica di Santa Maria della Salute, the gondolier in action: all contribute to my feeling that this is an unreal echo, reflection, or memory from the past. Truly, I am delighted that the image somehow occurred, and am very grateful the negative landed in my library of negatives. It is yet another magnificent gift to be thankful for.

MK

Gondolier and Basilica di Santa Maria della Salute, Venice, Italy, 1980

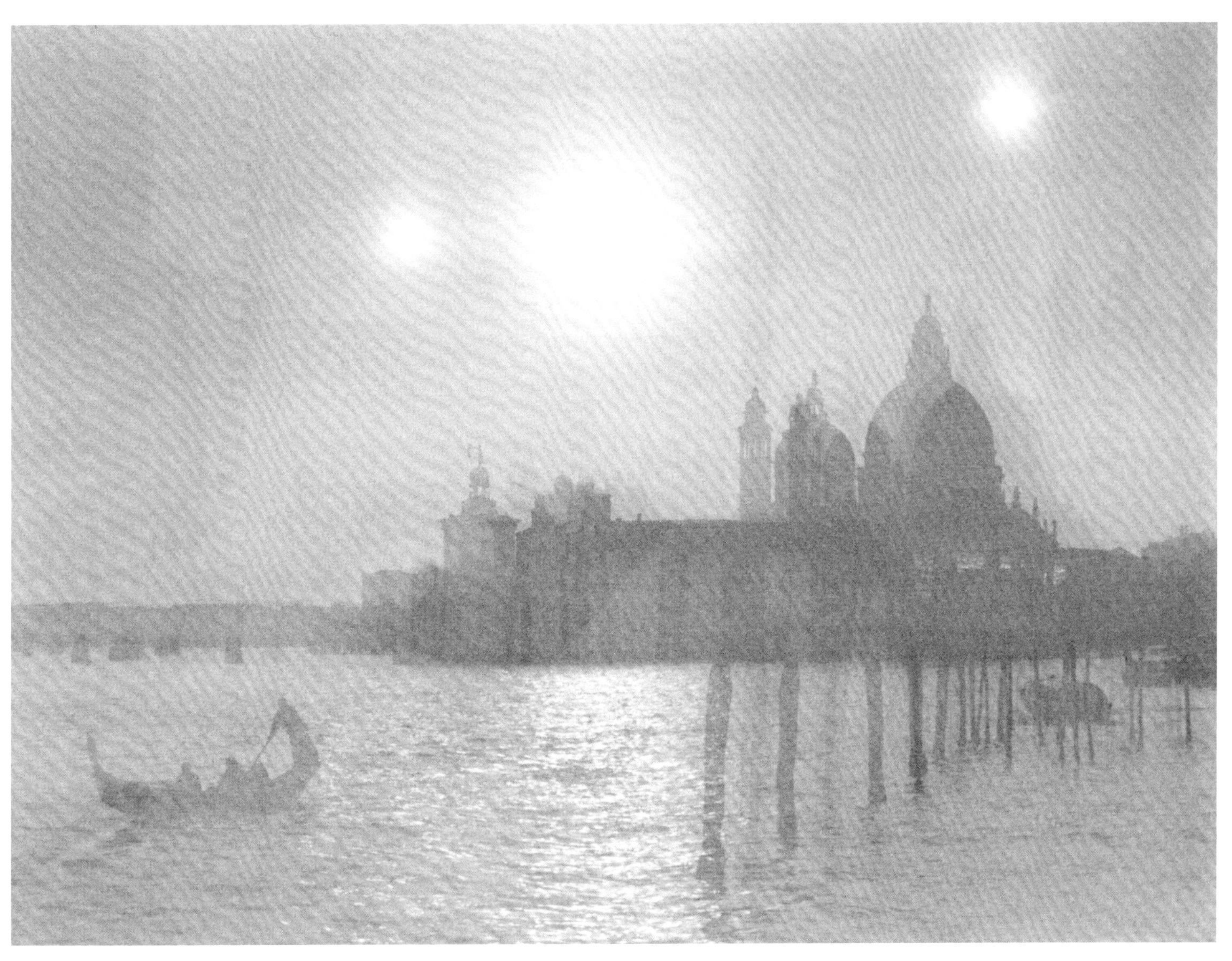

Our Backyard Treasure

Where could we go in 2021? The health club was closed. A quarantine hotel awaited me. Planes were mostly grounded. But always there remained the open road.

My wife and I woke up early, eager to take exercise, and walked up the narrow street behind my mother's house. The sun was just rising over the distant hills. The valley to one side of us was swathed in thick fog. Golden light began to flood the slopes in front of us.

We turned around and saw the Pacific shining in the distance. In the clear springtime air—no planes, so little smoke—we could almost count the ridges in the hills on the islands across the water.

Why ever think of flying to Cape Town or Capri or Rio when such wonders were right here? Down the road, twenty minutes from where my parents had been living for more than fifty years. I'd never walked to the end of that road till lockdown made it a necessity.

In the afternoons we walked along an empty beach ten minutes away and followed the flights of cormorants and pelicans, of sandpipers. Dolphins sometimes leaped thirty feet from where we strolled.

Michael drove down the road, too, and found this treasure not far from his home.

PI

Unmasked

The pandemic had us locked down, sheltering in place, isolated. Human interactions became reserved as we hid behind masks, kept our distance, and no longer recognized other people, except perhaps as potential contaminators. Travel was severely restricted. Cities and towns became strange, empty, and quiet. Pollution decreased. We were all startled and heartened by reports of dolphins returning to the empty canals of Venice. Nature continued on, even flourished in these few years where humans no longer trampled in their billions across the globe. A lesson to be learned and remembered: resilient earth is not so much at risk as we fragile humans.

During this curious time, I was kindly invited by the Portland landscape architects PLACE to visit the glorious Grandfather Oak on the empty Nike campus in Beaverton, Oregon. My wife and I drove from Seattle, Washington, almost alone on the usually busy freeways. It turned out to be a most welcome respite during that anxious period of virus paranoia. Unmasked, breathing freely, perhaps even smiling, the tree stood in all its glory, welcoming and open to a hug—not that I could even get my arms around its girth! After this first visit in 2021, Mamta and I made several more pilgrimages back to Beaverton, in all four seasons, to document this majestic Oregon oak (*Quercus garryana*), and I eventually made seventy-eight individual studies.

The pandemic changed, if only for a short time, our human dynamic. I like to think it brought us closer to nature, even if only for some brief moments. It brought me closer to the Grandfather Oak, for which I will always be grateful. I find it sobering to consider that this tower of sentient dignity had already been around for some three hundred years before I was born. It is equally comforting to imagine that, probably and hopefully, it will still be there, a noble symbol of longevity and strength, long after I fly with the angels.

MK

Grandfather Oak, Study 51, Beaverton, Oregon, USA, 2021

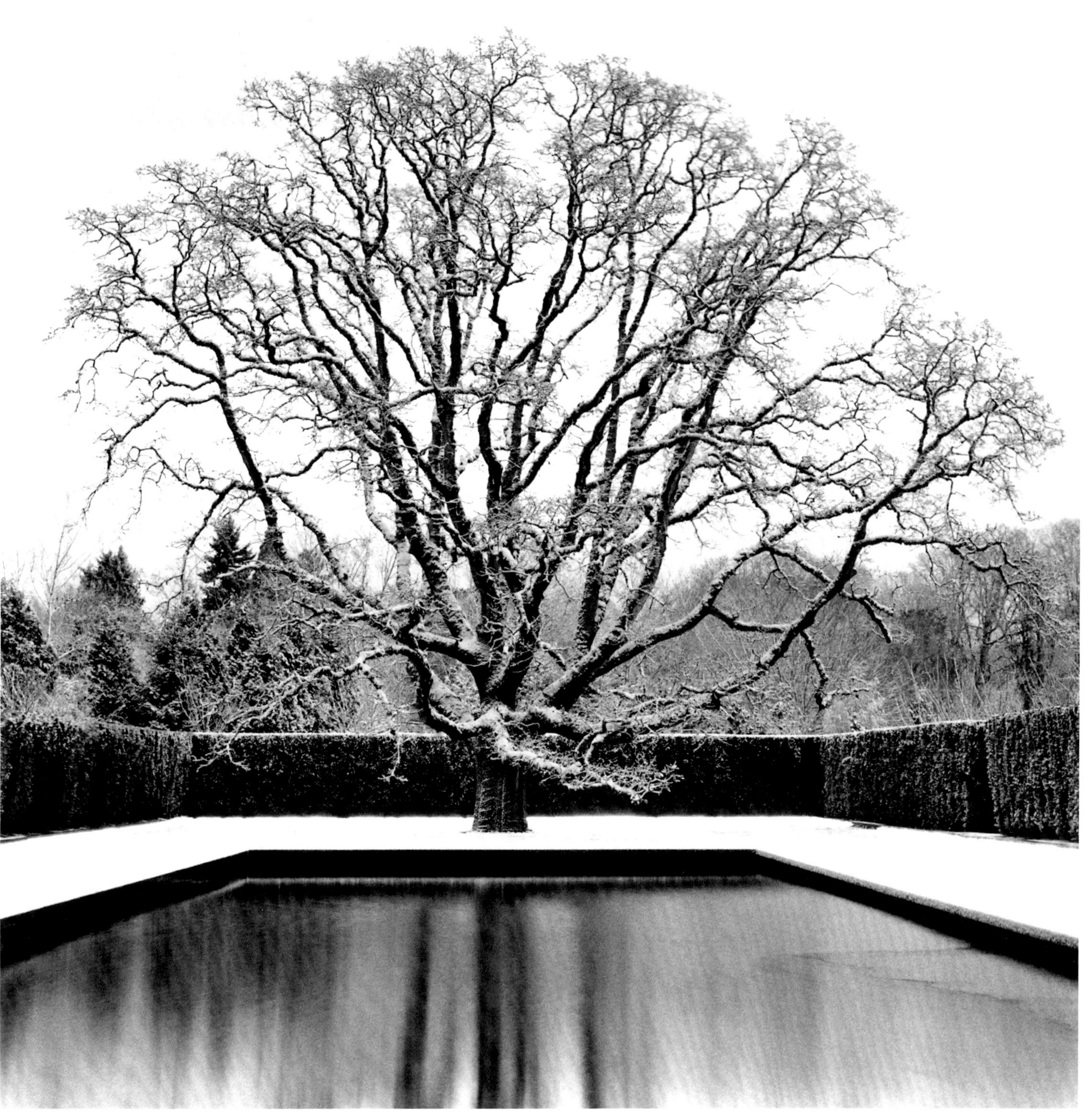

Waiting in the Dark

My wife and I like warm places. So, as good travelers, we flew up to Alaska in mid-January, when the high temperature was minus 40 (Centigrade or Fahrenheit, you ask? Please don't. The two scales converge at minus 40). We flew low over unbroken forests to stay in a lodge ninety-eight miles from the nearest road. We boarded a helicopter to fly out again, over icy rivers in the nothingness—auditioning for a Kenna photograph—after all planes out of the lodge were canceled. We learned that the little town of Fairbanks is crowded with Thai drive-thru restaurants, ensuring that every citizen can gobble down hot tom kha gai in the snow.

We visited a town called North Pole. We watched the first Trump inauguration. I recalled the time I'd stayed in a luxury camp next to Mount Denali that offered no electricity in its little cabins, no running water, and no indoor plumbing. I'd been told to keep an eye out for bears as I stumbled through the night to the outhouse nearby.

In the wall of the shack was a single heart-shaped hole though which I could see Alpenglow gilding the snowcaps.

Alaska, I saw, is a high chair for contemplating the lands below. It draws mystics, solitaries, adventurers, and misfits. People who long to live off the grid or at least at a safe distance from the madding crowd. The elements come to one there—in summer when the sun seems never to set and in the dark of winter—as almost nowhere else. From our high chairs, children again, we looked for the moon and waited for the coming of light.

PI

Distant Frontiers Close to Home

Visiting Alaska was a revelation. Flying from San Francisco to Anchorage I saw endless snow-covered mountains. Not daring to drive on icy roads, I had prebooked trains, boats, and buses to explore this vast, wild, frozen northern frontier. It was incredibly photogenic. White glaciers set against deep blue skies. Dark forests. Towering mountains. Roads that stretched to nowhere and everywhere. I observed wild bears out of the windows, and a host of other wildlife. I incessantly photographed, excited about what I saw through the camera lens. Looking back now, I am still bemused that the most interesting photograph was made just a few minutes' walk away from my hotel in downtown Anchorage.

There are many superb wildlife photographers, inspiring landscape photographers, admirable mountain photographers, all sorts of fine, skilled photographers. But, picking up a camera and making photographs doesn't necessarily translate into excellence in every field. Looking at my contact sheets, some months after photographing, I concluded that although I had made professional and competent black-and-white records of what was in front and around me, what I had seen was far more captivating, multifaceted, and attractive than my, dare I say it, boring copies. It was a humbling learning experience.

I try to photograph what I cannot see, suggestions more than detailed descriptions, the presence of absence, what is invisible, behind the veil. It is not for everyone. This dark tennis court netting, designed perhaps to shield players from cross winds, suggests a night sky. The crescent moon shape and line of white lights nudges us towards this metaphor. The vague outlines of an umpire's high chair gives an additional catalyst that helps us to imagine an alternate reality. This picture invades my mind, encourages questions, and continues to intrigue me. The other pictures I made, of the beautiful landscapes, gently invite me back to Alaska, to try again. Which, come to think of it, is OK too.

MK

High Chair, Anchorage, Alaska, USA, 1989

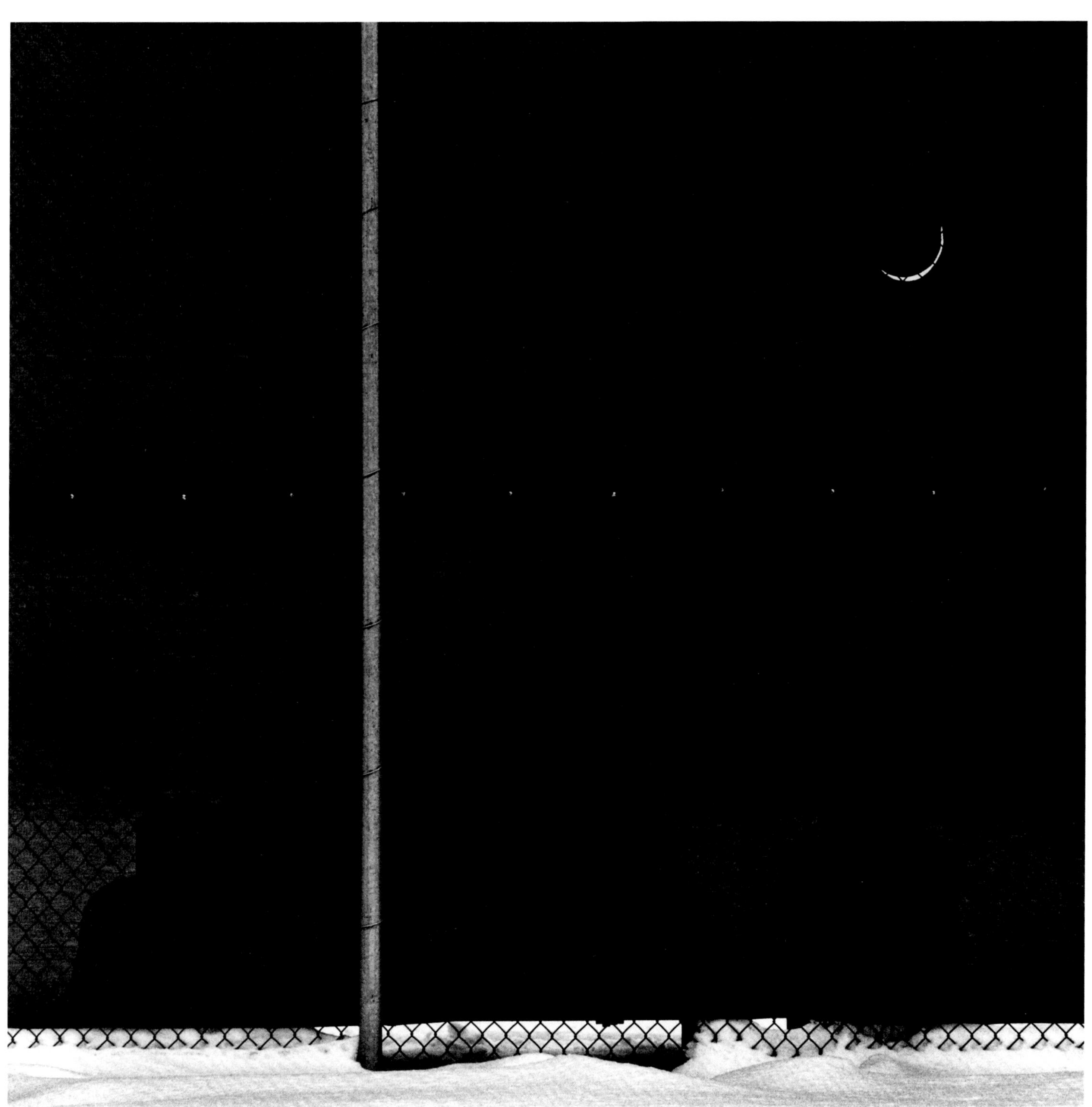

The Long and Winding Road

As I prepared to turn fifty, I assumed I'd begin settling down: I'd seen much of the world that summoned me, and it seemed time to explore the feathery fences within. How could I have guessed that I'd soon be in Jerusalem, its narrow alleyways winding this way and that like a never-ending argument? That, a year later, in a single month, I'd find myself for the first time in Varanasi, Jerusalem's Eastern cousin, and Mauritius and Galle, as well as in Beijing and Jaipur and (best of all) Narita, Japan, in the midst of its blue-skied New Year.

That I'd be walking across an Indian Ocean island with two untethered lions, wandering through the dark between bonfires burning bodies, that I'd be talking about Graham Greene in the middle of a bloody war, huge billboards on every side urging the locals towards slaughter?

Beauty and violence were chasing one another through the backstreets of Varanasi, the Old City of Jerusalem, Sri Lanka's tropical gardens like feuding sisters. Certainties were exploding like grenades.

Meanwhile, my life in Japan remained as calm and undisturbed as this field on the island to the north. If my twenties were a time of excited exploration, the second half of life, I saw, would be about stitching the moments together into something of a pattern, if never quite a meaning.

PI

The Ever-Giving Landscape

There was a time when I photographed in Hokkaido without a guide, in the middle of the winter. The wonder of it all is that I lived to tell the tale. Take this innocent-looking fence, climbing up a hillside in Teshikaga. I first saw it in 2002 when driving to see the famous Tsurui red-crowned cranes. Driving alone, I pulled off the main road and my car sunk deep into snow, the driver's side lifting off the ground. I struggled out of the car with my camera equipment and walked into the field for a closer view of the fence. In seconds the snow was up to my chest. I continued, but my cameras were soon soaking and useless. Then there was the scary 360-degree skid on an icy road, fortunately ending up in a snowbank, rather than off the side of a cliff. It is just not a good idea to photograph in a Hokkaido winter without the assistance of somebody who knows what they are doing. Enter from stage right Tsuyoshi Kato, kindly introduced by my assistant Mark Silva.

Tsuyoshi (aka Hokkaido Man) and I have worked together for over twenty years. He is the single reason why I can sing Yujiro Ishihara karaoke songs in Japanese, as well as continue to explore this wild and wonderful island of Hokkaido. Equipped with a four-wheel-drive vehicle and the know-how of what to do in treacherous conditions, Tsuyoshi has guided me to numerous remote and exquisite locations. If Hokkaido was Everest, he would be my Tenzing Norgay. *Domo arigato gozaimasu Tsu san.*

I continue to photograph this fence. One might think that little would change, yet each time something is different. Perspectives constantly alter, snow levels vary, and the light is never the same. Perhaps a new pattern and configuration appears, an arrangement of forms changes, distance contracts or lengthens to become ambiguous. The minimalism and sheer simplicity of the scene can transform three dimensions into two, and the sparse elements seem to make prints more like sumi-e ink paintings than photographs. I have printed nine studies so far, and fully anticipate a new one from this year's visit. It is a landscape that keeps giving.

MK

Hillside Fence, Study 6, Teshikaga, Hokkaido, Japan, 2007

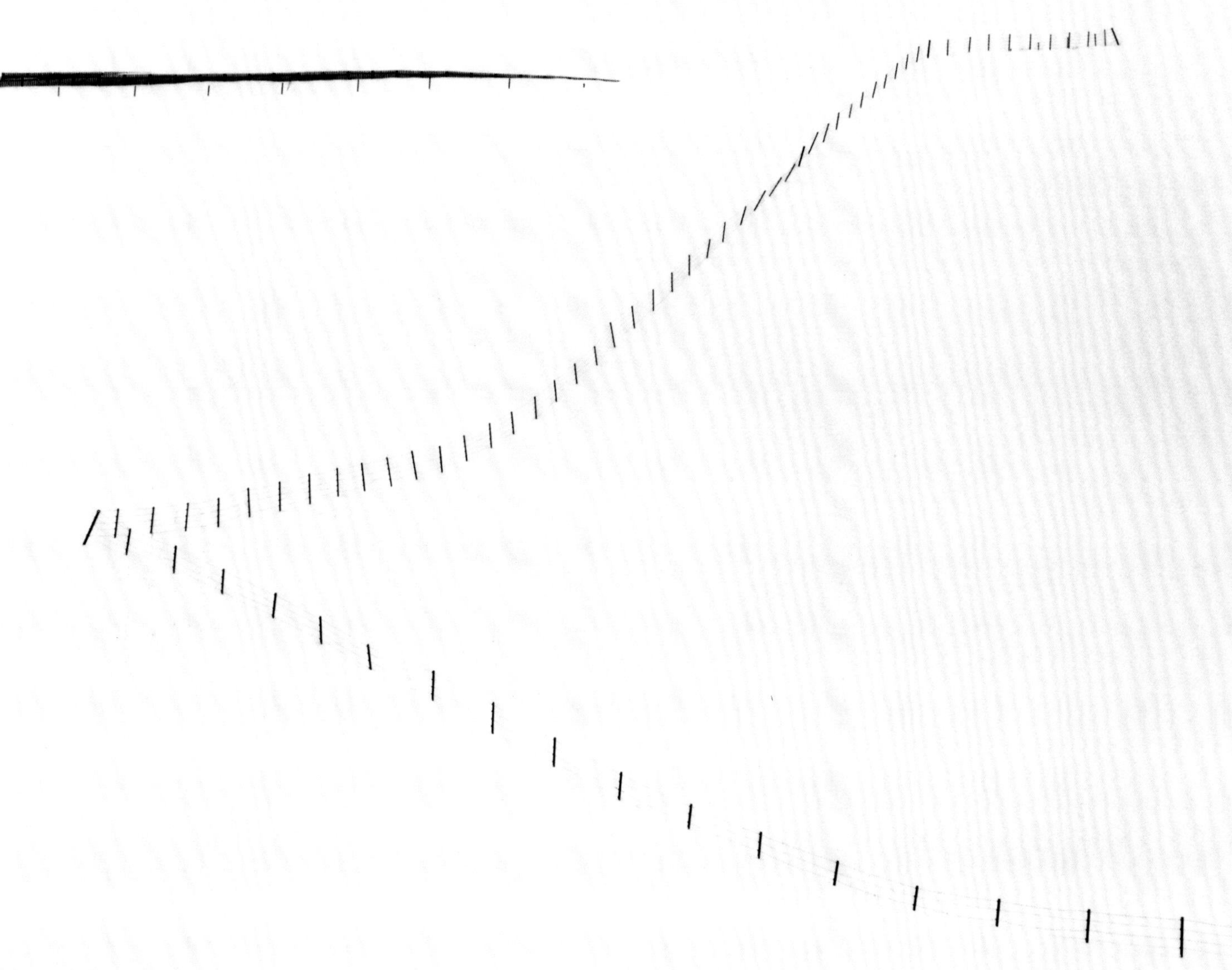

The Misty Path

This is the life I wish to lead: that's what I realized the minute I stumbled upon an exhibition of Henri Cartier-Bresson's work in Boston, in 1980. I hadn't known much about his photography before, but as I followed him around the world, a door swung open. I, too, could try to go to China, India, Japan, and if only I could keep my eyes open and fresh, I, too, might find wonders that last a second and forever. Even very close to home.

Over the next four decades, he was never far from my mind. I kept his address in the little black book I always carry with me, as talisman and protection. I spotted him once, at the annual Magnum party, and I came to know his photographer wife, Martine Franck, when both of us were spending time with the Dalai Lama. She pressed into my hands a little book, privately printed, showing the great observer of the twentieth century smiling irresistibly as he held onto one of the century's great figures of conscience, the leader of the Tibetans.

Cartier-Bresson referred to himself as an "accidental Buddhist," a perfect phrase for the other master who had also been educated at the Lycée Condorcet, Marcel Proust. He rejected fixed positions so he could remain open to what was in front of him. In many of his spirited, quizzical—elegantly shaped—transcriptions of eternity in an instant, I was convinced I could see an image of the man himself. One bright spring day in Kyoto, I pulled out from a shelf a huge collection of his immortal images. Right next to it were two books by another admirer—a fellow traveler—who here describes his own path between the trees.

PI

Don't Be Silly

When I first saw this road in France, with the tunnel of trees snaking off into a misty distance, I could only think of Henri Cartier-Bresson and his stunning 1986 Brie image of similar subject matter. I felt both the compunction to make an identical photograph, and the necessity to acknowledge the recognition. Looking through a maestro's eyes can be a fascinating way to see the world, and another perspective might take on a ring of familiarity if we follow in the footsteps of pathfinders.

Cartier-Bresson was one of the great masters of humanist photography, renowned for his astounding ability to capture split-second decisive moments of compositional grace from all around the world. For the most part, he photographed with a Leica camera and 35mm film, using split-second exposures. He had his negatives printed full frame and even included part of the black border as proof that he had not cropped the image. I dearly love his work, as do so many others, and deservedly so. I also choose to operate in a completely different way. For example, the famous Cartier-Bresson instant decisive moment is, for me, often an exposure of perhaps ten hours. I see the actions and movements of people as constant blurs, combining and accumulating into areas of tonality. I couldn't even imagine trying to photograph in the manner that Cartier-Bresson did. Which is all just a roundabout way of stating the obvious, that one can be profoundly influenced, indelibly impressed, in absolute awe of somebody's work and way of working, and choose to take a different path.

I should also add that standing on shoulders is one thing, lying in the middle of a country road on a misty morning is another. No matter how much you might love a particular photographer, there's really no need to be silly! Warmest thanks and kindest regards to you, Monsieur HCB.

MK

Homage to HCB, Study 2, Bretagne, France, 1993

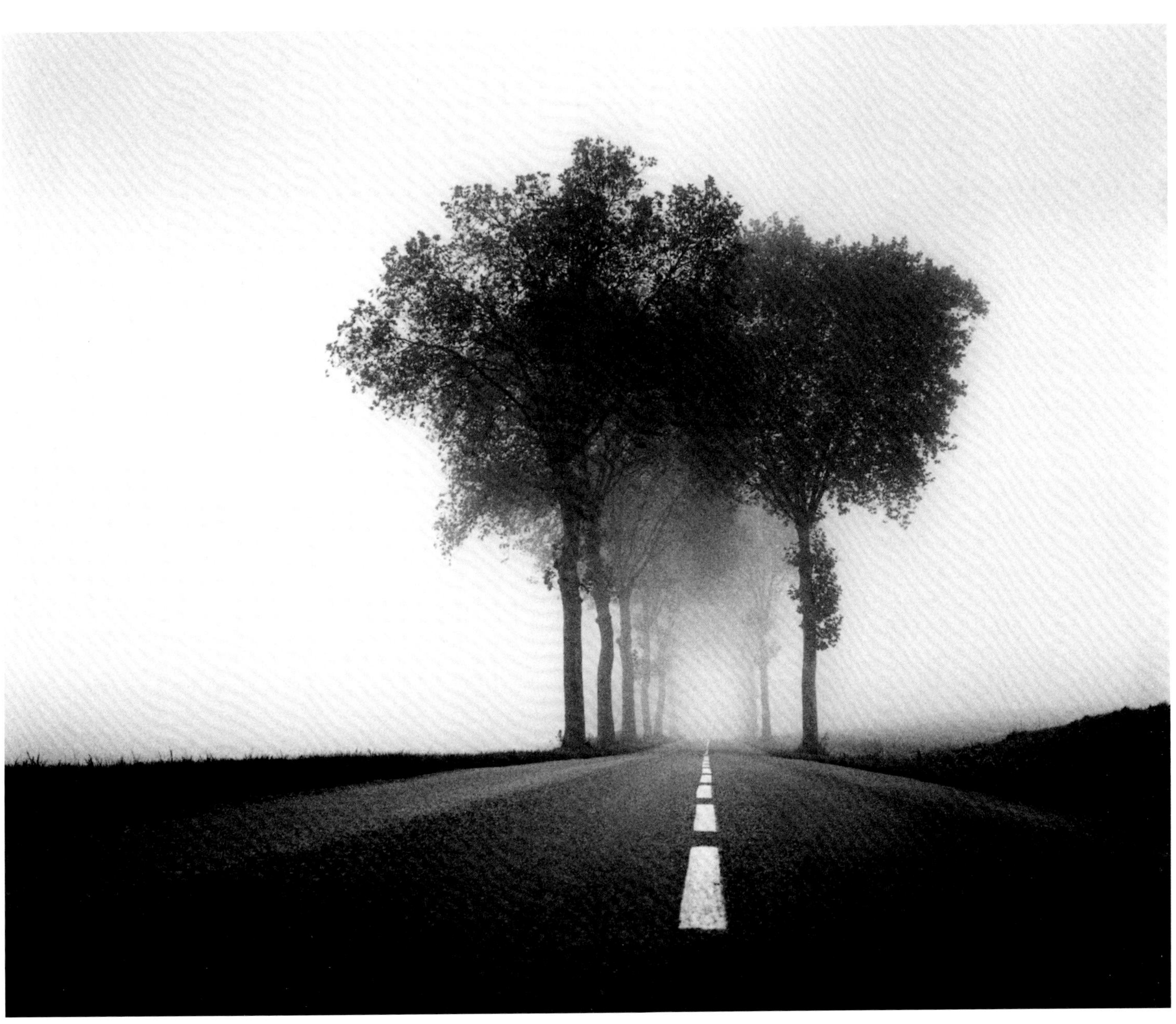

Journey to the East

This is a painting of a whole school of painting—or, rather, of a way of looking at art, a vision, an aesthetic, and an approach to life. I loved it the minute I saw it because all of East Asia lives here, in the mist, the negative space, the almost palpable silence of a landscape that looks to be nothing but mighty mountains, not a human in sight.

When viewers call Michael an Asian photographer, it's because of images such as this: he's not making pictures of Asia so much as images from within the heart of Asia. Of course he can give us very different portraits of streaking New York and swirling Rio de Janeiro and the dark concentration camps of Europe, but often he gives us an Asian perspective even when working in San Francisco or France.

When I began writing, I was full of words. You couldn't move in one of my pages for the torrent of allusions and ideas and references; there was no room for the reader, unless my poor victim consented to be spirited along by the bullet train of my prose.

But half a lifetime in Japan has stripped me of almost everything, so all I aim to write now is a version of this portrait: the emptiness wider than its subject, and almost everything left up to the viewer.

Not an assertion from writer or artist, but just the quietest invitation to a dance and an act of harmony.

PI

A Sea of Clouds

Huangshan, also known as Mount Huang or Yellow Mountain, situated in Anhui, China, rises 6,000 feet above sea level and has been the subject of innumerable paintings and works of literature. It is particularly known for its uniquely shaped granite peaks and the ubiquitous pine trees that grow right out of the rock faces. Cables cars now assist in the ascent, and thousands of tourists are able to visit. On my second journey there, the cable was unfortunately closed due to high winds and bad weather. My option was to climb close to 6,000 steps.

Fortunately, there were porters on call. Expecting a muscled warrior, I worried that the young, petite woman who proffered help would not be able to make the ascent while carrying my heavy cameras and luggage. There followed a humiliating lesson. Giving me a knowing wink, she picked up a long, thick wooden pole that became bowed on either end by the weight of my baggage, and began scampering her way up the mountain path. I followed as fast as I could, but would often hear her chatting and giggling away on her cell phone as she waited for me to catch up. She often had a lit cigarette in one hand and her phone in the other. I was in decent physical condition at the time, a marathon runner, but my legs would ache for days to come.

Once on the mountain, clouds and rain rolled in, visibility was limited, almost nonexistent at times, and I wondered if it was worth all the effort. As I climbed higher, above a moving sea of clouds, the scene suddenly transformed into a spellbindingly hypnotic, magical, once-in-a-lifetime experience. Clouds appeared and disappeared, constantly moving and changing. In this image, which reminds me of an ancient scroll, I imagine a vertical row of vermillion characters running down the right-hand side. What the writing says or means might be irrelevant, for it would be a suggestion or catalyst for a thousand and one magnificent possibilities.

MK

Huangshan Mountains, Study 6, Anhui, China, 2008

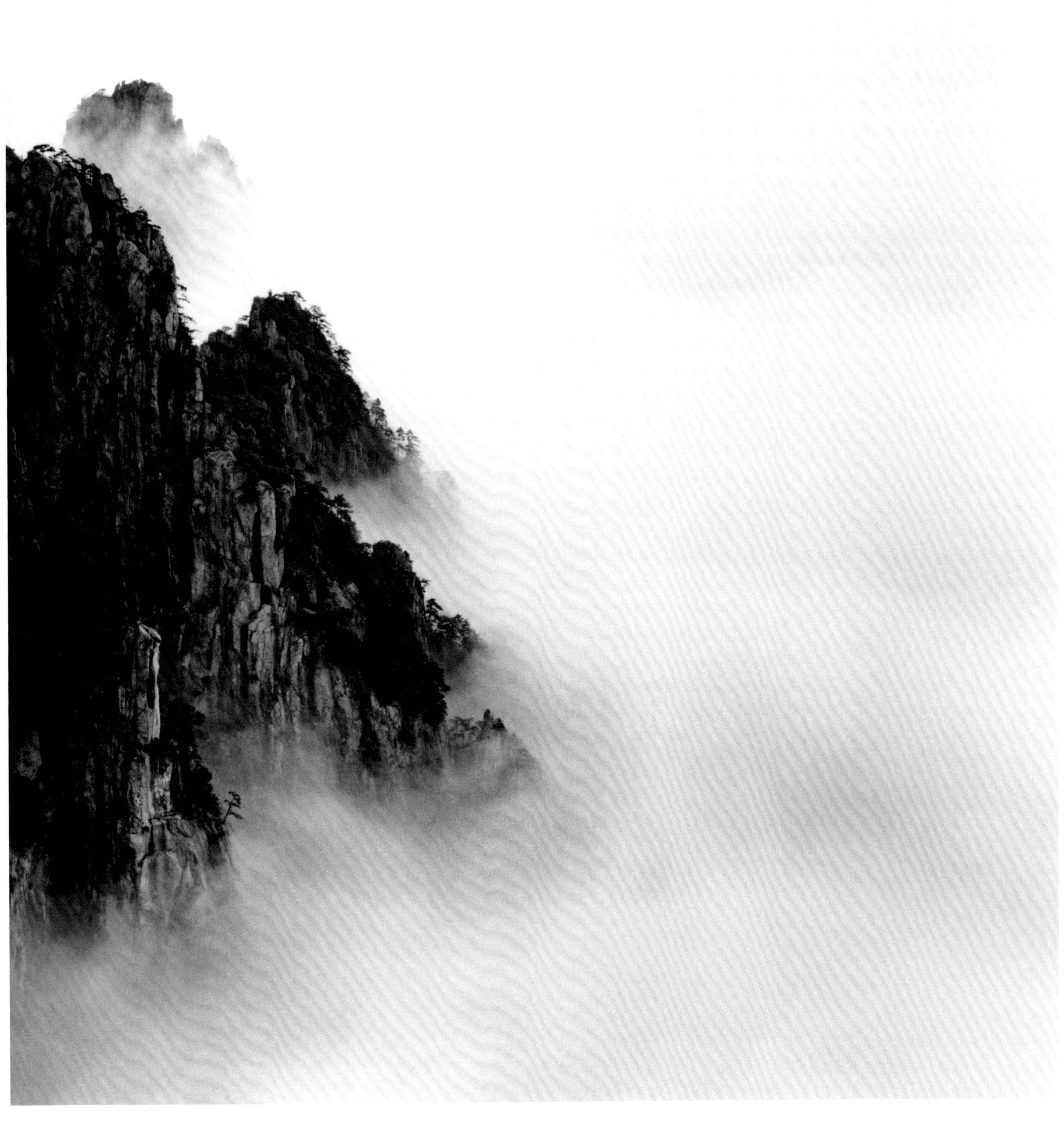

Taking Flight

To meet a Kenna photograph is to be spirited away to some forgotten land within, beyond the reach of words. It's to be stilled by the patience that lies behind the work, and to be moved, indefinably, by the geometry, the unwavering focus, the clarity, and the quiet from which such work emerges.

But in this case, I have to admit: it's the title that seizes me and makes this image take flight.

Like Michael, I'm entering the final act of life; I've completed almost seven decades and become ever more grateful for all I've been allowed to see and do. Were I to pray, it would consist of nothing but a sustained "Thank you!" and, perhaps, the silent hope that I might be permitted to live a little more.

Six weeks from now, I go to France and, this time, as never before, my hope is to travel at last to that magical church on its peak above the waters. I'll walk along the Paris streets I know by heart, remember the Vietnamese café outside of which I first set eyes on Michael and Mamta, see the sun sink above the Seine and watch elegant souls on their deck chairs with their books in the Jardin du Luxembourg.

But my prayer will be that I get to glimpse the cloisters that set the tone for the film *To the Wonder*. And, more deeply, that I never grow too old to see the world, or to watch a hope take wings. Michael's lens tells me that you don't have to go to a holy place to have a prayer.

PI

Silence Is Golden

In nomine Patris et Filii et Spiritus Sancti. In the name of the Father, and of the Son, and of the Holy Ghost. As a boy, this was the start of every prayer, the beginning of every Latin mass. It was recited at baptisms and pretty much every Catholic ritual I attended. It was also included in the catechism we had to learn, the staple of every child's church education. The concept of the holy trinity—three persons in one god—was accepted as divine dogma. The holy ghost, now more often referred to as the holy spirit, is/was often depicted as a flying white dove.

In the boarding school I attended, every night we had a long period of silence, Magnum Silentium, from the night bell at 8:30 p.m. until after grace before meals at around 8 a.m. I attribute much of my appreciation and requirement of quiet, solitary time to these enforced rules. I am sure they also greatly influenced how I photograph. On several later occasions, I have stayed in silent retreats with Benedictine monks in their monastery atop Mont-Saint-Michel in France.

On late afternoons, what resembles an extremely busy market village empties out very fast on Mont-Saint-Michel. There are only a few places to stay, so it becomes quiet, calm, dark, and solitary at night. The abbey and monastery are also closed to visitors, and if you are lucky enough to be on the inside of the locked doors, the place becomes a treasured and precious sanctuary. A small ascending walkway of steps leads from the monks' living quarters to the abbey's front entrance. On my first day there, I quietly closed the monastery door behind me, looked through my handheld camera viewfinder, composed, and made this picture. Not a white dove, but surely an invitation to prayer.

MK

 Invitation to Prayer, Mont-Saint-Michel, France, 1994

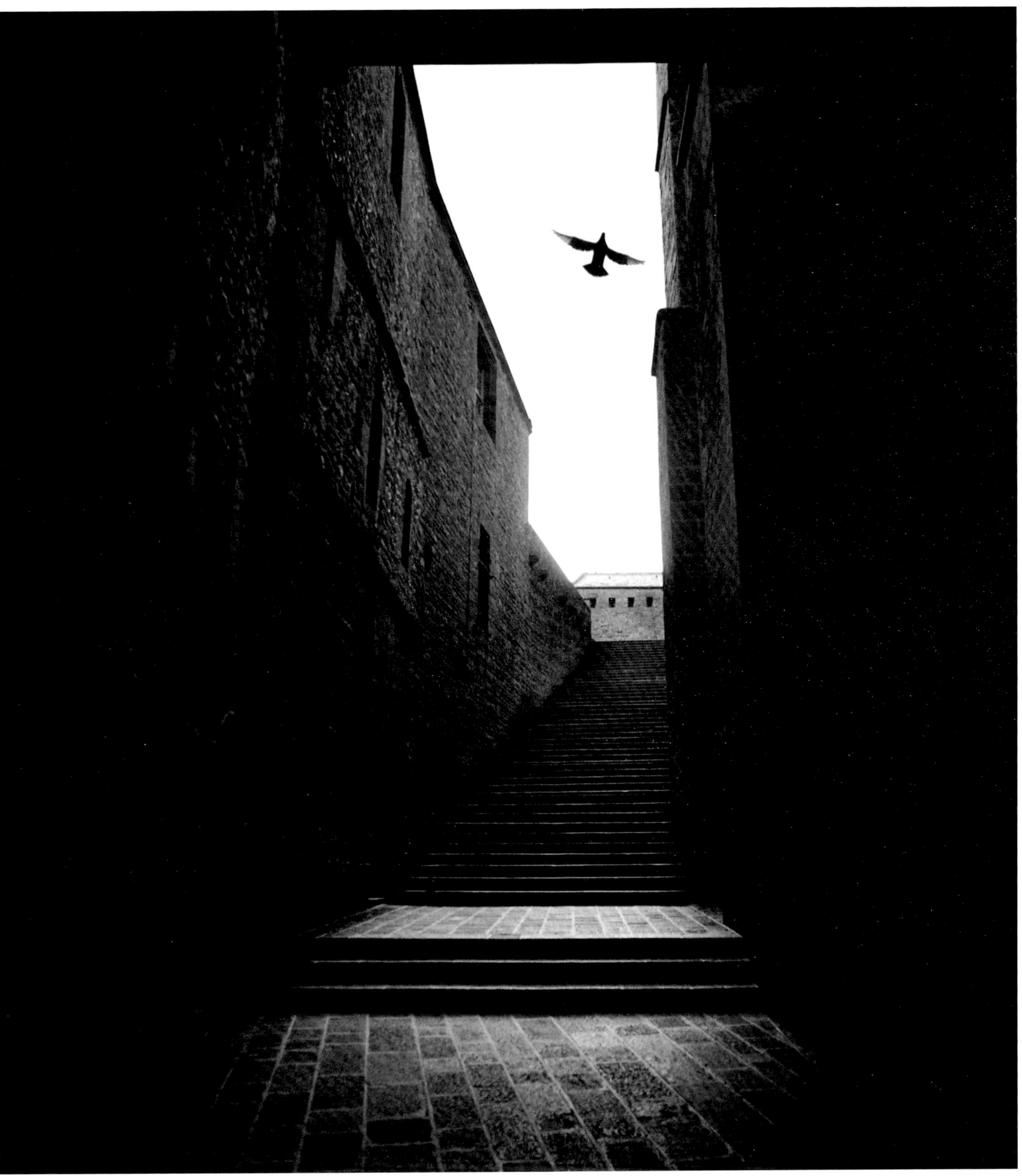

What Cannot Be Suppressed

Everyone will see a different outburst in this image—I like to think it reflects the birth of Michael's first grandchild, coming to life in Geneva, nine years after he made this effusive picture.

I recall the first picture I'd seen of the celebrated photographer: sporting a bright smile as he received his first Covid injection, glasses off, sleeves rolled up. Before long, he was writing to me from his quarantine in Geneva and walking the streets like the marathon-running contemplative he is. Then I heard the cry of this unmet friend's joy across the world: his daughter's daughter was out in the world!

A fountain expresses joy overwhelming as few things in life ever can: an uprush of emotion, an overflow of delight. For me, too, the pandemic brought many blessings: most of fifteen quiet months with my mother as she passed through the final seasons of her life. The chance to see wonders down the road. The writer's retreat of my dreams (no planes to board, nowhere to hurry to).

It was a time of worldwide sorrow and grief, but it reminded us that grief is never incompatible with causes for gratitude and moments of beauty.

A child is born, a ninety-year-old mother passes on. Life refuses to be reduced to one thing or another. The fountain keeps bursting out, even at a time of loss.

PI

Light and Dark Days

By 2019, I had photographed in over forty countries, with others waiting in my imaginary Green Room. The Covid pandemic changed everything. After over a year of sheltering in place, I flew from Seattle to Geneva for the birth of my first grandchild, Freya. Permission to travel arrived only after applying for special dispensation from Swiss authorities. I provided evidence of two Covid vaccinations and four Covid tests. The subsequent journey was strange and unique in an almost empty plane. The transit terminal in Frankfurt airport, usually packed, was deserted except for immigration control, and there were no passport or customs checks when I arrived in Geneva.

A requirement for entering Switzerland was that I would spend ten days of solitary quarantine in a rented apartment, wearing an electronic monitor at all times. Then, I would be allowed out, fully masked, keeping an appropriate social distance from others. My daughter Olivia and her husband Joachim left plenty of supplies on my doorstep, and every day, via Zoom, my wife Mamta would guide my cooking to make sure I had excellent dinners. For exercise, I walked endlessly around the apartment. During this time of isolation, I wrote about my seminary school experiences, subsequently published by Prestel as *St. Joseph's College, Upholland*. Looking back, I found it all quite magical.

On the eleventh day, and after another Covid test, I was finally allowed to hug my very pregnant daughter and her husband. We enjoyed a hilarious and happy dinner together, perhaps laughing a little too much, for later that same night, off they went to the maternity hospital. Dearest Freya was born the next day and I began my next period of quarantine, for I was not allowed into the hospital due to Covid protocols.

While the excitement and drama unfolded, I took long walks, each one inevitably leading to the conspicuous *Jet d'Eau*, which I regarded as an old friend, having photographed it on many previous occasions. Someday, I hope to print all the studies I have, but in the meantime, this one, made seven years before Freya's arrival, serves to remind me of those surrealistic days of dark and light, sadness and hope, tragedy and celebration.

MK

Jet d'Eau, Study 1, Geneva, Switzerland, 2012

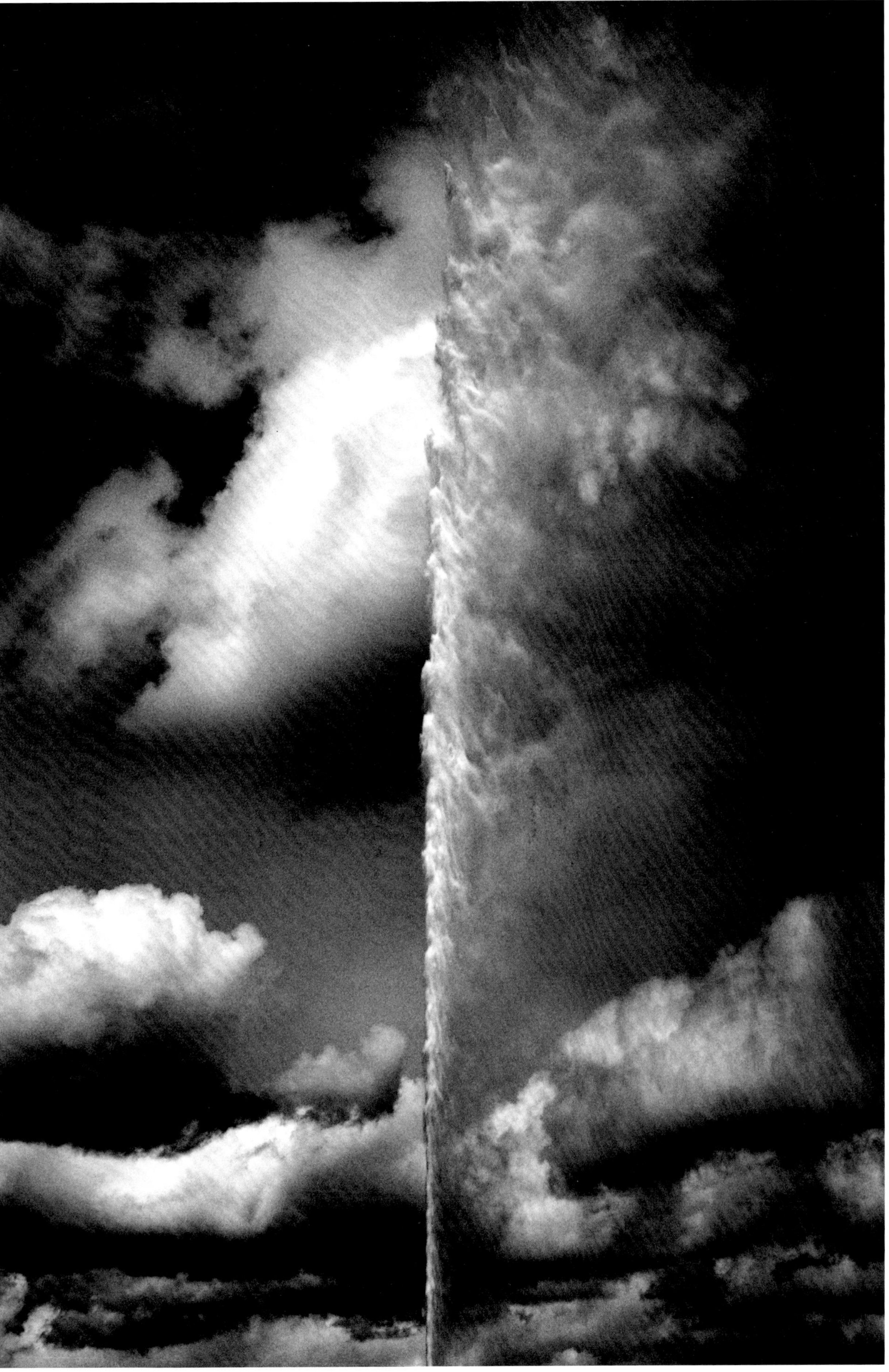

The Journey Is the Destination

A Michael Kenna photograph teaches one proportion. This image is, in its way, a sibling to the other one here of two tiny figures reduced to almost nothing as they walk above that commanding boulder at Avebury Stone Circle. My life as a traveler is defined too often by the ship I'm waiting to board, the plane at the gate, the car idling outside the house. The places that await me obscure the places at my feet.

But here all our attention is drawn to the stones that lead up to the ship. The days of preparation, which can sometimes become the highlight of a journey. The sights to be seen as you're planning for your takeoff. The jagged path that leads to what you hope will be a straight line.

Sometimes, as here, those plans give out. You never reach the ship. But no time has been wasted. Ask me about the trips I had to cancel—or postpone—and you'll hear about some of the treasures I found in their place. They may be as textured, as real, even as striking as these stepping stones that lead towards a vessel of adventure you never reach.

PI

Balearic Sea Dreams

Pathways, boardwalks, roads, railway lines, fences that lead you over a hill. I imagine them all as invitations to move forwards, sideways, even backwards, to discoveries and experiences, as ticking clocks measure a day unfolding into night and back into day. I am a sucker for these elements, as well as any suggestions of visual and/or physical travel. I find lines of trees disappearing into the distance to be irresistible. Add a little mist into the equation, and I'm gone, lost in my imagination.

These giant rocks point out into the Balearic Sea and then turn a little to the left, inviting us to follow, to perhaps leap from one stone surface to another before diving into the inviting water where we could swim over to the waiting ship on the horizon. That is one of the many ways we could interpret this photograph, although I can barely stay afloat in water, never mind swim that distance, so the reality might be completely different for me. That's OK. Imagination is all.

Mallorca is well known for tourism, but here we see no people. Photographers, after all, have no necessity to record and/or describe what is actually in front of them. They are, or can be, like the writer I am privileged and honored to share this book with, also storytellers who choose to observe and select vignettes of life, before weaving personal interpretations, suggestions, and extrapolations in and out of their worldly tales.

MK

 Jetty and Waiting Ship, Palma, Mallorca, Spain, 2017

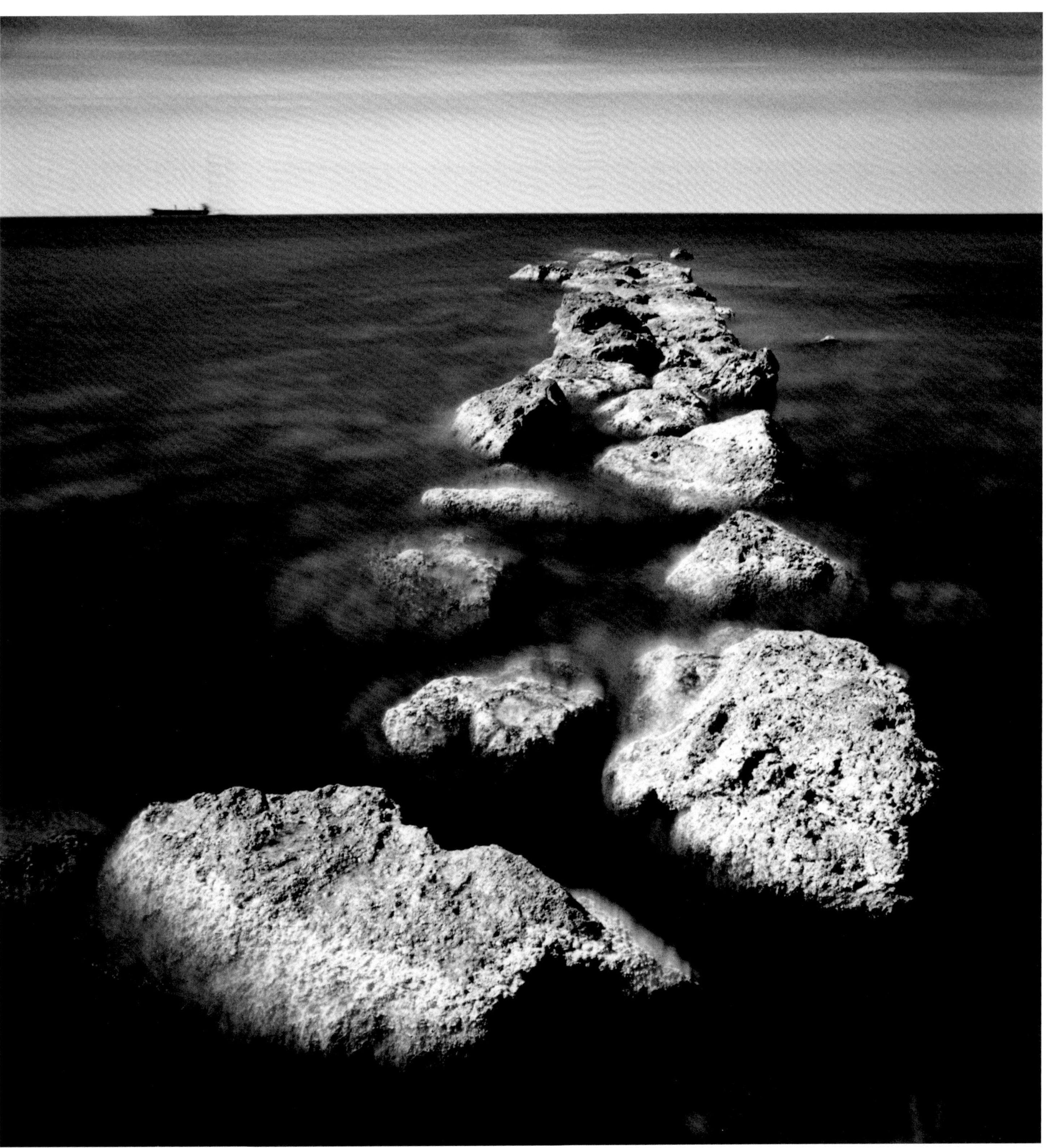

The Branch of Unknowing

One hot summer night, my grandmother-in-law was walking home from the public bath near her home under the fox shrine known as Fushimi Inari. She was feeling carefree, cozy, warm as she glanced at a willow tree along the lane. Underneath the willow stood a ravishingly beautiful woman.

She wondered, entranced, why the woman was standing there, almost beckoning, until she glimpsed, at the woman's back, a tail. This was a fox-woman, the legendary creature of Japanese folktales who lures people towards who knows what.

She was so startled that she ran back home, leaving her sandals in the street.

Trees are our friends, especially in Japan. But last week, in Kanazawa, I saw one that resembled a witch; impossible not to see in its branches the gnarled hands of someone old whose presence bodes no good.

Many of the most celebrated cherry trees in Japan seem to be weeping, as do the willows along the canals of the entertainment quarter.

This tree may be completely innocent. But it's a tonic to remember that spirits, like gods, wear two faces. Their power lies in the fact of all we cannot know or see.

PI

Kenna's Tree

When I was a wee boy, my brothers and I had our favorite trees in the local Victoria Park, right across from where we lived on Birchfield Road. Some of my first memories are of being pushed in a pram through this park by my sister Pat. My brothers, Peter, Francis, Anthony, and Vincent, climbed these trees and spent time in their branches. They called out to each other and made up imaginary scenarios from which we could not escape without being eaten alive. I befriended trees at an early age.

I first met this Japanese oak in 2002 on the banks of Kussharo Lake. It reminded me of the stooping old ladies I had observed in the Japanese countryside who spent years in fields, picking rice or other crops. I made a first portrait of the tree and returned on many subsequent years to visit and make further pictures. Sadly, the tree was cut down in 2009. Situated in a campground, it had lured people to climb it for years, to sit on branches and look out at the lake. I suppose the manager of the site decided it was unsafe. The demise of the tree was reported in a Hokkaido newspaper. Somehow it had become known as "Kenna's Tree." Despite my sadness, this association still makes me smile.

Time passes, change inevitably occurs, friends come and go, and yet, in a curious way, things stay the same. I have such fond memories of the secluded winter hideout where the lovely Kussharo Lake Tree lived, that I have since returned many times, to walk, listen, remember, and photograph. The Dalai Lama tells us that it is only after we accept death that we can fully appreciate life. I understand that trees have their own lifespans; they come and go, and it is the way of the world. I am equally sure that certain trees, as certain people, never really leave us.

MK

Kussharo Lake Tree, Study 17, Kotan, Hokkaido, Japan, 2007

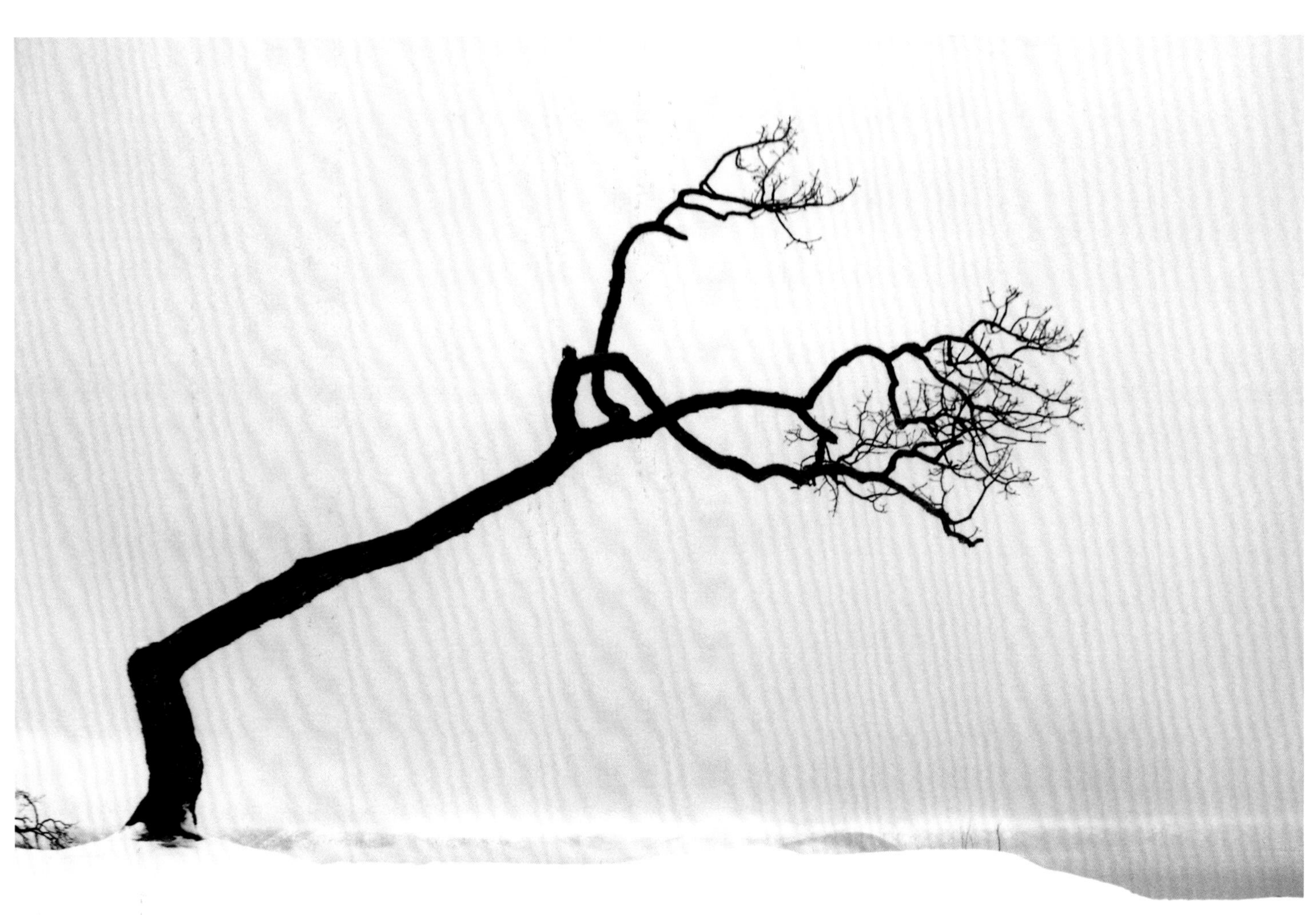

The Other Direction

Whenever I go to Hong Kong, I make it my practice to walk along the waterfront in Kowloon as the sun sets. Over more than forty years, I've seen the city through a torrent of changes; the showpiece spectacle of the lights across the harbor seems the perfect way to register all that shifts, the constant surge of energy.

Lovers from every continent pose and click in front of the illuminated high-rises, the discreet blackness around the Peak suggesting that the real power lies in the shadows. Vendors shuffle past, knowing there's no more lucrative open-air market to be found. Workers on their day off take dinner together on the steps, telling themselves their lives aren't entirely bad; the city can still put on a dazzling show, whatever furies it's covering up.

Very soon every inch of space along the walkway is claimed, excited couples posing for selfies, proud families commemorating their moment of glory in a flashbulb's blast. Here is the life so much of the world aspires to, even if it can be grasped, only for a moment, one night in a foreign city.

The year of protests in the streets, I saw two local men, cameras on tripods, with their backs to me as I walked up and down beside the water. They were looking in the opposite direction from every other lens and eager clicker. Not towards the sparkle of blue and red and yellow on the corporate headquarters, but towards the grimy clamor and chaos of the streets of Tsim Sha Tsui. Just as Michael says above, quoting from Ansel Adams: the point of art is to look and stand before what the rest of us hurry past. To face the opposite direction.

PI

Kowloon to Cotton Tree Drive

The rooms were tiny and the walls paper-thin. Nylon bedsheets were emblazoned with all-too-familiar Disney characters. The shower was a hose pipe sticking out from the wall, and drinking water was supplied in recycled plastic Coca-Cola bottles. Arriving in Hong Kong after a fifteen-hour flight from San Francisco was surrealistic. The Nazraeli Press publisher, Chris Pichler, had assured me that he had booked rooms for us in a charming guest house. We were there to press check *Monique's Kindergarten*, our first book together, in 1997, being printed in nearby Dongguan in mainland China. Now we were on the fourteenth floor of the Mirador Mansions in Kowloon, and it was Hong Kong noisy and stiflingly hot. Sticky, disheveled, and jet-lagged, after a short, sleepless night we met outside the one rather aromatic corridor toilet, and decided to do a runner. Finding a hotel close by, Chris and I agreed to meet for breakfast. After luxuriating in a long hot shower, I dressed and left my room. Chris looked at me strangely, appearing a bit surprised, before gently pointing out that my hair was still full of wet shampoo...

Hong Kong incites vivid memories of singular sounds, smells, vibrant colors associated with this twenty-four-hour city, jampacked with buildings, roads, traffic, cranes, and construction, teeming with humanity. My association started with that first visit. Fourteen years later, I married my lovely wife Mamta at the Cotton Tree Drive Marriage Registry, which certainly added to an already extensive collection of memories. Of course, it is always possible to discover another side of Hong Kong—quieter, calmer, more meditational, away from the constant hustle-bustle of the familiar industrial/financial metropolis. It can be discovered under the giant Buddha, or at the Peak in the early morning, or on the various sparsely populated islands dotted around Hong Kong. I hope this photograph, made on Lantau Island at dusk, helps point the way.

MK

Last Light, Tai-O, Lantau Island, Hong Kong, 2007

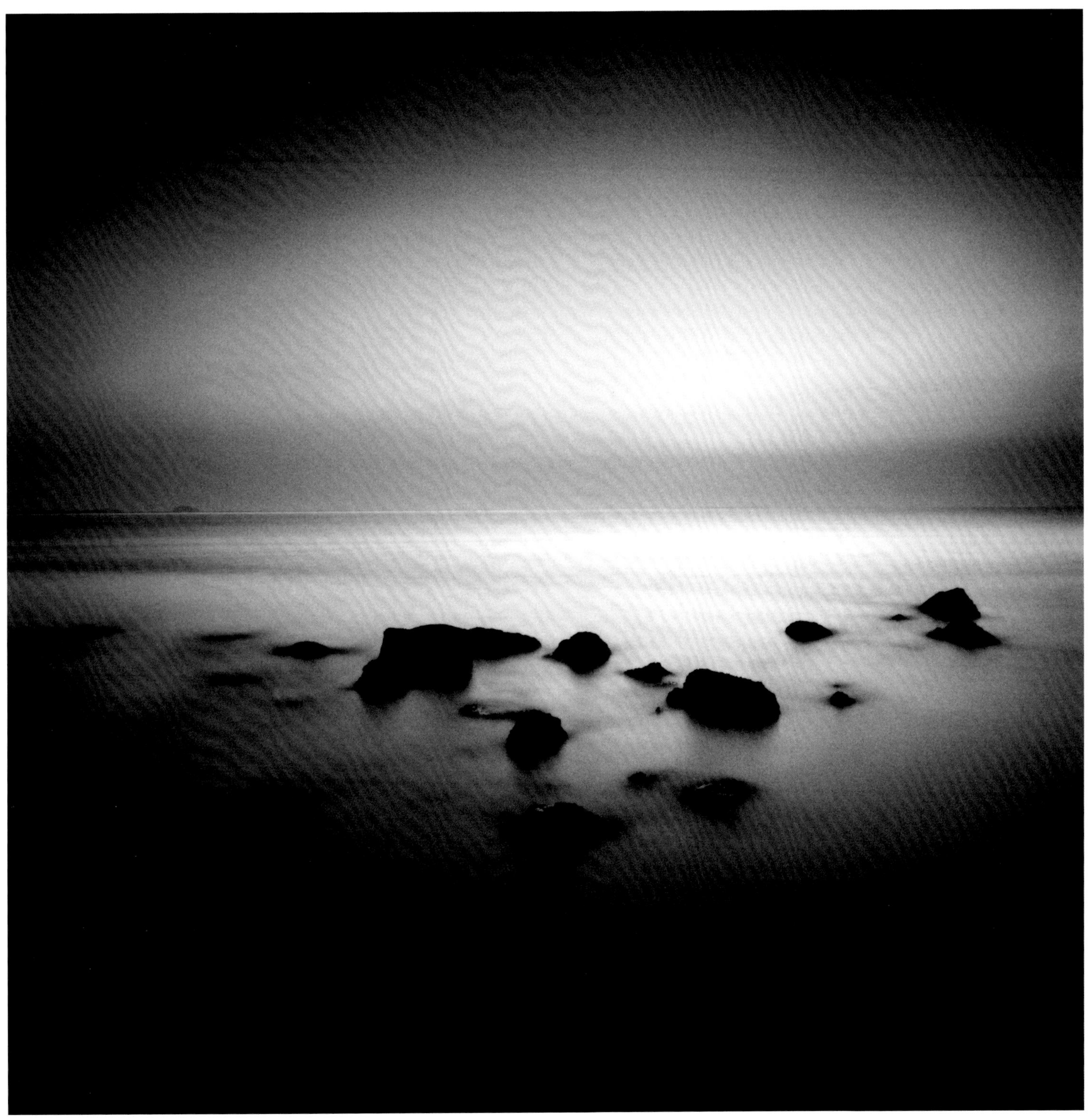

The Search for the Beyond

What do we seek in all our travels? Often, I think, it's that point of light, a small explosion, where the rainbow touches the earth again. That legendary spot on the distant horizon where rumor likes to place a pot of gold.

The "unknown," as we call it, or the unexpected. The inapprehensible. The fact we can't lay eyes on it gives our imaginations infinite scope. I knew what I wasn't looking for every time I felt the wings of a plane begin to turn and the engine begin to rev up, and it was simply everything that I might have known already.

To come upon a modern society where there was no television on Thursdays (Iceland) and a remote Himalayan kingdom, Bhutan, where there were no traffic lights in the capital; to sail around an Antarctic Peninsula where I am just a dot—or to alight in a place, in almost any country, where I am an exotic: in every case, I'm reminded that the world is much larger than our ideas of it, or our expectations.

Now that I have been lucky enough to see quite a bit, I realize that maybe the rainbow is enough. Just to witness that occasional miracle, even outside my home, moves me to gasp. Nothing at the far end of it can ever match what I'm gazing at right now.

PI

Alchemists, Conjurers & Magicians

Rainbows are so incredibly colorful and beautiful, fleeting and fragile, treasured gifts when they appear, full of promise, inciting wonder and awe in any lucky viewer. I have photographed many, with limited success. However, I do feel as though I have spent my whole photographic life chasing the metaphorical pots of gold associated with rainbows. If we agree that a fundamental principle of photography is the suspension of rational belief in favor of an acceptance of illusion, then I think it is reasonable to regard whatever we photographers track down and photograph to be—well, pots of gold.

A photograph of a tree is, of course, not a tree. It is a reference and catalyst for us to imagine a tree, and the same is true no matter what the subject matter is. René Magritte spelled this out clearly in his famous quote: "Ceci n'est pas une pipe," regarding his painting of a pipe. Similarly, an arrangement of black and white silver salts, suspended in gelatin and coated on a two-dimensional paper surface, is precisely what it is, not what it suggests. I sometimes think it takes a degree of hubris to purposely reduce our five-sense multidimensional world into a monochromatic two-dimensional rectangle and expect others to be interested. Yet, this is what I do for a living, aided and abetted by a little darkroom alchemy to help the process along. Perhaps photographers should be reclassified as practicing conjurers and magicians, for we essentially deal in illusions, which require an acceptance between photographer and viewer to see imaginary pots of gold rather than mere pieces of paper.

I remain extremely appreciative that I accidentally entered a puzzling and fascinating profession, and ever so grateful that viewers continue to freely participate in this curiously odd magic show.

MK

Late Afternoon Rainbow, Dunalley, Tasmania, Australia, 2013

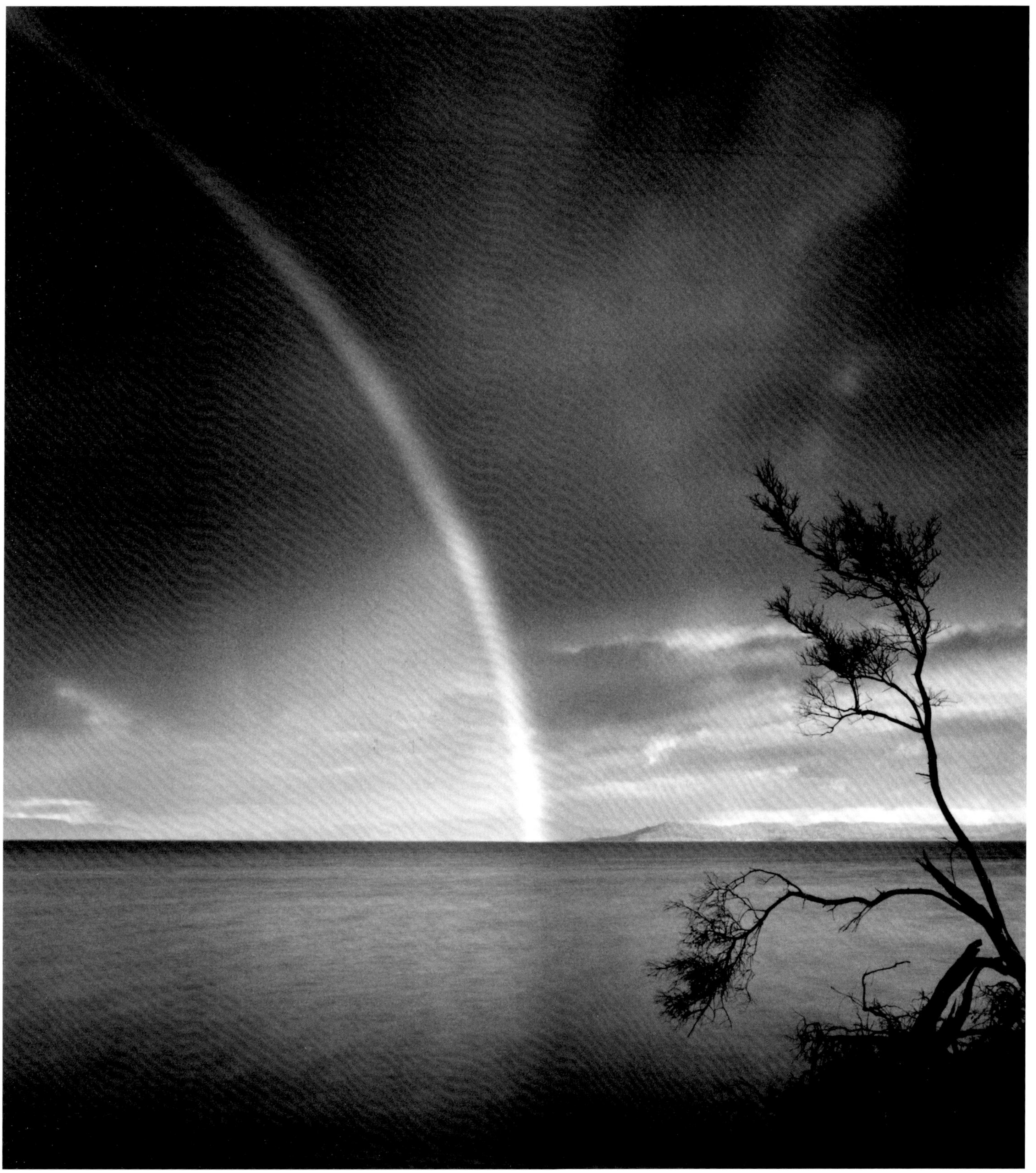

The Hideout in the Woods

This image is for me one of the priceless, timeless works of Michael Kenna that gives us a world within. All my life, I sometimes think, has been spent searching for this pavilion in France, the lost paradise that the “grand Meaulnes” keeps seeking out in the novel that held me captive at sixteen.

To write, I often tell friends, is to make a daily commute to a cabin in the woods. You sit there, in silence, alone—it might almost be your darkroom—and you prepare yourself for the day to come, process the hours just passed, gather your resources. It hardly matters what, if anything, issues from the stillness; this is your meditation hut.

In time—not long after Michael found this sanctuary—I came upon a small space above the sea in California. Far from the empty room I sought out in Kyoto in 1987, but full of what the Buddha meant when he spoke of seeking out a refuge from anger and confusion and greed.

My two homes, in a life of movement, have become the hermitage in the wilderness that stands above the busy highway, apart from it, and my two-room apartment in the middle of Nowhere, Japan, a secret monk’s cell. What do they look and feel like? I refer you to this picture.

PI

Presence of Absence

Le Désert de Retz is a unique eighteenth-century folly garden, situated in Chambourcy, France. It was left abandoned for years before being renovated and restored in the early 1990s. I had the opportunity to visit before that restoration began. The buildings and monuments were still derelict, the gardens and trees overgrown, and it was not yet open to the public. I felt a strong presence of absence. Maybe ghosts still lived there! The place exuded atmosphere and I happily and eagerly photographed.

Returning a few years later, after the restoration, I saw and felt a difference. Structures had been rebuilt and the gardens manicured. But, it wasn’t just the outer appearance that had changed. More palpably, the overall atmosphere of time suspended had as well. The past felt brushed away and the spirits of Le Désert de Retz had moved on. Or perhaps they were just hiding. In any case, I did not feel the same enthusiasm.

More recently, I attended a book signing event at Paris Photo, an annual international gathering of photography print dealers, galleries, photographers, and interested people. It was housed in the refurbished and resplendent Grand Palais. The whole place was jam-packed. I left feeling exhausted and depleted. Perhaps it was partly due to jet lag, as I had just flown in from Seattle. The morning after, I took a long walk along the Seine, finding my way to the glorious church of Saint-Gervais-Saint-Protais. I entered this quiet space and subsequently spent a solitary hour, listening to silence, observing shadows, and experiencing its charged atmosphere. When I went back out onto the streets of Paris, I felt recharged and renewed. I do not like to make generalized conclusions, but I suspect these contrasting experiences might shed some light on my photographic interests and proclivities.

MK

 Le Désert de Retz, Study 21, Chambourcy, France, 1988

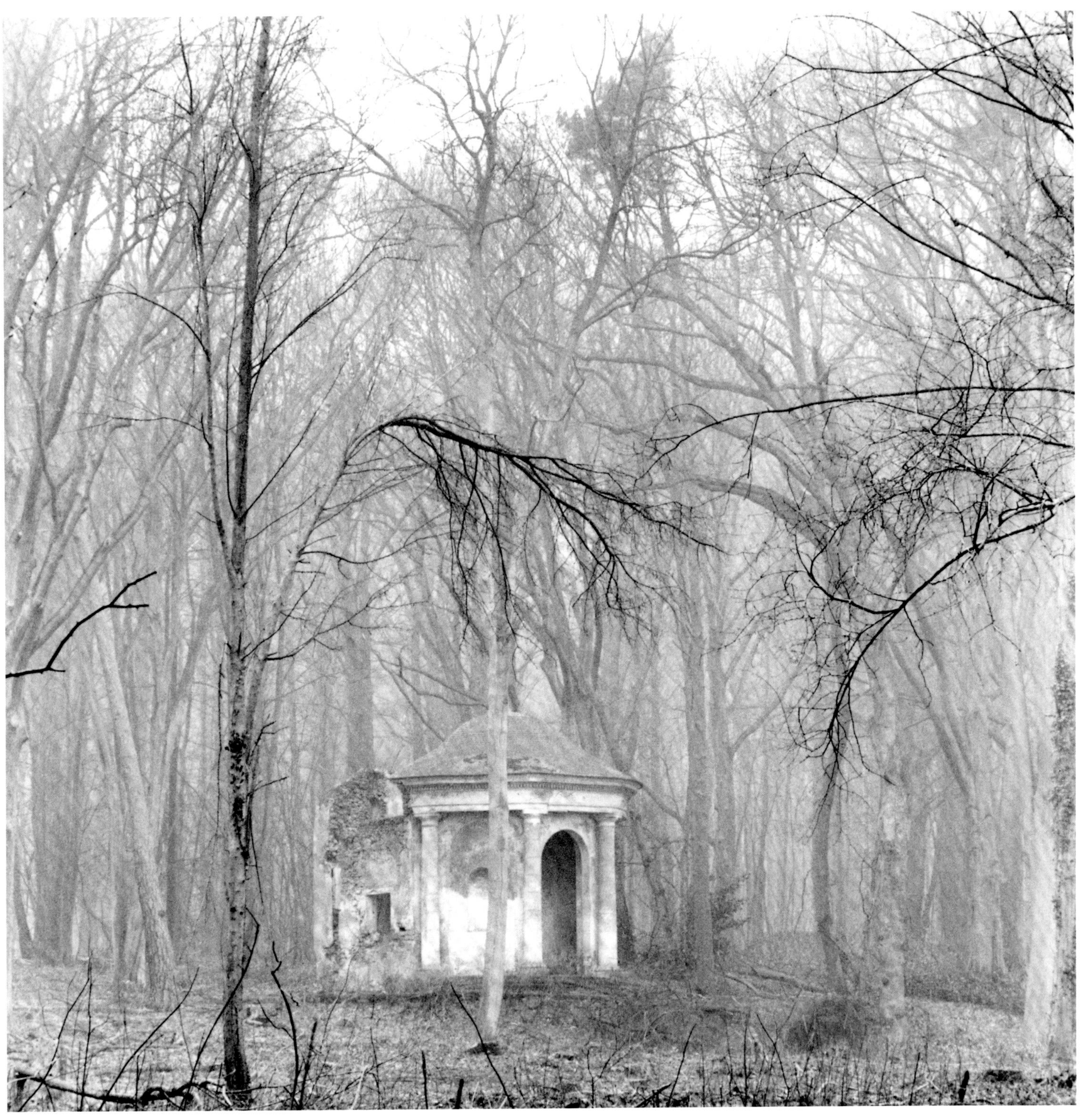

Holy Island

The artist, conventional wisdom tells us, is the one who makes the familiar strange, who finds the magic in the everyday. But sometimes he or she can walk in the opposite direction: taking a place of legend and making it look like somewhere down the road. When you come to the 1,600-templed city of Kyoto, I tell visiting friends, head to the convenience store and the department store; there you'll find more surprising grace notes and places of beauty than you could ever discover in the Golden Temple or the castle with floorboards that squeak like nightingales.

Lindisfarne is one of the magical names of my boyhood. It referred to the silvery folk-rock group that brought out the most popular album of 1972, when I was fifteen. It spoke to a faraway place I'd heard of called Holy Island, not far from Scotland, where an illuminated version of the Gospels was found, from the eighth century, fashioned by one Eadfrith in honor of Saint Cuthbert. And much later, when I made it to Edinburgh, it was the place my wife got to see, on a radiant day trip, and came back singing about, while I had to work in the city.

Now I wonder what it is I didn't see. Because even if I had gone there, I'd never have found this perspective, in black and white, caught by very special eyes. I'd have brought back just the postcard version, a British Mont-Saint-Michel, failing to glimpse what an artist can retrieve as he makes even places of magic seem, wonderfully, part of the neighborhood.

Call the subject of this image "Holy Island" and everything is transformed.

PI

Vague Vignette

"Sittin' in a sleazy snack bar sucking sickly sausage rolls." I always loved those "Fog on the Tyne" lyrics from the 1960s band Lindisfarne. In that era, my friend Cuthbert Jackson's name came alphabetically just before Michael Kenna in our many boarding school lists. Our sleeping cubicles, desks, boot racks, sinks, etcetera, were usually next to each other, which is probably how I first heard about a cult of the medieval Saint Cuthbert on Holy Island, along the Northumberland coast.

Born in 635, the same year that Lindisfarne monastery was founded, and living a holy life, on Holy Island, Cuthbert the monk became a hermit, and then a bishop. After his death, it is said his body did not decay for a hundred years or so and was a focal point for pilgrims. Then the Vikings came, pillaged the monastery, stole whatever they could, and took the monks as slaves. The Lindisfarne monastery was later rebuilt as a priory and the ruins still survive. The castle was built as a defensive structure. That's the quick version, with the bottom line being that Holy Island has an extremely rich history, and is well worth visiting.

There are many places where I still want to photograph. Holy Island is a place I intend to revisit, having only photographed there on one brief morning. Fortunately, it had been a low tide, so the three-mile causeway to the island was accessible. I quickly photographed the most dominant feature, the castle, as it rose through the mist, along with these fantastic pieces of wood rising from the shoreline. Then I had to get back to the mainland, rather than be marooned in the North Sea for the next six hours. My time there now feels like a fleeting, distant dream, something from the pages of *The Mists of Avalon*, and this image a vague vignette, proof that I was there. I was, wasn't I?

MK

Lindisfarne Castle, Northumberland, England, 1991

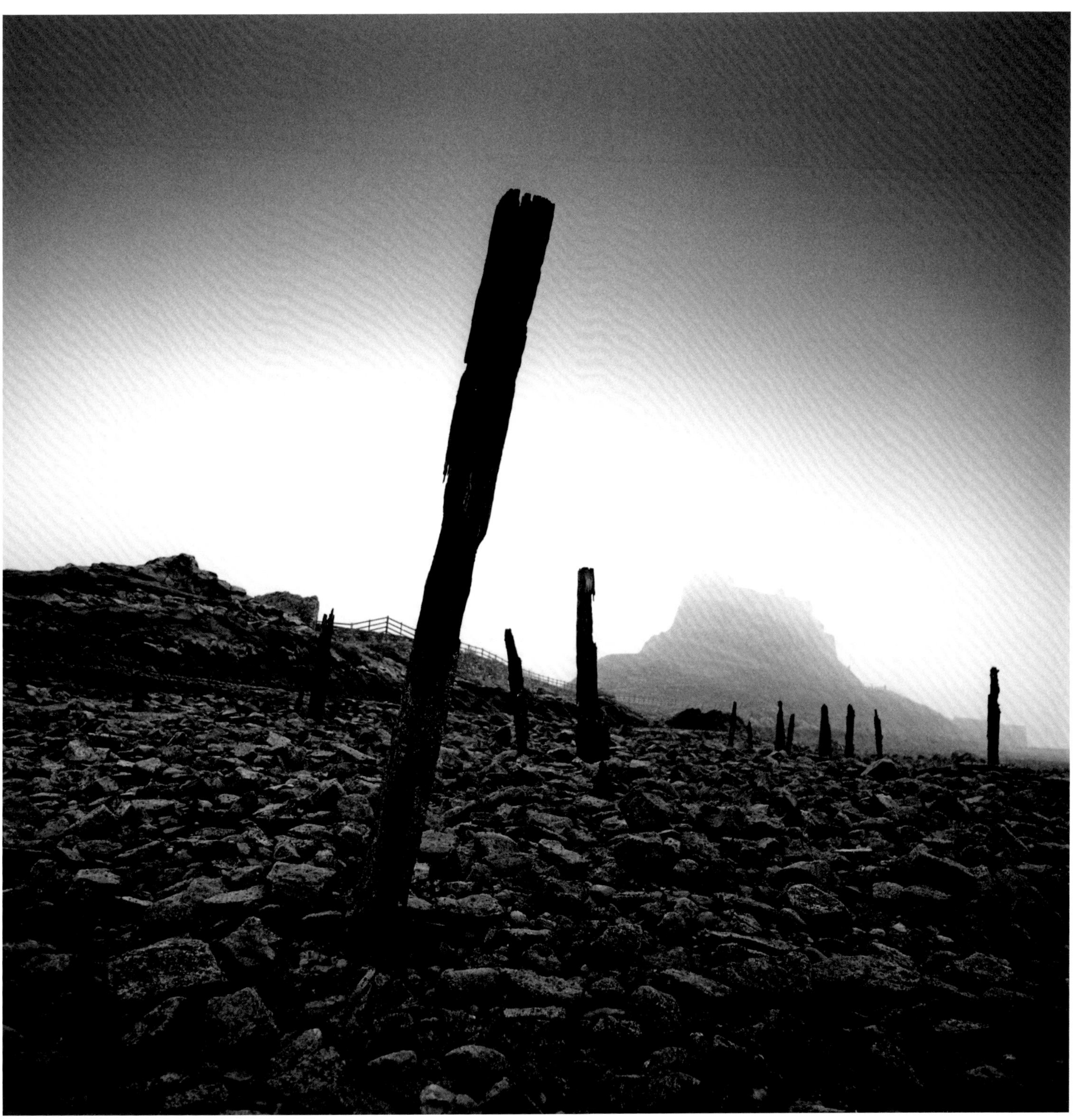

Electric Jungle

One of the greatest gifts any artist can offer us is unexpectedness. So I let out a cry of delight when I saw this image of urban density and repletion, so very different from the hushed and minimalist work I associate with Michael. I can almost hear the noise pulsing through these blocks, feel the ambition urging each new structure to go higher, higher. How could it not capture me at the tender age of twenty-five?

But the heart of life—and therefore of Michael's work—is contrast, the dance of shadow and light. So I rejoice in an image that complements—and rounds out—the silent trees and the weathered chapels I more often see in a Kenna. I remember the fact that, save to a very discerning eye, this picture is actually of something not on any map, and found across the globe. It could be Hong Kong, Shanghai, Pyongyang. It could be a portrait of an era.

I remember when I lived in the midst of this concrete clutter, commuting every morning, in a boxed subway car, from my one-room apartment on the eleventh floor overlooking 20th Street, to my barely smaller twenty-fifth-floor office overlooking 50th Street. After twelve or so hours in my little box, I returned to the subway car and to my studio apartment above the grind. I look at this image and recall exactly why I fled the shining towers for an empty room along the eastern hills of Kyoto where I had nothing but space and time and the chance to be anything—or nothing—at all.

PI

Flying Ms. Poppins

I didn't wait for my final graduation at the London College of Printing and took a plane to New York's Kennedy airport instead. Arriving in Manhattan after over twenty-four hours of travel, including an emergency stop in Keflavik, Iceland, my first impression was that of a volcano about to erupt. It was night, boiling hot, the humidity was high and steam belched out of manhole covers. People were everywhere and the city vibrated with energy. I was shouted at by a street vendor when I questioned why he had shortchanged me for a hot dog—I'd never heard of sales tax before! I was duped into giving money away while purchasing a bus ticket at Port Authority. Riding a Greyhound bus on the New Jersey Turnpike made me almost faint with emotion after years of listening to Simon and Garfunkel songs. It was 1976, the bicentennial year, and I, like so many others, had come to look for America.

I am so envious of Mary Poppins who always arrives on the ground with such grace and elegance before folding up her black umbrella and getting to work. I refer somewhere else in this book to the one time I jumped out of a plane and parachuted. It remains embedded in my psyche as being a truly terrifying and amazing experience!

The New York photographer Garry Winogrand once remarked, "I photograph to see what something will look like photographed," which encapsulates the philosophy of photography as a means of discovery and transformation. Sometimes I only discover elements in the frame long after the photograph is made. Indeed, I often open the camera shutter for long exposures at night, perhaps say a little prayer to the photo gods, and hope for the best. An echo of life, for in the big picture I must admit that I have little idea of what we are all doing here.

I certainly don't recall seeing the enormous wall poster of Ms. Poppins when I made this picture. Perhaps she might have magically floated into the frame while I was looking elsewhere. I could see her doing something like that, for surely I would have been seduced and distracted by the buildings and night lights, the geometry and perspective, and the always present potent atmosphere of this gargantuan metropolis. Thirty years after my first visit, I was as impressionable and impressed as ever.

MK

 Mary Poppins over Midtown, New York City, New York, USA, 2006

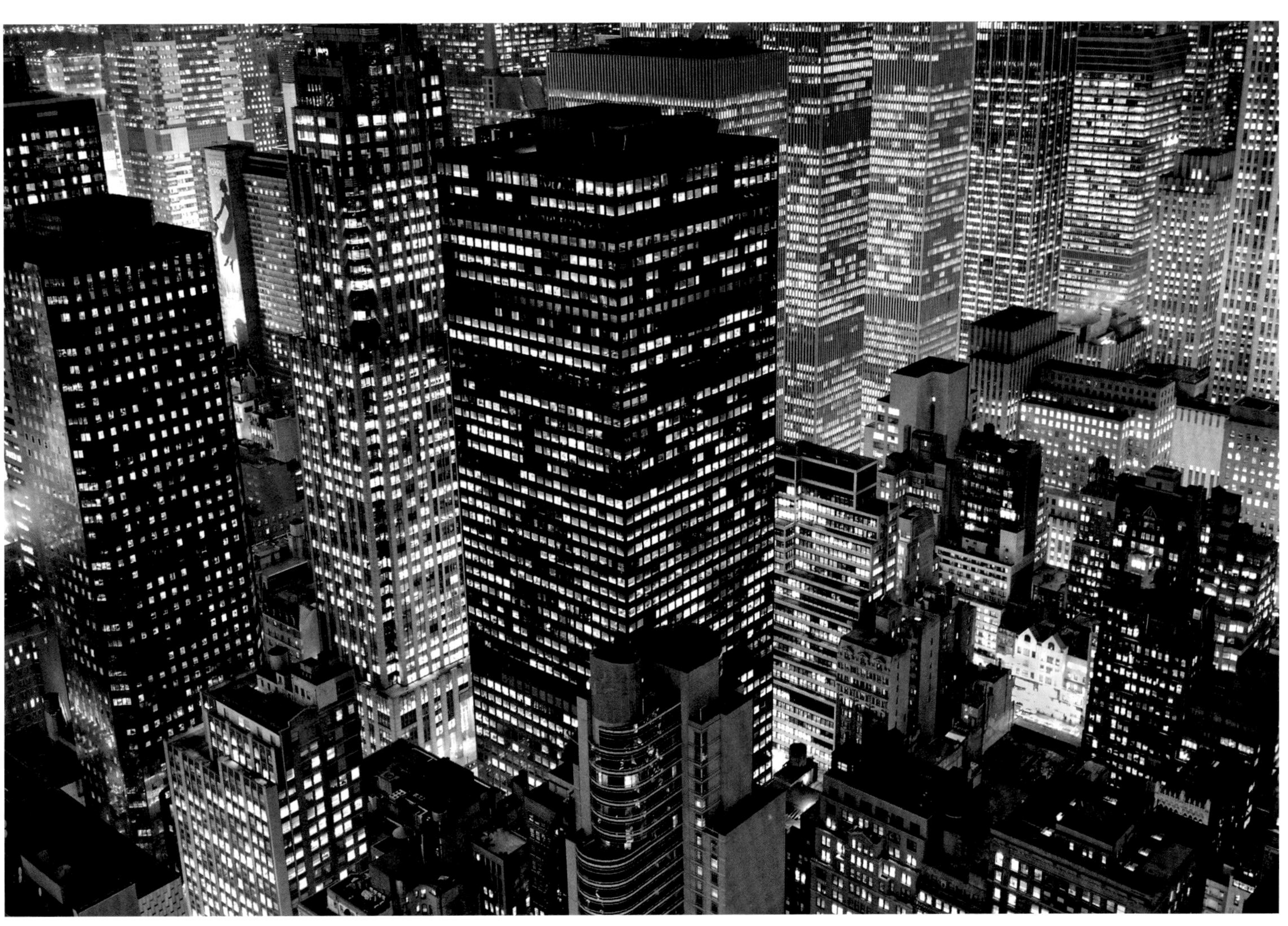

The Cave of Secrets

I stepped out of a rickety train in northern Burma, on my first, life-changing trip to Southeast Asia—October 1983—and into a scene much like this. A boatman standing with immemorial grace above a calm body of water. A stillness that shook the tumult out of me. A past that never seemed to shift.

Yet the beauty of Southeast Asia, I would find, is that it's never quite what it seems. When, many years later, I found myself on this very stretch of the Mekong, drifting down from the city of temples, Luang Prabang, I got out of our small boat and walked into a cave. There I found a tall Egyptian-looking statue on either side of a central statue of the Buddha. Feminine figures, perhaps serving as attendants, guardians in the candlelit quiet.

I stood before them, and soon found that I couldn't move. My wife left the cave and I remained where I was, transfixed. I had to. She came back in and told me it was time to go. I couldn't stir. She pulled me out into the daylight and I shook myself free and said, "I'm so sorry; I have to go back."

This time, my wife came with me and recited the Heart Sutra so the enigmatic powers would not take away my soul. Later we heard that hundreds had taken shelter in such caves during the bombing campaigns of the Vietnam War, never to come out. But in some ways I barely worried; my wife, like this region of bottomless calm, had stolen my soul many years before and kept it in safekeeping.

PI

The Universe Conspires

For many years, the organization Friends Without A Border held annual auctions to help fund the Angkor Hospital for Children in Siem Reap, Cambodia, and I happily donated prints to raise funds for this worthy cause. After all, the photographer and driving force behind the hospital, Kenro Izu, asked me to. How could I possibly refuse? In 2014, Kenro also asked me to photograph in Luang Prabang, Laos, as part of a book project to help raise funds for a new children's hospital there. I was exceedingly glad to accept his invitation and went the following year.

Laos is one of the poorest countries in the world, with a population of almost seven million people, of which over half are under twenty. As a first-time visitor, awaiting me was a beautiful sense of calm and quietness. The people and landscape emanated serenity, equilibrium, and contentment. The ubiquitous children smiled, played, and laughed. However, the reality is that widespread and unnecessary suffering is rampant in Laos and a high mortality rate ravages the population. Doctors are few and far between, and most local people cannot afford to pay for them. Miraculously, the Luang Prabang Hospital for Children did eventually open, offering free medical services for children, and I even had the privilege to visit—a humbling and eye-opening experience.

Compared to the above mission, my photography commitment in Laos pales in importance. I observed and photographed this scene on the Mekong River while visiting a Buddhist temple. It felt as though the beautiful sunset, the mountain scenery, the framing of undergrowth, and the performance of the fishermen casting their net in the foreground was all masterfully stage-managed. It is said that the universe conspires to make good intentions manifest, and it certainly did a masterful job that evening.

MK

Mekong River Fishing, Luang Prabang, Laos, 2015

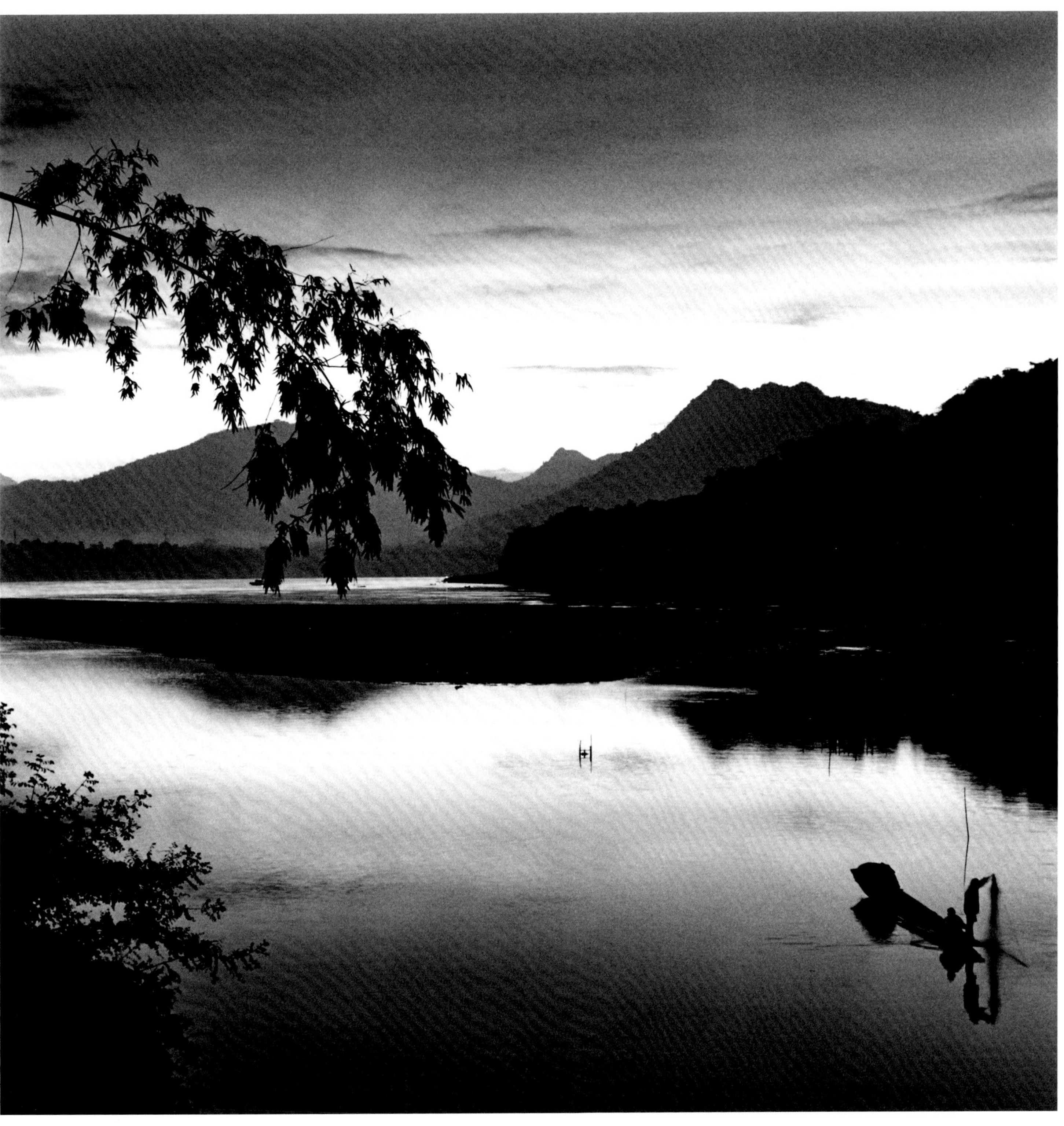

Our Constant Friends

Soon after I met my Japanese wife-to-be, she led me off to the large park outside the Imperial Palace at the center of Kyoto and pointed out two trees. "That one's you," she said, directing my gaze to a red-barked oak, "and that one"—she drew my attention to some neighboring branches, all but intertwined—"is me." I didn't know what to say; I'd never been likened to a tree before.

Now that I'm married to Japan, I can see that all the trees around me—the cedars, the maples, the golden ginkgos, and the pines—are the trustiest neighbors I could imagine, as well as the steadiest anchors. They never go away. For all their changes, they always come back again, newly splendid in the spring. A pair of thousand-year-old camphors in Kyoto have been designated National Living Treasures; a whole lexicon of *hanakotoba* expresses everything through flowers.

It was after I saw how he took trees to be his deepest friends that I knew beyond a doubt that Michael Kenna was Japanese. This image happens to come from Myanmar, home to the most blue-skied, engaging, unfallen souls that I have met. But Michael can find a different kind of soul, more abiding and no less eloquent, in these gracious, living, intertwined presences with whom he's been conversing, silently, for fifty years. Under such a shade the Buddha found peace—and all the truth he could ever need.

PI

Fortune Favors the Birds

Learning to distrust my creative decision-making, my mantra these days is: whenever you think you know it, you don't! I scouted this location in the hill town of Pyin U Lwin one afternoon and arranged with the gatekeeper to come back early the next morning before the park officially opened. Long before the sun rose, I was ready and in place. It turned out to be a lovely dusk with beautiful light and rising mist.

In my mind, I wanted to photograph the silent and special conversation between the trees and lake. After I began, two birds flew into the frame and settled by the waterside. I found them to be distracting. After a few quick exposures, I clapped my hands to shoo them away, before recommencing what, for me, was the more serious work of five- and ten-minute exposures.

Over the next hour, the mist floated by and the water became like a sheet of ice. Sunrays and shadows constantly changed. Each photograph was different and it was a hugely delightful experience. I continued to photograph from pretty much the same spot, making variations of framing and exposure as it was never possible to predict what would happen next.

Months later, I saw the processed film and contact sheets. It didn't take me long to realize my mistake. The long-exposure images were good, but not as I had hoped. They seemed a little predictable. The few initial images made with split-second exposures, with the birds included, appeared far more spontaneous and engaging. I had missed the obvious: the birds echoed the trees, and their presence was a fortunate bonus. On this occasion I was lucky.

MK

 Morning Mists, Pyin U Lwin, Myanmar, 2019

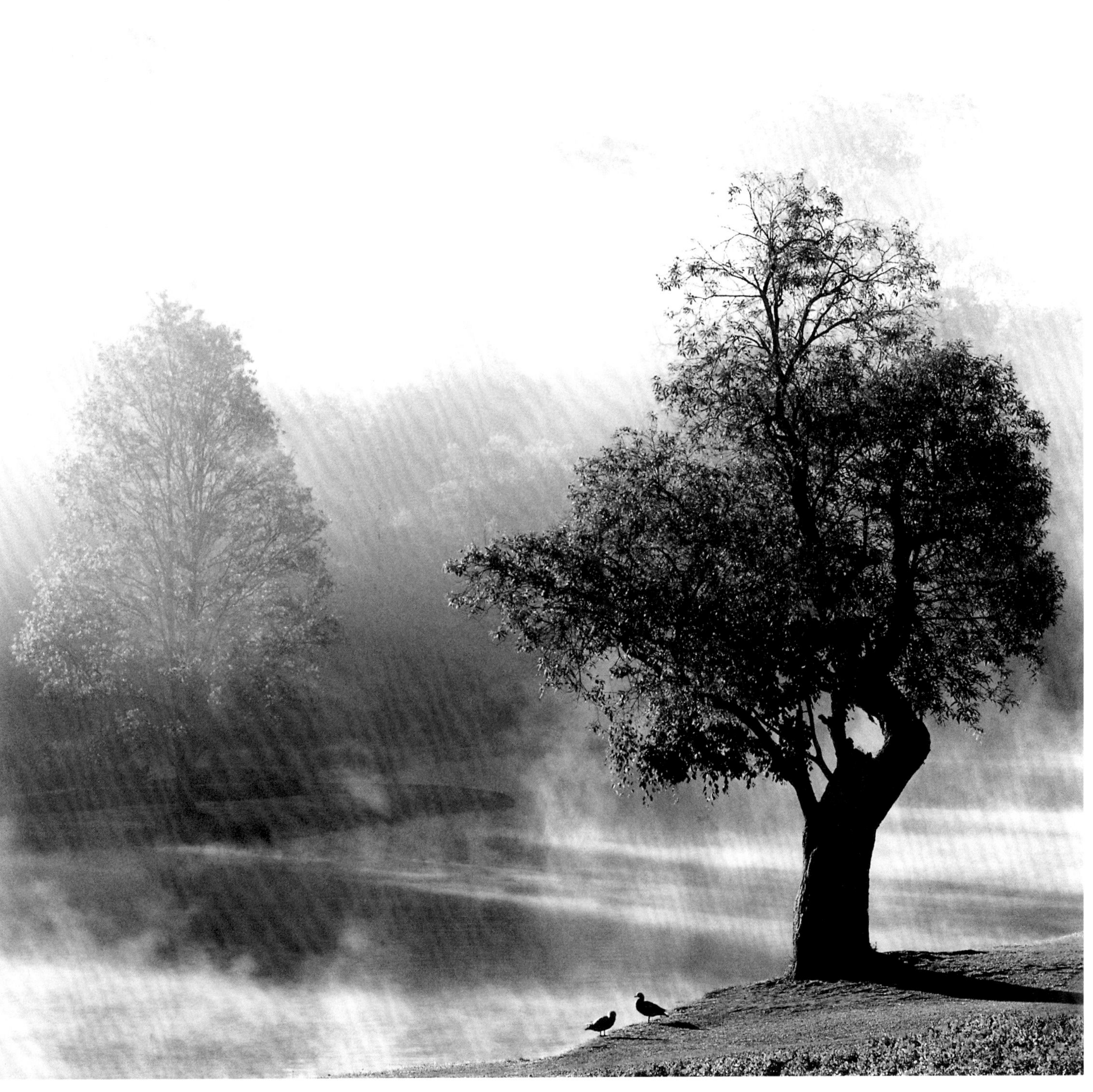

Our Designated Dreamer

Because Michael's photographs take us to places inside ourselves, they're never afraid of terrors. Of spooks and storms and all those dreams from which we awaken relieved because they were the opposite of consoling.

They give us the inner world in all its variety, which is never so different from the outer one, but has a rare power to shake and startle us because we see it so rarely.

I sit at my desk and every kind of weather passes through me. An unruffled ocean. Storm clouds blackening the horizon. Radiant spring light. What looks—as here—like a Gothic nightmare.

The artist performs a kind of conscious dreaming on behalf of us all, making his or her way through the storm, like the characters around King Lear, so as to emerge on the other side. Making manifest our dreams, not all of them golden, so we're reminded of the thunderclouds within. Passing through the darkness to remember that it's never the end of the story, any more than the light is.

I shiver when I look at this image, but only because it looks like what visited me in the depths of the dark last night.

PI

Things That Go Thump in the Night

My camera had been mounted on its tripod, calmly and quietly accumulating light during a long time exposure on the grounds of the Dom Pérignon estate at Hautvillers in the Champagne region of France. I had been asleep on the grass, as it was around 3 a.m. People often ask me what I do during night exposures. Sleep is one option, counting stars another, watching what moves a third. There are many others, but why should there be a necessity to do anything? A rumbling of distant thunder woke me up from my dreams. Better, I thought, than the sprinkler system coming on, as it had the night before, soaking me and my cameras.

Fast-forward thirty minutes. The thunder was now overhead, the lightning all over the place, scary, but an opportunity not to be missed. I composed the image, opened the shutter, held up my umbrella, and hoped, wished, prayed. The camera stayed dry, I got drenched, and the lightning performed as if sent by Central Casting. Of course, I have other exposures without these wonderful graphic lines, but the spontaneous and unpredictable aspects of this image make it more appealing.

The negative is ridiculously difficult to print. Dazzling lightning ensured a backlit, silhouetted church. I have spent hours in the darkroom wrestling with the negative, with most prints ending up in the dustbin. The few acceptable prints are all different from each other, as the burning, dodging, and light manipulation is so extensive. Impossible to duplicate, each print becomes all the more precious. Looking back, it was an amazing night, a great adventure with fantastic weather conditions in a gorgeous location. Worth a glass or two of champagne, perhaps?

MK

Night Storm, Hautvillers, France, 2001

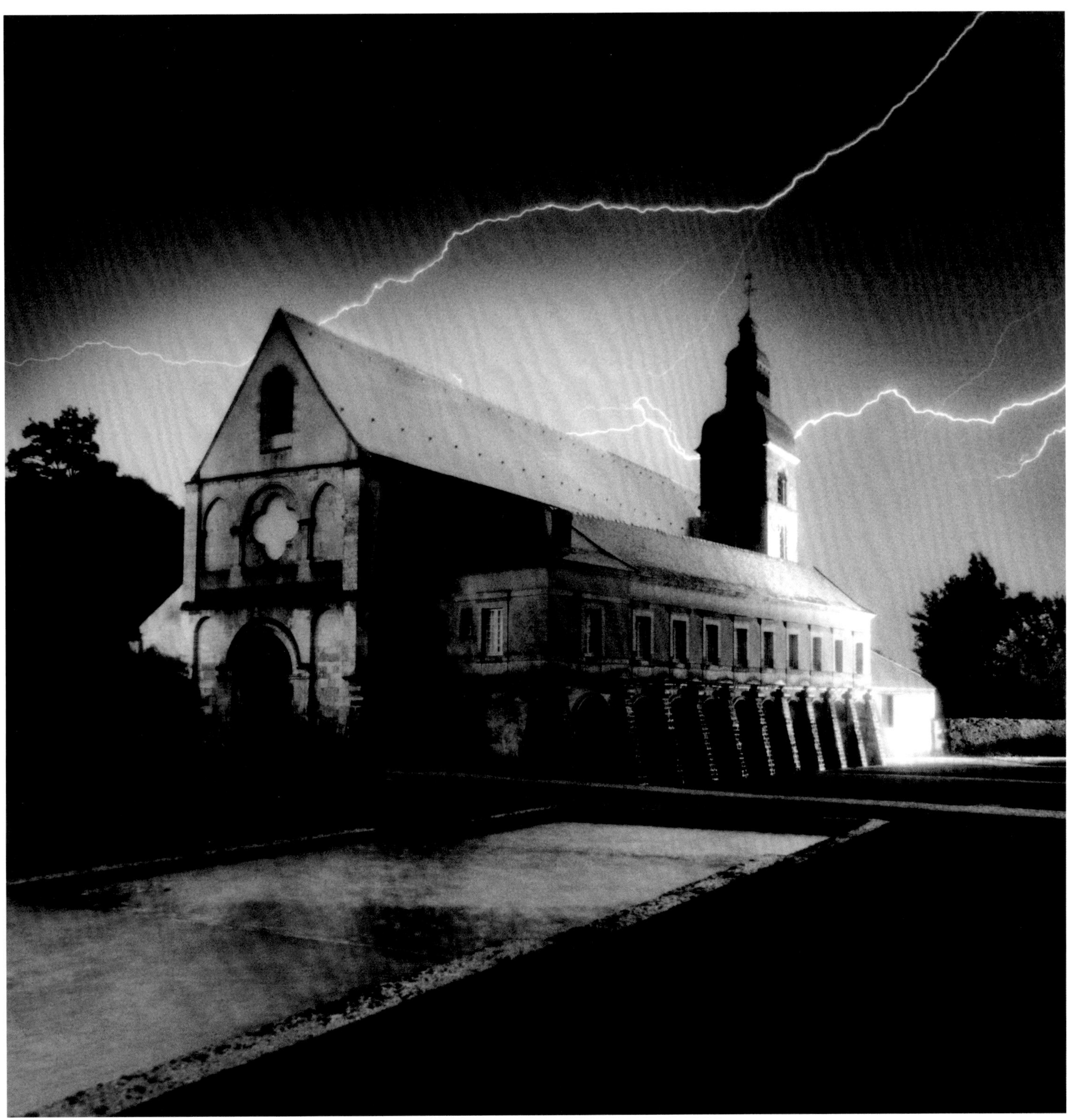

The Overcast Dream

As ever, I was on Easter Island in exactly the same year as the photographer named Kenna, and as ever it was he who found beauty and Polynesian lyricism while I was plodding around the empty streets trying to find vegetarian food for my sari-clad mother. It was New Year's Eve 1999, and the whole world was scheduled to collapse at midnight—or turn into a pumpkin at least—thanks to Y2K, the anticipated glitch that would render all computers inoperative. It felt right to be in a corner of the planet where a twenty-first-century luxury was a piece of wood.

Yet there's no question that the unexpected pleasures of Easter Island lay all in its South Seas languor and not, I thought, in the stone statues that I was coming to resemble as I learned that even our hotel offered no items a vegetarian could enjoy. For me at least, the *moai* that draw visitors to the remotest island community on earth—1,300 miles from Pitcairn (population 65)—looked not so different from what I might see on a travel agent's poster, or at the nearest branch of Trader Vic's Polynesian restaurant.

But the *South Pacific* pleasures of the place—the bare-chested man riding his chestnut horse down the barely paved main street, the young beauty with flowers in her lustrous hair—were a wonderful incitation to Polynesian ease of the kind I didn't find on later trips to Papeete or Mo'orea. This photograph beautifully extracts the dreamy otherworldliness of Easter Island precisely by removing it from specifics and rescuing it from clichés. Here is a picture to serve as chaperone to W. Somerset Maugham's unforgettable story "Rain." Here, too, is a reminder of how images may give us faraway places as the places themselves seldom do.

PI

Cheese Sarnies and Lucky Snaps

When in Paris, I photograph the Eiffel Tower. In Giza, I try to capture the magnificent pyramids. In London, it's Big Ben, and then there's the Empire State Building in New York. All these subjects could be considered clichés. And on Easter Island, of course, the *moai*. I am a big believer that no two sunrises are ever the same, and every sunset is unique. I cannot resist photographing irresistible subject matter. Is the result ever original? Does it matter?

Originality, I feel, is akin to beauty and in the mind of the beholder. I visited the outrageously inexplicable Easter Island on two occasions, each for about five days. Sometimes I walked. At other times, I rented a small jeep to drive around the island. I photographed the *moai* at every opportunity, while never seriously believing that I could do justice to these stone figures. The statues embody such unseen, unknown, unfathomable mystery and wonder that it seems inconceivable to transmit this in a single image. Of course, any photographer worth his or her salt must be forgiven for trying.

In one rare moment on Easter Island, the skies opened while I was photographing. I rushed back to my little jeep to stay dry and eat the cheese sandwich that I had prepared at breakfast. While turning around to find it in the back seat, I noticed the rear window with rain drops obscuring the few palm trees on the island. It reminded me of the famous *Apple Tree* photograph by Ruth Bernhard. I made a few quick handheld snaps before munching my sarnie. This exposure turned out to be one of the most memorable photographs of my time on Easter Island. Now in my seventies, I accept more and more that ignorance is often bliss, and supposed clichés are also very much in the mind of the individual beholder.

MK

 Palm Trees, Anakena, Easter Island, 2000

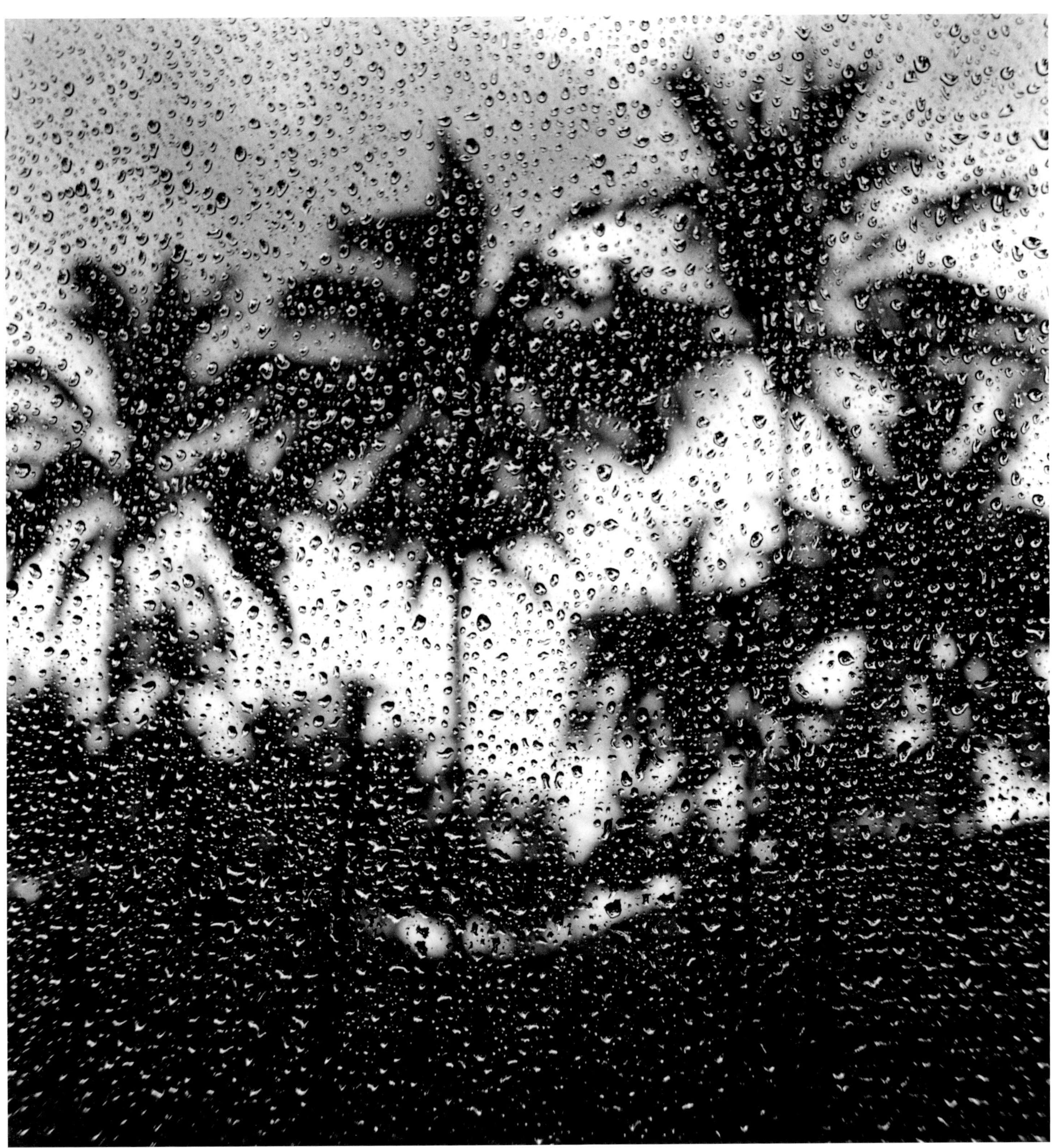

Journey's End

Nobody ever told me that, as the adventure draws towards its conclusion, life would become so calm, so free of pressure, so full of joy. The psychologist Daniel Kahneman, after sixty years of studying the human mind, found that the end of any trip is disproportionately important to the way we remember it, and therefore experience it, till the end of our days. A happy reunion on our last day makes up for—erases—sixteen days of bumpy buses filled with screaming children and squawking chicken.

Maybe that's one reason Michael's images have come to be such a friend to me in the autumn of my life. They clear away inessentials, they dispense with what's passing, and they take us to the heart of things, what lasts. A tree in the snow that outlasts all our hopes and words.

We revisit old friends; we make new ones. The years contract, the horizon expands. That fresh, unexpected brother is striding towards me now with a cheerful wave.

What lies through that torii gate? Another bridge, I'm sure, a new mystery, perhaps a journey that never ends.

I give thanks for the undeserved graces that keep coming my way, unexpected.

PI

Collective Consciousness

The Japanese Shinto religion, animistic in nature, espouses that deities reside in the land, trees, rocks, and water, as well as in shrines and temples. It is a belief system dear to my heart. Respect, reverence, and honor is symbolized by the ubiquitous torii gates, often integrated into the landscape as focal points, giving us the opportunity to stop what we are doing, perhaps to pray, think, rest, and escape from our everyday existence for some moments. Shrines and temples throughout Japan are regarded as communal places to ritually commemorate and celebrate the various stages of our lives.

My guide, Tsuyoshi, was surprised that I had not previously visited this shrine in Hokkaido. He was convinced we had been there before together, but I didn't remember. Considering there are approximately 80,000 Shinto shrines in Japan, I wasn't overly worried at my inability to recollect. It is true, though, that I like to return to the many shrines I am familiar with. One of my favorite activities is to spend hours at dusk or dawn close to a torii gate, preferably alone, sitting, watching, waiting, and/or perhaps photographing. I always come away refreshed, inspired, renewed.

Since photographing the Peoppe Hill shrine, I have already revisited it a few times—and now I can even remember! Like everything, it has changed. On different occasions snow levels have increased and decreased. Vegetation has grown or been cleared away. The weather has always been different. And yet the torii gate stands, calmly, as if it has been in the same place for an eternity, and will be there forever more. I wonder how many pilgrims and other visitors have been to this shrine, how many prayers have been said, and offerings made to the gods. These shrines are the receivers of our collective memories and emotions. They embody our experiences. No wonder they have such a powerful presence.

MK

Peoppe Hill Torii, Hokkaido, Japan, 2024

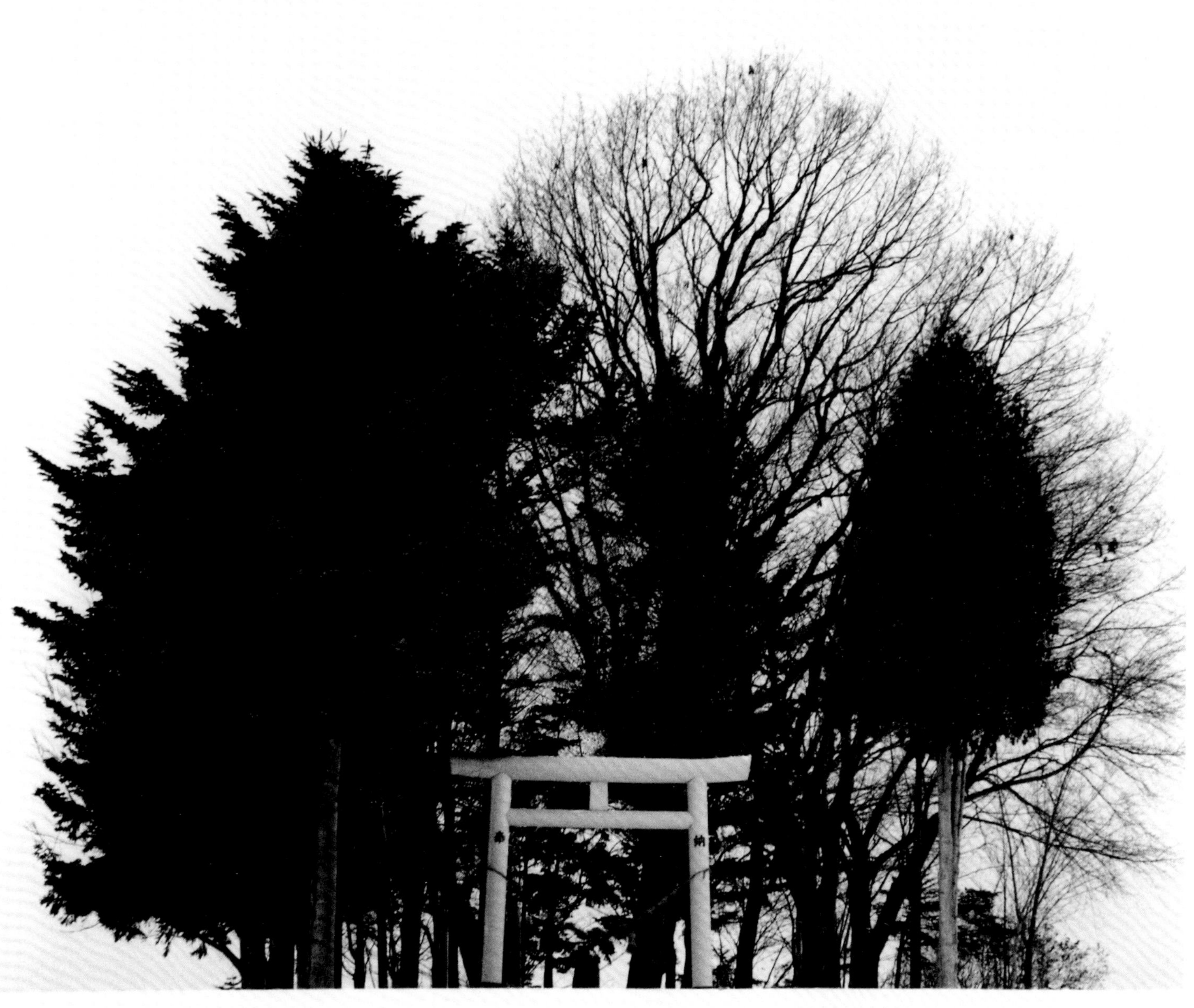

Taking Flight

Soon after I left school, at seventeen, I got onto a bus in the scrappy border town of Tijuana, with an equally clueless classmate, and bumped across Mexico and Guatemala. We made our way to Panama and then Cartagena, and there boarded a bus to jounce us through the jungles of Colombia, along the 15,000-foot passes of the Andes—nothing but llamas and snow for day after day—past the Incan ruins in the sky to the city named for peace two miles above the sea in Bolivia. I might have been the plane in this picture. I couldn't catch many details, I didn't understand much that I was seeing, but I sensed the presence of the mountains, the outlines of a city, a world I could never have guessed at, months before.

On arrival in Rio, we drove along the beaches, past lagoons, in and out of rainforests, to where my friend's father's friend lived amidst this miracle of natural beauty calling itself a city. A hundred days of no-star hotels were erased in an instant as we settled into a capacious villa with a tropical garden and our generous host began pouring two visiting teenagers some drinks.

I've returned to the city again and again since then—to watch soccer matches, to launch books, to share the beauty with my wife. I walk along the beach all day and stop there between flights, or linger at the juice stands for a week. Yet still it has the airy, featherlight quality of this image as if it's never been crass enough to touch the ground.

PI

Hip-Hoppers and Running Interference

Between 2006 and 2009 I was commissioned to photograph in eighteen countries, many for the first time, including Brazil, China, Egypt, India, and Turkey. All was not wine and roses, for I was chased by flying cockroaches, eaten by swarms of hungry mosquitoes, sucked on by bloodthirsty leeches, "cleansed" by intestinal bugs, and frozen, baked, drenched, and sleep-deprived into submission, often while precariously dangling off high buildings or harnessed onto the side of helicopters. But, what a fabulous journey!

In Rio de Janeiro, our team had ascended, predawn, to photograph the vista from a prime vantage point. Another film crew arrived in the same place to record a hip-hop music video. Hoping for a quiet environment, which always helps my concentration, it was not to be. Loud music blasted out and dancing was filmed. We tolerated each other and worked side by side in the small space.

A hallmark of an excellent assistant is the ability to know what to do without being asked. Such is the case with Mark J. Silva, who has been my "wingman" for over twenty years. I often make long time exposures, and when people are around Mark will gently confide to them that I am counting seconds, hence I should not be disturbed. Counting becomes both a form of meditation and a useful device to ward off distractions.

That morning, Mark was assisting and doubling as a bodyguard. Planes occasionally appeared to the side of where I was photographing, before they circled slowly in order to land. Seizing the day, I left our group briefly, with the excuse of saying hello to the hip-hoppers. Instead, I made several quick exposures of a descending plane, while Mark ran interference. Of all the photographs from that morning, this was the most interesting. Thank you MJS!

MK

 Plane and Sugar Loaf Mountain, Rio de Janeiro, Brazil, 2006

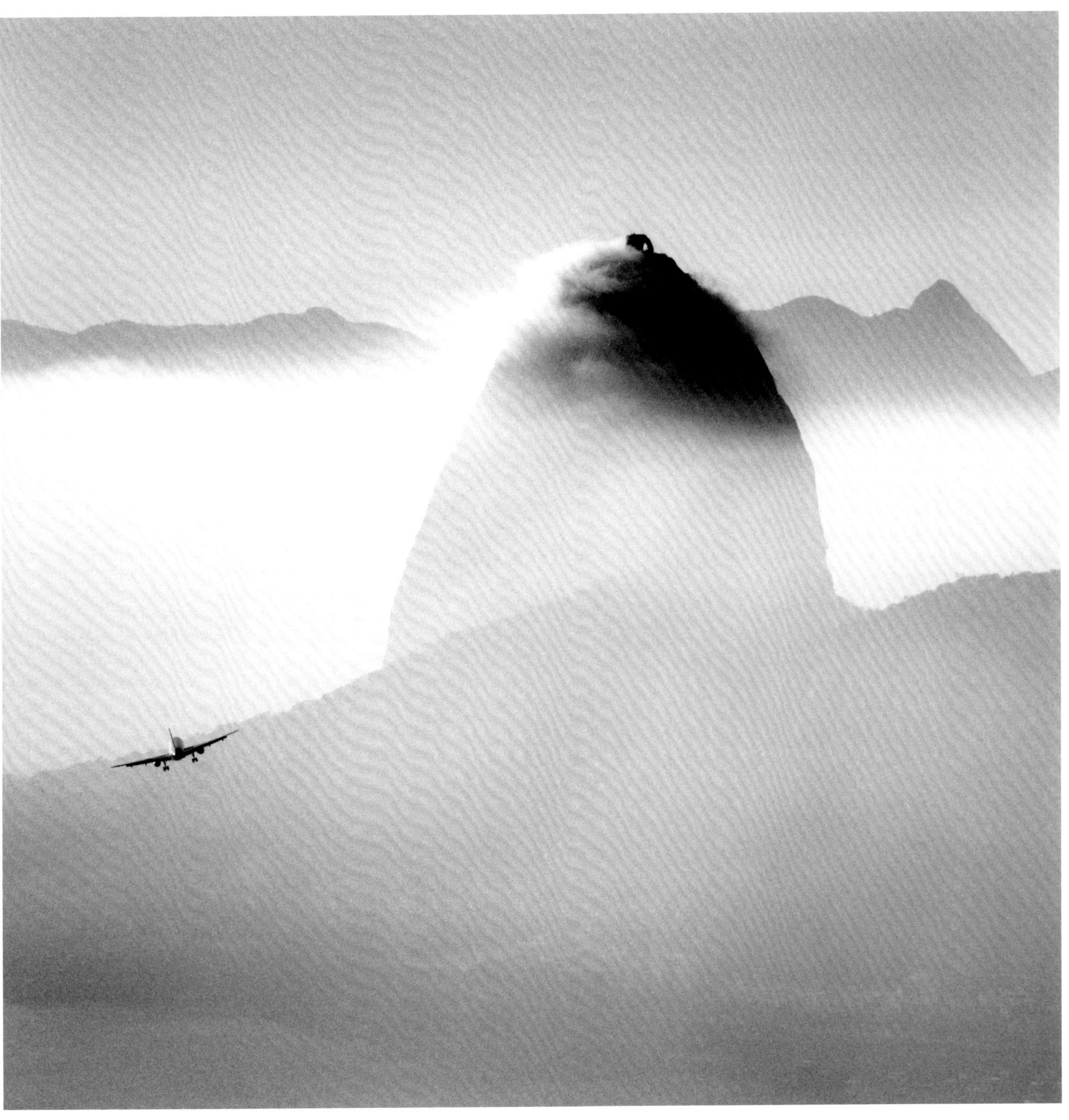

The Playing Fields

All my boyhood seems to hide within this image: the damp meadows, chill with dew; the low gray skies; the challenge of having to make sense—a life—out of the trudge across unpromising lawns. Muddy games of rugger in November drizzle, boys in shorts, bruised knees above grimy socks; the cold plunge into freezing water, clutching onto an unstable riverbank and being urged to thrash our legs around with greater vigor. The forever damp dormitories of the Dragon School, five minutes from this field on foot, all named after long-extinct animals; neatly folded pajamas on iron beds.

If only there had been some instrument of escape, as Michael gives us here: for me it was a public telephone—in the masters' house—into which I stole to call my father, in California, and cry, "Get me out of here!" But nine years later, there I was again, on those same fields, at university, working hard to fall in love and inhabit all the poems, by Keats, by Yeats, I was learning to dissect.

I look at this image fifty years on and think: "black and white" is just how the sludge and perpetual rain of England always struck me. But another, happier thought: Michael knew these very streets, in the very years I was tromping across this field, and knew how to find magic, art—surprise—even there!

PI

Flights of Fancy

My mother died when I was fifteen. The train of consequences set in motion was unforeseeable and unpredictable. For me, it involved a two-hundred-mile move south, from a predominantly working-class, Caucasian, Widnes in the northwest of England, to Southall, a vividly colorful and spicy Southeast Asian community in Middlesex. I was transposed into another world, and loved it.

Later, my father and stepmother moved to Banbury, Oxfordshire, where I enrolled in the Banbury School of Art. Being young, enthusiastic, and new to a world I had yet to experience, I would from time to time bicycle the twenty-four miles to the more cosmopolitan and glamorous city of Oxford, to spend hours at the Radcliffe Art Gallery looking at and absorbing their collection.

Perhaps if I had not been so focused on paintings and sculpture, and instead had looked around at the local Oxford populace, I might have noticed a young Pico Iyer wandering around those same streets during that same time. I like to imagine that perhaps there could have been a moment or two of synchronicity where our paths might have first crossed there, without us being aware.

Eastern philosophy refers to an invisible red thread, believed to connect people who are destined to meet. Pico and I have almost met far more than we will ever know, or will ever find out. Both born in England, brought up in boarding schools, moved to California, married Asian women (both with two children), inveterate travelers, hypnotized by Japan, solitary in nature, devotees of convenience stores; well, the list goes on. This playground plane from the distant past somehow says it all. An empty field. A hazy horizon. All to play for.

MK

Playground Plane, Oxford, Oxfordshire, England, 1979

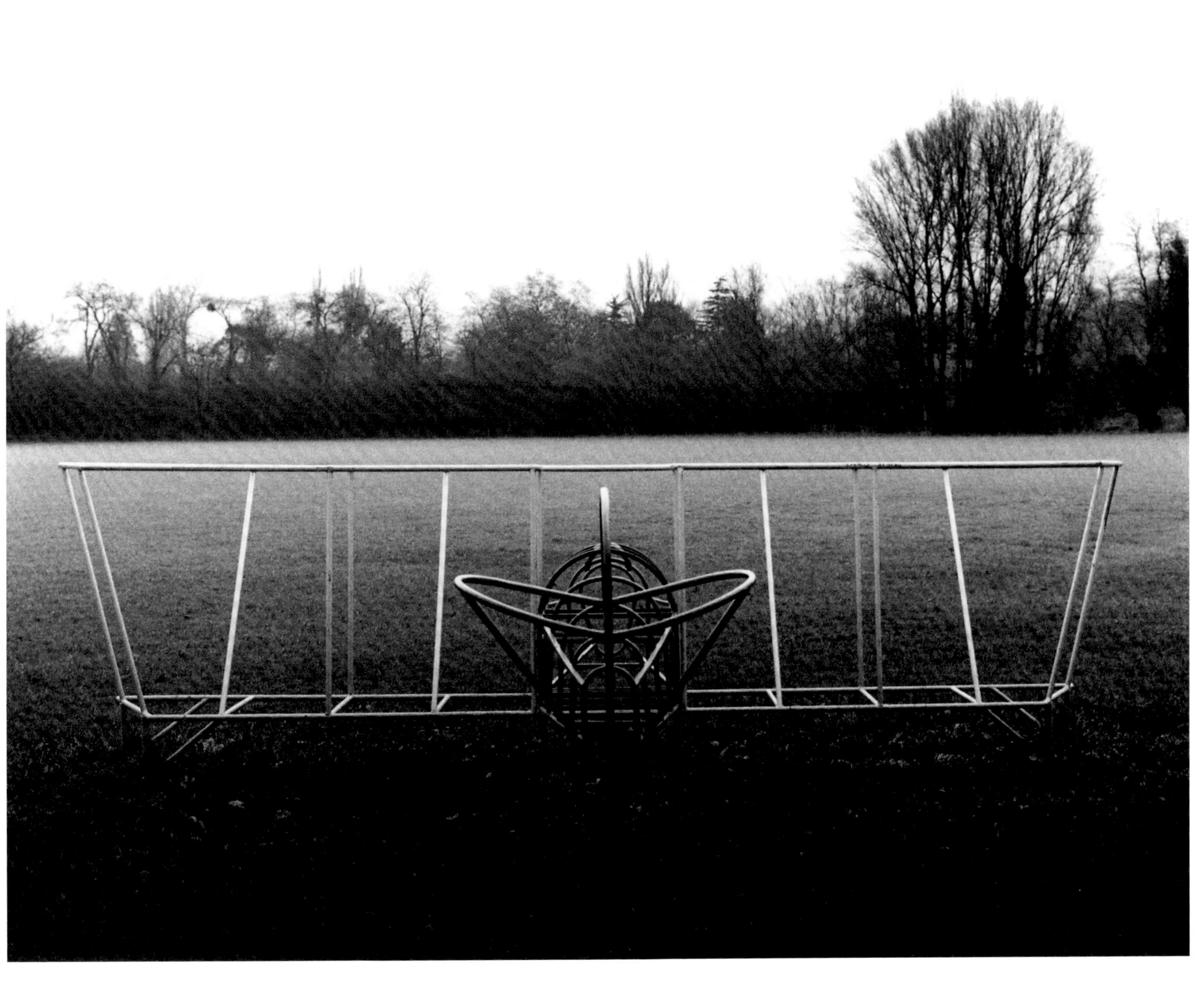

A Trick of Light

When falling in love, I learned very early, it's the difficult moments that count. The heavenly grace of your beloved, your wild and secret laughter, the moments of perfect union—they can all take care of themselves. The one you truly love is the one you can stay with even when she is foggy or cold, or you are.

Nowhere is more famously made for love than the City of Light. I love it for the sun glinting off the white-stone buildings as I walk along the river in the lingering brilliance of a summer evening at 10 p.m. Bright explosions through the glass pyramid at the Louvre, lovers' faces gilded as the last light catches them in their sauntering. The special quiet of a golden morning when only bakeries are open.

But it's on a day like the one pictured here—chilly and gray as the England you might have just fled—that asks you how deeply you really care.

The first time I took my wife-to-be to Paris, it was late December. Both of us were as bleary and overcast as the city around us, having flown in from California and Japan respectively. I fell asleep in the Musée Rodin, she did the same on the romantic nighttime cruise down the Seine I'd so excitedly planned.

Now we return to this very bridge every summer and never grow tired of the stunning light. But only because, perhaps, we survived, thirty-three years ago, long days of dark and clouds.

PI

Amour and #LoveWithoutLocks

Glance one way and see the Île de la Cité, never changing, except perhaps for the recent temporary post-fire scaffolding on Notre-Dame. Look the other way and lights twinkle over the distant Eiffel Tower. Glance down, and barges, bateaux mouche tourist transports, and other sundry boats glide underneath. The Pont des Arts pedestrian bridge connects the left bank Institut de France to the right bank Louvre. Ongoing dramatic, comedic, and romantic productions unfold and are reborn day and night. Selfies abound. Painters and photographers use it as a studio en plein air. Musicians and buskers park themselves for the day. Whole families have picnics, and scammers are constantly in play. This is the bridge where it all happens.

One Bastille Day, my wife Mamta and I jostled for space to watch jet planes fly over, leaving red, white, and blue plumes in the sky. On another evening we waited for the Strawberry Moon to rise, along with the beating drums of a Midsummer following. Mamta kindly pointed out to a group of slightly inebriated people, mesmerized by the Eiffel Tower spectacle, that they were missing the already risen moon in the opposite direction.

When I made this photograph, it was long before the love locks craze threatened the structure. By 2015, over a million locks, weighing about forty-five tons, had been attached to the grated side panels. Paris is, after all, *the* city of love! The locks were subsequently removed and a #lovewithoutlocks campaign was launched with a government recommendation that selfies were a more preferred way to express *amour*. Like good tourists, Mamta and I follow these protocols on every visit.

MK

Pont des Arts, Study 3, Paris, France, 1987

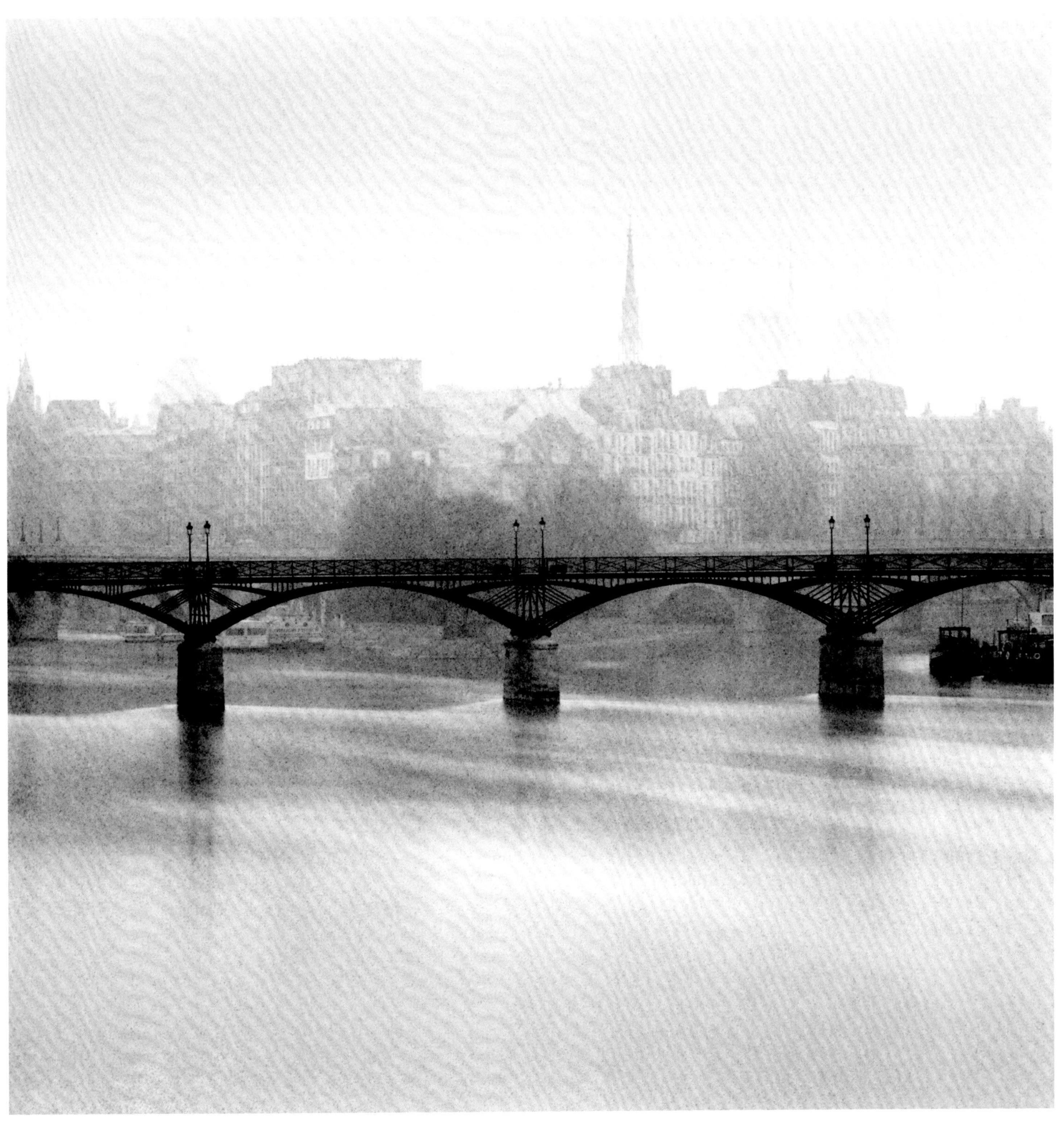

The Hidden Heart

Hanoi is where Vietnam stores its tradition, its learning, you might even say its soul. Saigon, far to the south, is a brassy, go-go Miami, all sultry heat and racy fashions. Hanoi stands apart, a stately and reserved New England. The capital of Vietnam is, beneath its crowds and motorbikes, a textured world of rain and chill, the wisp-bearded scholar who steeps himself in the wisdom of the centuries.

There is a Temple of Literature in the city, from almost a thousand years ago, honoring Confucius. Hoàn Kiếm Lake, in the center, always seems to be posing for calligraphers and brush-stroke paintings with its evasive mists. The backstreets of the Old City are thick with traditional crafts—water puppets and lacquer boxes, shimmery white *áo dài* and books of poetry. The house where Ho Chi Minh lived is made to look like a contemplative retreat perfect for a Tang Dynasty sage.

So of course it's in Hanoi that one finds these books of prayers all carefully preserved, much like the complete set of sutras to be discovered in Tibetan temples. The world may buzz and beep and race into a digital future, but somewhere along the shaded streets of Hanoi, what's old is never out of date. Ho Chi Minh's name may be remembered in the raucous city to the south, but his spirit lives on most deeply amidst the tamarind trees, behind thick walls, in the glass cases of Hanoi.

PI

Stay Still and Be Happy

There are probably predictable consequences of a seminary boarding school curriculum filled with hours of meditation, prayer sessions, rituals, and the nightly ten hours of complete silence. Despite my current state of unknowing and agnosticism, I am still irresistibly drawn to shrines, temples, churches, synagogues, mosques, any and all locations of worship, reverence and respect for the gods and things we do not know and cannot see. Hanoi is replete with these places—empty, calm, quiet, welcoming spaces.

In one such temple, I found these books, stacked and stored behind glass. They suggested a certain yearning for connection to an existence outside of our everyday lives. They must have been held and read by countless individuals. One had been separated from the rest, so I picked it up and glanced through it, thinking that, by osmosis, perhaps some words of wisdom might reach me. While the books contained sentences and prayers comprehensible and full of imagined possibilities to a Vietnamese reader, they remained wholly mysterious and incomprehensible to me.

This experience reminded me of the 1970s when the Latin Mass and other Catholic rituals were translated into English. I found that I no longer enjoyed or even agreed with what I was reciting. Since then, I have preferred services in any other language than my own. When praying, I never know what to say, and end up repeating, thank you, thank you, thank you, for everything. I am now resigned to not understand literal meanings of the rituals I attend. It helps, as my tendency is to run away from dogma of any and all kinds. Mystery allows me to sit still and be happy. Having listened to Pico's brilliant TED Talk, "The Art of Stillness," I think he might concur. I must remember to ask him some day.

MK

Prayer Books, Tay Pagoda, Hanoi, Vietnam, 2019

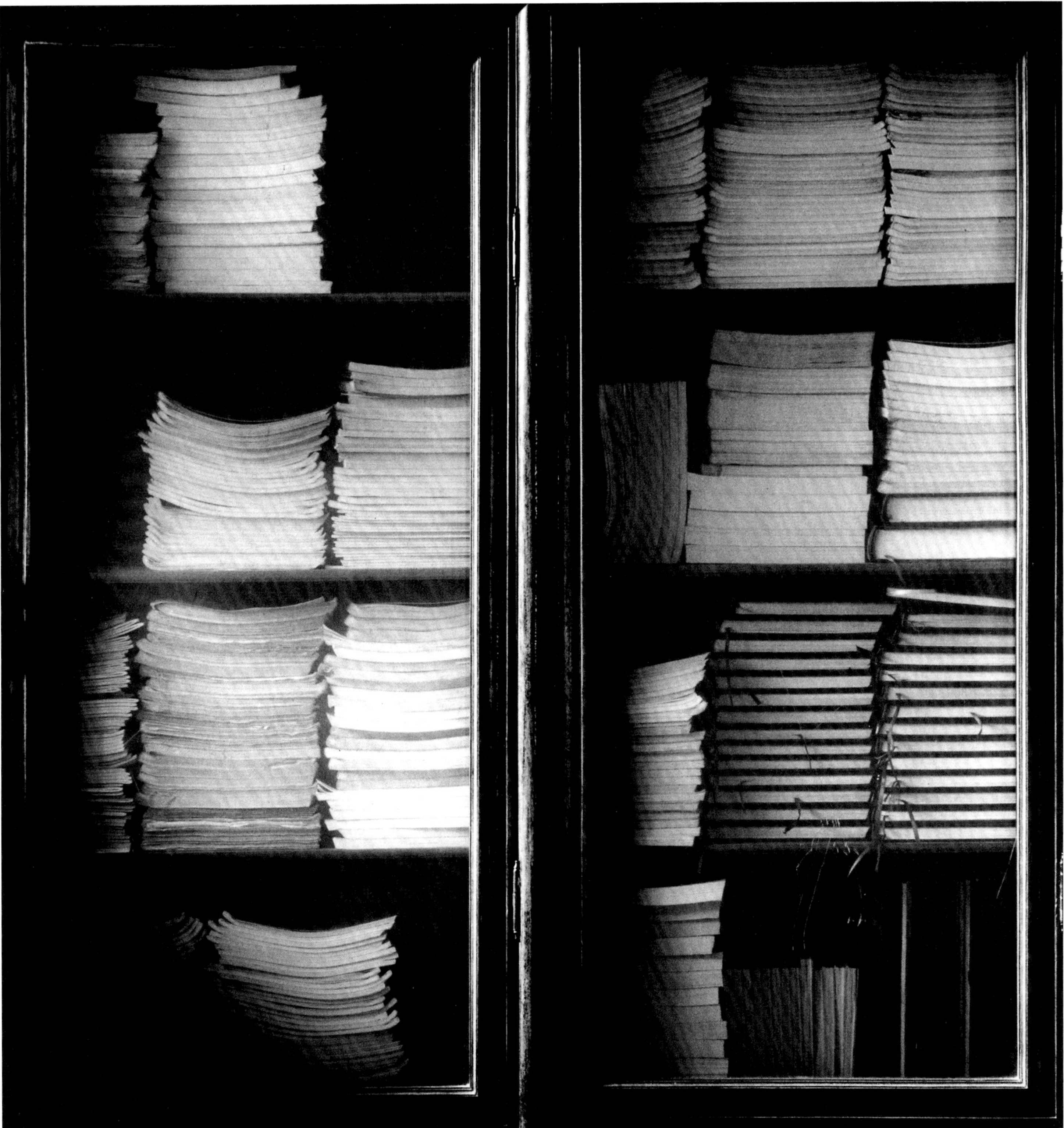

Tilting Against Windmills

I write this in the little apartment that I share with my wife in an anonymous Western-style suburb in Japan. We've spent more than thirty-two years here in these tiny two rooms, so cramped we can't open the bathroom door completely, so crowded that when our two kids were here, I had to sleep on the couch next to the TV while our poor son watched baseball on headphones.

We have no car or other mode of transportation, very little media comes here, and I have to rustle up $500 a month to pay the rent. It all feels quite luxurious.

My kindest friends often worry that I'm tilting against windmills. Books seem about as up-to-date as horse-drawn buggies and writing resembles a hobbyist's pastime akin to making ships in bottles. The book review pages in most American newspapers have disappeared; libraries these days are filled with DVDs and computer screens.

What kind of Quixote would devote all his time to producing works that few people will ever read?

Only someone who believes that writing is the richest and most delightful adventure I have ever discovered, a madness that feels like passionate romance. I've been lucky to enjoy many glorious pleasures across the planet in my almost seventy years, but none can match the one of tilting, with high spirits, against the windmills of time.

PI

White Windmills, Golden Saffron

I have been very fortunate to have had parallel and connected careers in photography, working as both a commercial advertising photographer, undertaking commissions around the world, and also pursuing my passion for more personal landscape work. I remain extremely grateful for the assignments that have taken me to places and countries I might never have dreamed of on my own. The opportunity to photograph windmills in La Mancha was wholly unexpected.

In 1996, the photographer Helmut Newton was selected to photograph for an international Spanish Tourist Office campaign. Just before the campaign began, he came down with the flu or some other malady. My clever commercial agent at the time, Tiggy Maconochie, persuaded the advertising agency to send me at short notice in his stead. Having just read *Don Quixote* by Miguel de Cervantes, I suggested that the surviving windmills of La Mancha might be an interesting subject matter. The idea was accepted and off I went to Spain accompanied by my then-wife, Camille, who spoke fluent Spanish and acted as interpreter and guide. For a week, we scoured La Mancha, searching for surviving windmills. Few were still functional, but some had been preserved and were usually situated on hilltops for the best wind conditions. While photographing them, I imagined Don Quixote charging across the fields on Rocinante, gallantly attempting to fight with them.

I printed eleven different images for the agency to consider. Study 10, photographed in the town of Consuegra, was eventually chosen and used in a worldwide advertising campaign. Some months later, I received a letter from the mayor of Consuegra, informing me that the town had conferred on me the honor of the Golden Saffron Award for services to the Consuegra community. I still treasure this letter and the golden saffron lapel pin I received.

MK

Quixote's Giants, Study 10, Consuegra, Spain, 1996

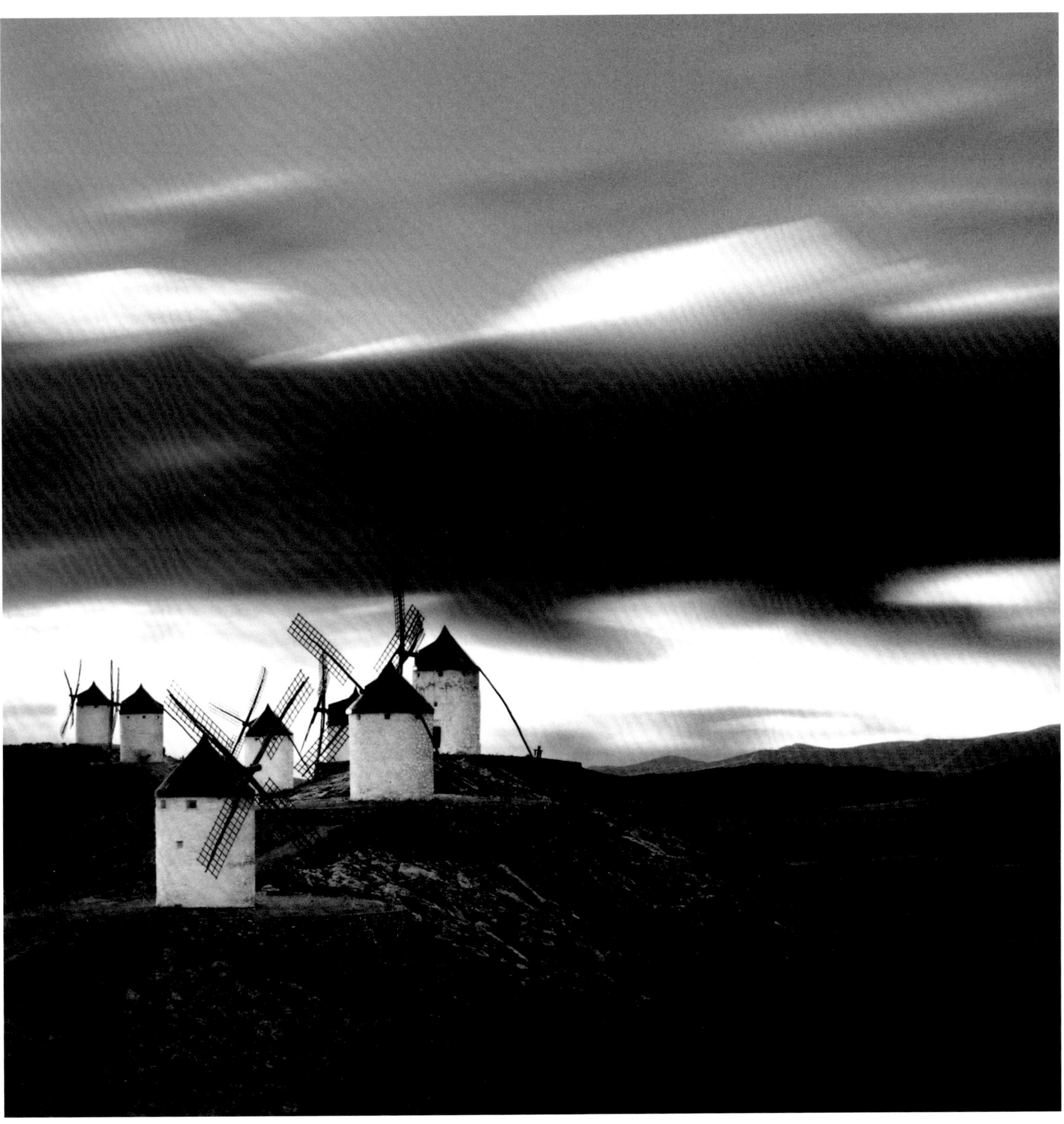

Recharging

I look at this image and realize I have nothing to say; I've never been so interested in power as in the powerless, and in how we can gather the power within to withstand the power without. And I have even less to say about Nottingham, since the only time I've visited that city was to see an uncommonly sweet and unfallen schoolfriend who was ending his days much too early.

As I saw Richard, always associated with summer days in Berkshire, hobbling into the house, barely able to move, I felt I'd arrived in the powerless station.

But 1985: what a world of wonders is hidden inside that date! I began that year with another friend from school—Bertie Wooster aspiring to be James Bond—and drove across the Atlas Mountains in the high winter sun before losing myself (and much of my mind) in the souks of Marrakech and Fès. I told my bosses, at my dream job in midtown Manhattan, that I was taking seven months off to travel across Asia, and soon found myself being turned around—and around—by Tibet, Burma, Brunei, Bali. One day the Royal Astrologer of Nepal was telling me to meditate every month on the day of the full moon (he was right, alas, and I was wrong to ignore him), the next I was losing my heart to a trishaw driver on the back-streets of Mandalay.

True power, I saw, lay not in the New York or London that I knew, but in Kyoto, Bagan, Kathmandu. And even as Michael was fixing his remarkable gaze on this structure, I was stepping out under the cobalt skies of 10,000 feet onto a sunlit terrace in Lhasa.

PI

Powerful Neighbors

I first saw the Ratcliffe Power Station while driving on the M1 from London to the North of England, having just arrived at Heathrow after a long flight from San Francisco. The eight cooling towers, with their clouds of steam rising into the sky, and a 650-foot chimney, guaranteed that the station dominated the landscape.

In my 1970s work, I looked for images consistent with a romantic vision of the arts. I was drawn to trees, misty castles, swing sets at night, waves rising from harbor walls, empty beach chairs, and the like. In the 1980s, more industrial subject matter interested me. Just a few years before, I would have spurned the power station in favor of the beautiful Nottinghamshire landscape. Now, I ignored the landscape and focused instead on this monolithic industrial construction. I would continue photographing Ratcliffe for almost twenty years.

Just twelve miles away nestled Mount Saint Bernard Abbey, along with its Cistercian order of monks. My father and stepmother used to visit and stay there, and soon I was also invited, made friends with the monks, and prayed alongside them in the abbey. I still keep in touch with the community and from time to time visit my parents' ashes that now rest peacefully in the monastery's graveyard.

Two neighboring power houses, so close together. The ostentatious, loud, fierce Ratcliffe closed in 2024. It was the last remaining operational coal-fired power station in the United Kingdom. The quiet, unassuming, almost hidden Mount Saint Bernard's calmly continues on. I wonder if there are conclusions to be drawn?

MK

Ratcliffe Power Station, Study 17, Nottinghamshire, England, 1985

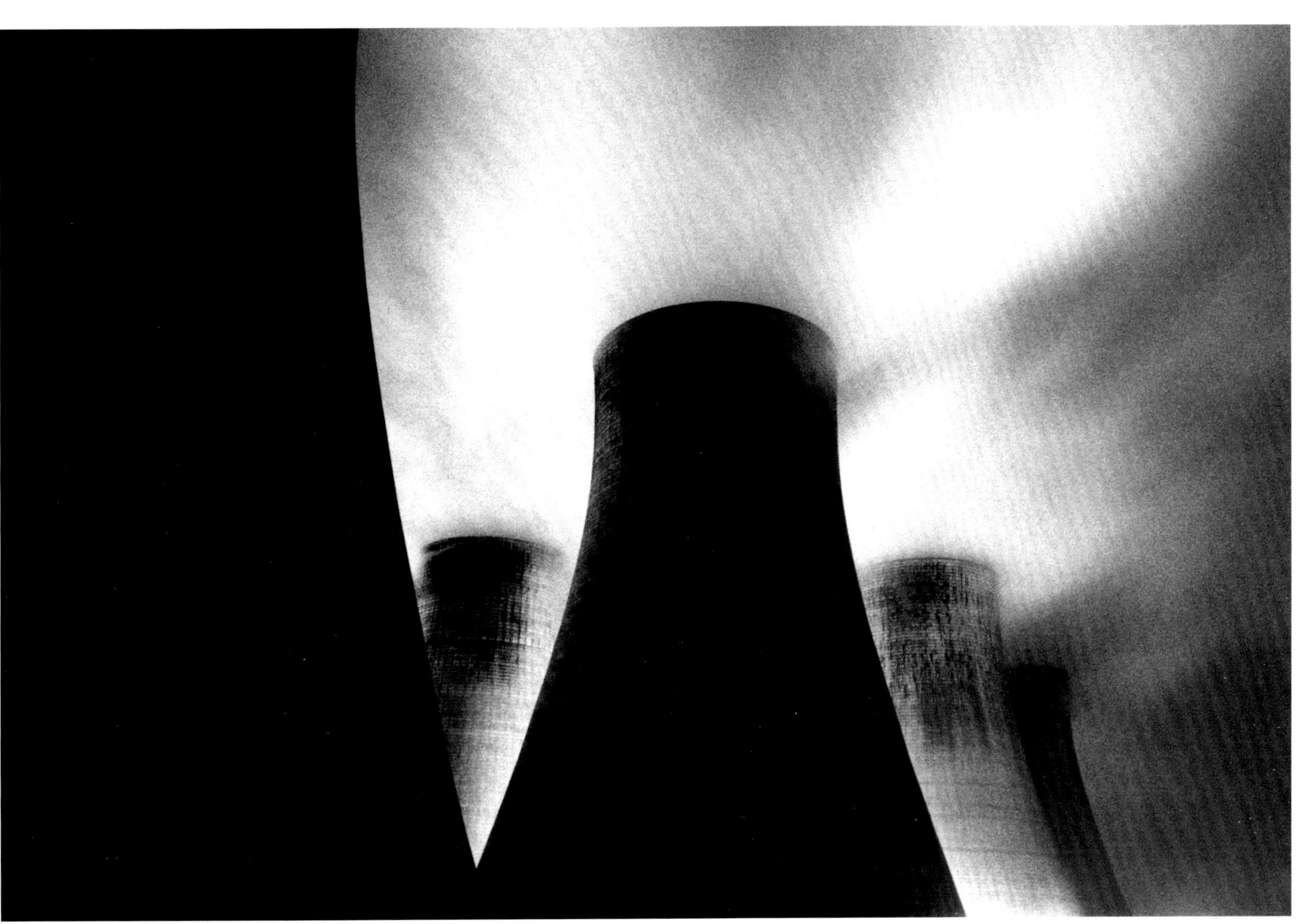

Bridges over Troubled Water

I'd never heard of Widnes until I met Michael Kenna, on the page and in real life; I'd seldom stepped, in the land of my birth, beyond the cloistered classrooms in which I served time for one long decade after another. But as I look at this image, I see the bridge that brought Michael down from his friendly home to the Oxford where I lived. Across from Oxford to the West Coast that we share, famous for its golden bridges. Over from the Far West to the Far East. And that bridge that somehow links both of us, however different we may be in skin color, origins, and sporting affiliations.

"A student of Buddhism should have no attachments," a Zen Master in Kyoto, overseeing 375 temples across the land, told me soon after I arrived in Japan. "So I have only five. Godiva chocolates. I really like. Häagen-Dazs ice cream. Starbucks coffee. Joan Baez. And"—he paused—"the image of a bridge."

Whenever he came to California he stayed in a high hotel room so he could look over at the Golden Gate. He'd made his life mission the building of bridges. To link the home where we are born to the one where we will be reborn, in a sense.

And back again.

It was in his temple, three weeks after I arrived in Japan, that I met my wife-to-be. And another bridge began to take shape, even as the night was falling.

PI

Late Afternoon Stroll

My eldest sibling, sister Pat, had told me when I saw her at the bus stop close to our family home at 49 Birchfield Road, that she was now living near the Widnes Bridge. Widnesians referred to the local bridge that crossed the River Mersey as "our" bridge—the Widnes bridge. I would only find out years later that the rest of world knew it as the Runcorn-Widnes Bridge, Runcorn being the "other" town. In the interests of full disclosure, it is now better known as the Silver Jubilee Bridge. Nothing stays the same. The year after I made this picture, maps were redrawn and Widnes was displaced from its ancestral county of Lancashire and moved into Cheshire. It didn't and still doesn't seem right!

One day, I decided to walk to my sister after school, not knowing that it was three miles away. It would be an adventure, thought I, and forgot to let my parents know! The bridge was visible on the skyline so there was little danger in getting lost. An hour and a half later, with traffic rushing this way and that, and the late afternoon light already fading, I looked out over the many rows of terraced houses visible from the bridge. I had absolutely no idea where my sister lived! There was nothing to be done—except cry.

Fortune, apparently, favors the unprepared as well as the prepared, for just then Pat looked out of her front room window at exactly the right time and recognized her little brother, bawling away, some two or three hundred feet from her. She quickly fetched me into her home. How wonderful to have a big sister!

I don't remember too much else. Surely there were hugs and kisses, a cup of tea and some biscuits, a drive home in her husband Keith's old Ford. Now, I wonder how my mum and dad felt when I didn't turn up as usual after school. This was in the days before we had telephones and tracking. They must have been worried, upset, even angry. I just don't remember, which is perhaps just as well. Selective memory comes in delightfully handy sometimes.

MK

Runcorn-Widnes Bridge, Study 2, Lancashire, England, 1973

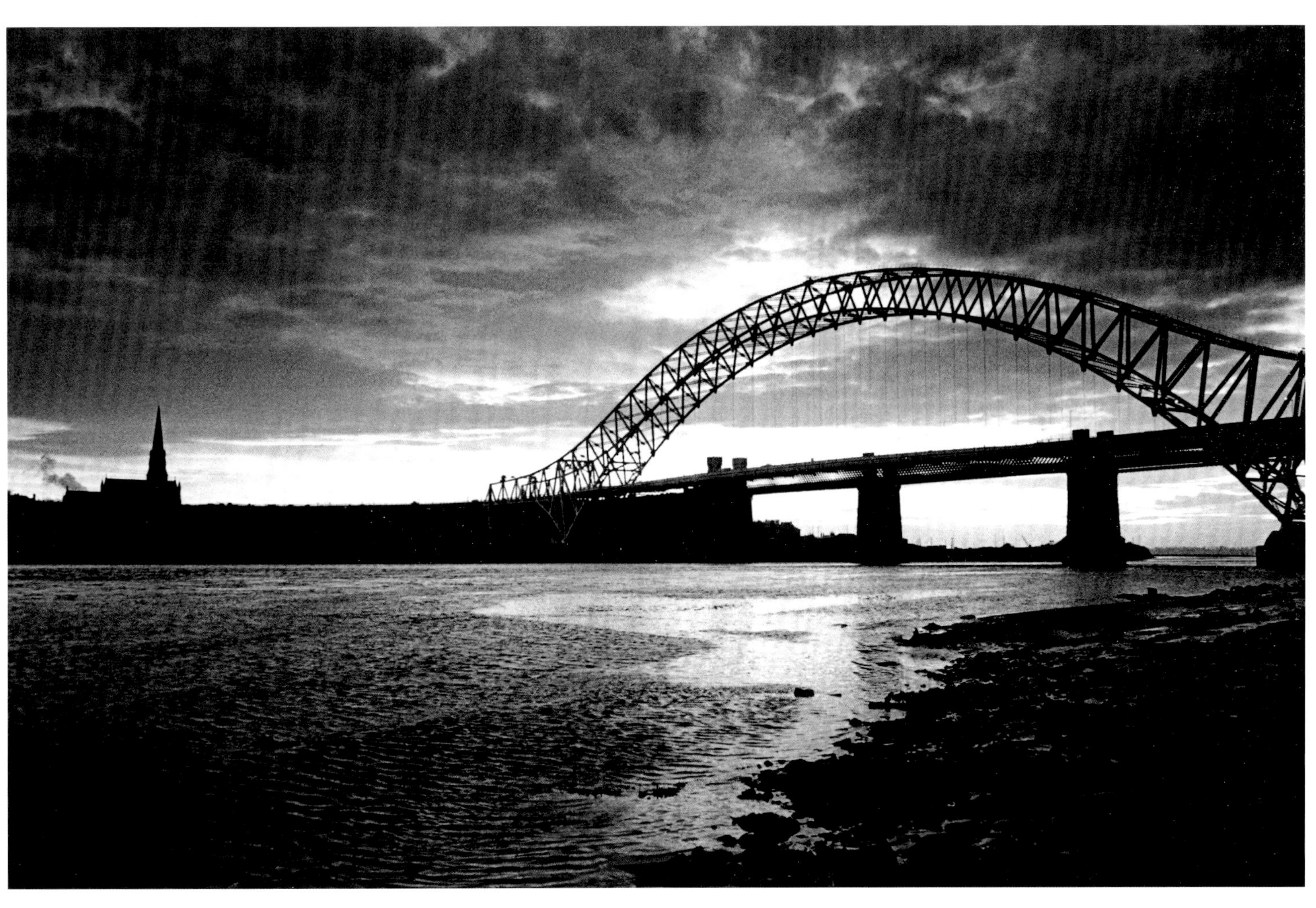

Ghosts

As soon as my fiancée and I set foot in Venice, in the last year of the last century, we found ourselves encircled by ghosts. White-faced wraiths loomed up beside us as we sat down upon a bridge; we walked through the Ghetto and living specters haunted our every step. Who was that uninvited phantom in that photo I took of Hiroko in the winter cold? Why was that man sporting a death mask, and would it come off once Carnevale was over?

In Florence, we were surrounded by specters of a different kind; memories haunt every corner, even around Michelangelo's famous sculpture. But when we stepped inside a church, Hiroko had to hurry out. Her heart was pounding, she could barely breathe: the blood, the caskets, the foot of that man otherwise shrouded in black cloth as he whispered secrets to an unseen priest.

Later that same day we walked around the fifteenth-century Dominican convent of San Marco and came upon a simple bedroom. Hiroko, long an intrepid traveler, burst into unexpected tears. Who had lived here, we asked? Oh, just a fellow called Pico, the Renaissance heretic who had published an oration on the dignity of man.

Actually, he had died in this bare room.

We shivered; my philosopher parents had been thinking of this man when they gave me my name. But not of his death, only his enduring life. The past is never gone, as it's easy to feel along the Arno and the Grand Canal; the centuries dissolve till it's unclear which of us is living and which of us is not, quite.

PI

The Audacity of Creation

I look at this image and applaud the artist who created this standing sculpture. The photograph was made in the Palazzo Vecchio when I was traveling in Florence over fifty years ago. I only recently identified the sculpture as *Samson Slaying a Philistine*, created during the years 1551–52 by Pierino da Vinci, a nephew of the more famous Leonardo da Vinci. Printing the photograph, I was reminded of what I have known for a long time, that I record, interpret, and share work created by others. Whether it is a landscape, a cityscape, a still life, an industrial scene, or even a dark image from inside a concentration camp. No matter what I photograph, I have not made the original subject matter. Each photograph is a collaboration.

Looking at the process objectively, I clicked the camera shutter on my camera (built by somebody else), while focusing on a piece of sculpture I walked by (created by somebody else). The image exposed on film (manufactured by somebody else). It was processed in a laboratory (by somebody else). Yes, I made the eventual print in my darkroom (on pre-coated paper made by somebody else), and then I had the audacity to sign it. I am mindful that when I publish or exhibit an image, protocols dictate that I stamp "copyright Michael Kenna" on the back of every print. In reality, I doubt this claim to ownership or authorship, and think of myself more as a roaming postal worker, finding, acknowledging, and transporting packages of mystery and beauty. Let's face it, in this and in other photographs, I was and remain a supporting actor in an enormous cast of giant characters, and I'm absolutely fine with that.

MK

 Sculpture Study, Florence, Italy, 1974

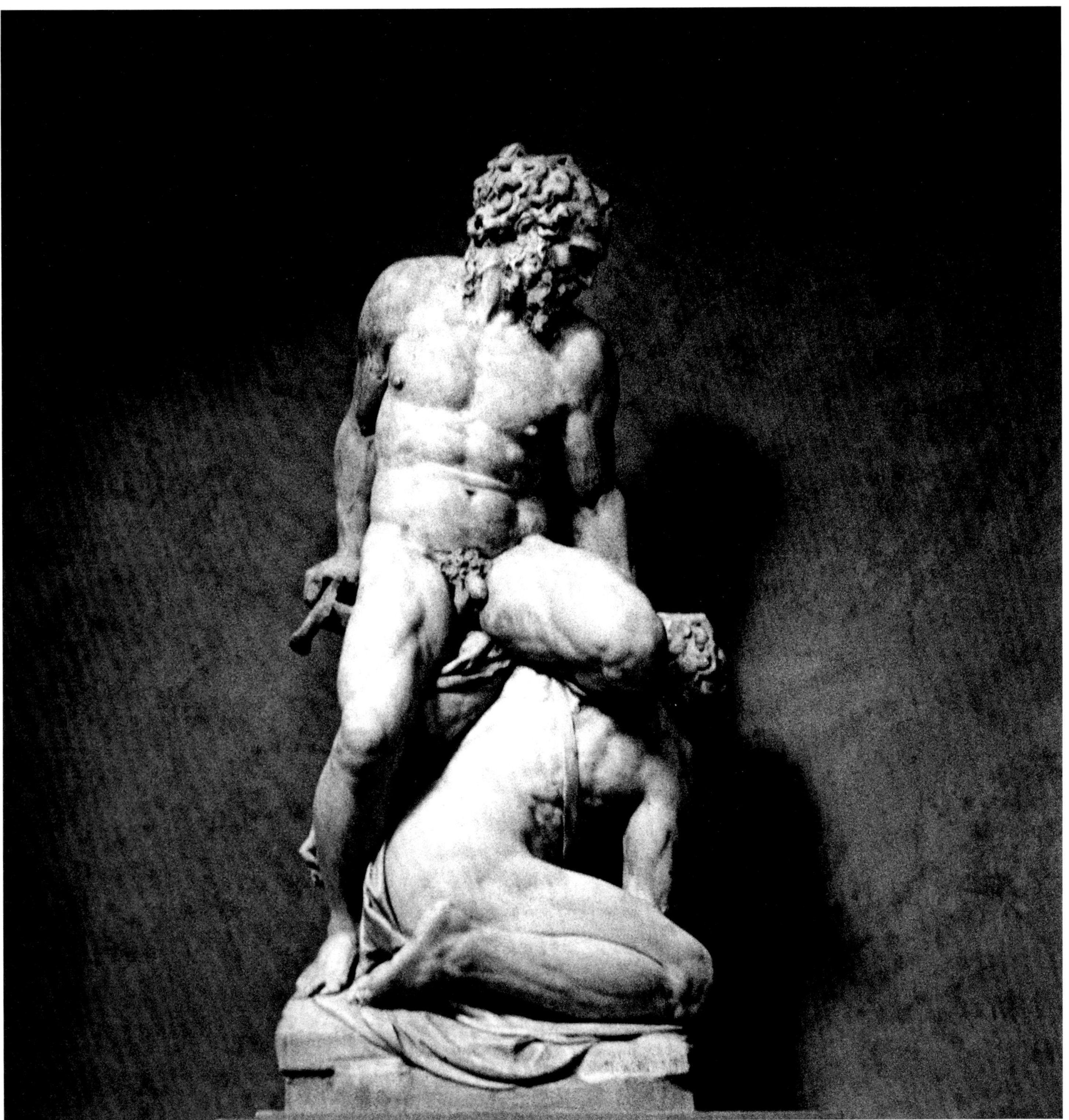

Moon Above the Mountains

In the simplicity of youth, I divided the two places that I lived between celestially: California was the sun, of course, and Japan had to be the moon. California was freedom and youth and play, the welcoming invitation of outdoors; Japan was an altogether quieter and more inward place, less bright, more subtle, protective. Across the world, the Far West was known as the Land of Eternal Summer; the Far East I came to associate more with the rice cakes and breath-held festivals of the harvest moon, celebrated each year as summer surrendered to the deepening shades of autumn.

But living in the East quite wonderfully frees one from all simplicities. The beauty of the Japanese winter is how blue the skies usually are, and how invigorating; California, meanwhile, suffers through more and more winter storms that wash away roads and trigger flash flood warnings. In Japan people feel compelled to put on a sunny face and offer public cheer regardless of what's happening in private; in California few people have qualms about sharing their shadows and even their darkness with strangers.

And as I sit in the golden light of early December here in Japan, I think of the moon above Mount Tamalpais: in so many ways, California remains a world of heavenly bodies and forests and distant peaks, all that must have quickened wonder in the earliest foreign settlers and that the native population have long known to love and to respect. There's a big moon high above those charged woods named after John Muir today, even as sunlight floods through my mock-Californian suburb, here in the eighth-century capital of Nara.

PI

Sun and Clouds, Mt. Tamalpais, California, USA, 1978

If I Had Wings

Sometimes, I have dreams in which I can fly, and they feel so liberating. It all seems so easy when asleep, a simple matter of mind over matter to rise above the ground, float, at first just around the room, and later above roads, houses, trees, and farther into the sky. I feel like a kite, able to hover, swoop, and look down at the ground below.

As a photographer, on several occasions I have been harnessed to the side of a helicopter, flying above New York City, the Swiss Alps, Panama, and Punta Brava, Mexico. They were amazing and sometimes very cold experiences. I have only ever parachuted once in my life. It was probably the single most terrifying thing I have voluntarily done. Scrunched up in a small plane, I thought my heart was going to beat out of my body. But, once I jumped from the plane and the chute opened, it was divine. Quietly floating, three and a half thousand feet in the air, nothing separating me from the sky, the distant horizons, the landscape, far below. Landing was another matter entirely, but let's not spoil things.

Back in the day, when twenty-four hours stretched further than they do now, I would sometimes drive to Mount Tamalpais, just north of San Francisco, on a late afternoon, to hike, sit, and watch the sun float above the clouds, as in this photograph, before it disappeared and sank into the beautiful blue Pacific Ocean. Or, I might read a book, that most luxurious of endangered pastimes. Occasionally, I even photographed. It was a location for hang gliders, flying humans who would soar overhead, glide past in front of me, with elegance and grace. How I wished to be one of them, with their elevated perspectives, freedom from gravity, and the wind in their hair. Flying in dreams is one thing, another when awake.

MK

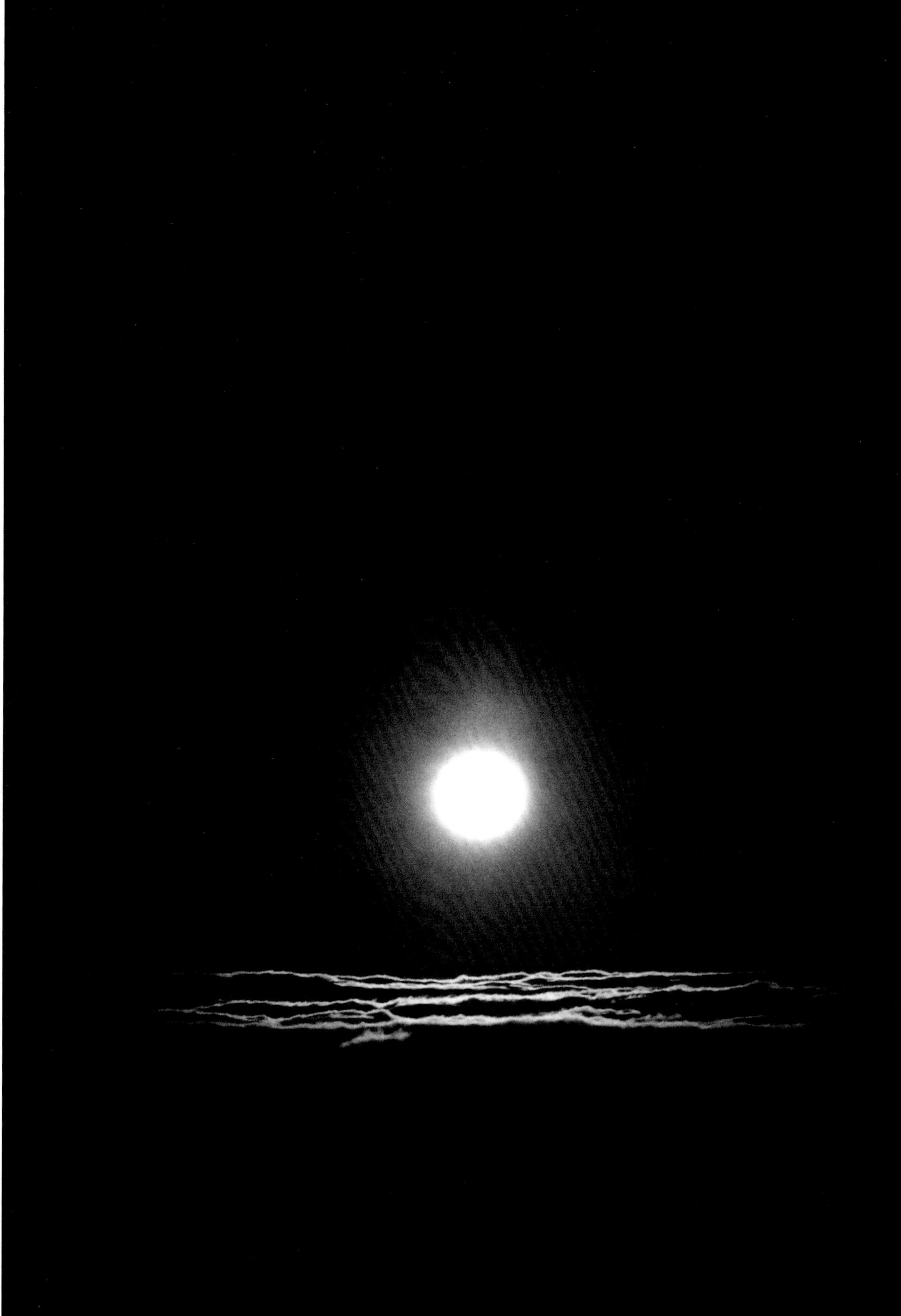

Sunset, Sunrise

The sun never set on the British Empire: that was the slogan my parents grew up on in Bombay, at a time when Britain controlled a quarter of the world. The Brits had given my mother and father English—their only common language—as well as Lord Tennyson and the Bible and cricket and fast-moving trains; I always felt they'd received the fruits of a double inheritance—all the wonders of their native India combined with something of what Britain exported.

Yet the year I came into the world, Empire began coming apart; by the time Michael looked out on this scene, the land of hope and glory was a thing of the past. Britain had come to seem a vespers place, its might of not many years before gone, its spirit and confidence vanished.

What we couldn't always recall then was that a setting sun always gives way to a rising one: I look at this image half a century later and see a Widnes boy remaking, for my Japanese neighbors, the land they thought they knew. I see myself, released from school at the end of 1974, in a year that brought me Bangalore and Dharamsala and Titicaca and Cartagena and La Paz.

I see a Britain that's infinitely younger and fresher, spicier and more brightly colored than it was then. One where the national dish is chicken tikka masala and, not long ago, the prime minister looked as foreign and improbable as I do. We could never have guessed, as the sun set over Northamptonshire in 1974, that, within our lifetimes, the Queen would be celebrating her Platinum Jubilee with a scruffy but well-meaning bear from Darkest Peru who pulled a marmalade sandwich out of his hat as she extracted one from her handbag.

Sunset is never the end of any story.

PI

After the Fox

At the start of my photographic odyssey I had more time and less money than now. I would buy film in bulk rolls and load it into individual 35mm canisters in dark rooms or cupboards. But I was never fully sure of the number of exposures I had on each roll. I often double-exposed either purposely or by mistake. Even early on, I was not so much interested in making copies of what I saw, preferring instead to attempt interpretations and variations. I experimented with grainy films and harsh processing, sometimes photographing the subject and re-exposing with the camera pointed to the ground, occasionally processing film in print developer, just to see what would happen.

As a student, I did what I could to earn my keep. This photograph was made in the Northamptonshire countryside while I was documenting a foxhunt for a local magazine. I remember riders in red jackets galloping their horses across fields, with an occasional horn sounding. The yelping hounds made lots of noise. It was all a bit alien to me, and most of the time I spent waiting and watching for them to ride by where I could see them. This photograph was made in one of the many intervals when the foxhunt was far away, and I was looking in the opposite direction, in this case at sunset.

After I processed the film, one frame at the end of the roll was so overexposed and possibly overdeveloped that it was almost black. Fortunately, I didn't snip it off and discard it. A few years would go by before I even noticed there was a hidden image. When I finally printed the negative, in my London College of Printing darkroom, the first time on Kodak Kodalith paper because of its innate contrast, I was startled to discover such a beautiful and delicate scene. I have reprinted it many times since, but due to its density, it takes hours, and then I have to hand-retouch. Much patience is required. I have no doubt that the finished and final print is well worth the extra effort and hard work. And always, in the back of my mind, I hope and pray that the fox got safely away.

MK

 Sunset, Middleton Cheney, Northamptonshire, England, 1974

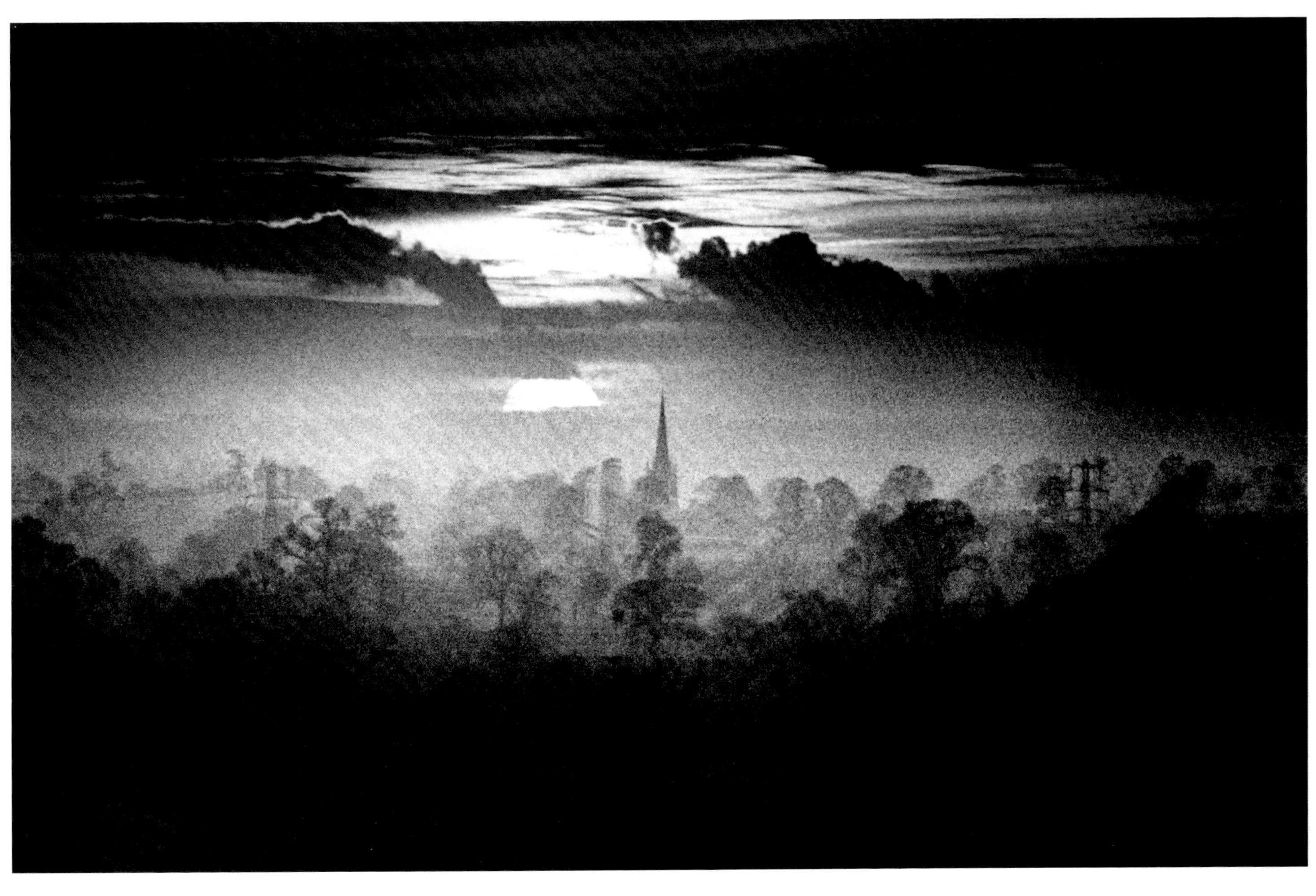

The French Lieutenant's Man

One day at college I decided to pay a visit to the living novelist who transfixed me most. I was a budding writer myself and he had enchanted me with his tales of a young Englishman, fresh out of my university, who goes to teach English on a Greek island. Before long he is being bewitched by two elusive young women and a magus who seems to shimmer enigmatically at their center.

The author had gone on to write a masterful epic about an Englishman in California, as if he were composing the next few acts of my life. I tried to type out a review of it and only fifteen years later realized that I was tapping out a memoir, or secret diary. In time I'd pay a greater tribute in a novel that, subconsciously, and to my surprise, echoed his work again and again, right down to its sentences.

As a friend and I pulled into Lyme Regis, we thought nothing of the unprepossessing coastal town in Dorset, unaware that our host would live there till his death—and that Meryl Streep would soon be swanning across its fields, in the writer's passionate nineteenth-century romance, highlighting everything that's kept out of most passionate nineteenth-century novels.

John Fowles greeted us cordially as one who'd once been where we were sitting, and spoke patiently to our tape recorder. The day became a treasure to me, a piece of magic I'd never forget, only deepened and made more haunting by this natural wonder, disclosed the year of my trip to the seaside town, and reminding me how nowhere is immune to the discoveries of clear sight.

PI

Random Sparkles and Propositions

A year after my graduation from the London College of Printing, I bought an old, secondhand twin-lens Mamiya C330 camera from my landlord and friend, Peter Espe. The camera took 120mm film, and the square format later become a hallmark of my way of working. Driving down to the south coast of England, in search of places to photograph, one of my first stops was at Lyme Regis, Dorset, the home of the Cob, a stone pier that curves out into the Channel waters. Walking along a raised seaside wall in the town, I was attracted by sparkles of light dancing on the surface of the unusually calm water. I made a series of handheld instant exposures, more to get into the groove of photographing and become comfortable with the camera than any serious work. I was not particularly excited about these photographs and continued on. It was a few weeks later, after I processed the film and made contact sheets, that I discovered this rather astonishingly beautiful swan shape that seems to float in and on the water. I regarded it then, and still do, as a whimsical gift, a kind blessing and treasured discovery.

In those early years of my photography career, I often deliberately and consciously imitated the work of the many masters that appealed to me; Atget, Brandt, Brassaï, Giacomelli, Stieglitz, Sudek, etcetera. I tried, as much as possible, to visit the places they photographed, in order to better understand their vision. I did not study the surrealistic work of Jerry Uelsmann until I met him years later, so it is difficult to imagine how I could have been influenced by him. But, looking at this image now, I regard it as a direct and conscious tribute to this great teacher and photographer who produced such imaginative and often humorous work. I am a big fan of his words: "The courage to believe we don't know what we think we know is the first stage of the discovery process." Who knows how creativity works? Perhaps if we did, it wouldn't be such an attractive proposition.

MK

 Swan Reflection, Lyme Regis, Dorset, England, 1977

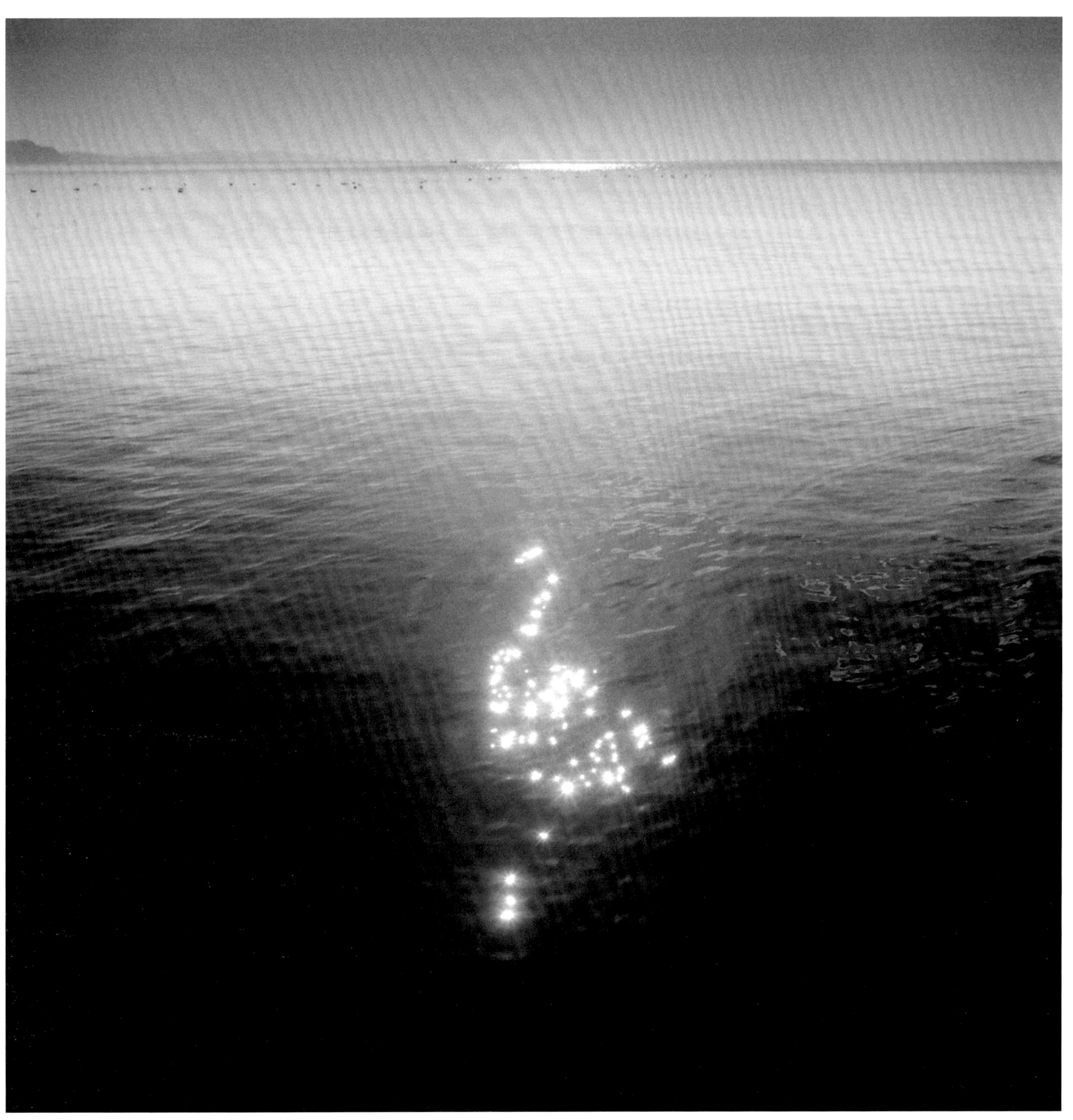

Guardians of Kyoto

I'm not sure I'd know what to make of this image—or the troubled skies above the serene curves—other than its geometry, and the way it draws our attention, though in a less emphatic, pointed way than any steeple, to the heavens. But then I read a caption of sorts—“Kyoto, 1987”—and I'm carried back to my arrival in Japan's ancient capital that very year, and maybe in the very season when this image came to light.

They say that each of us has two homes: the one in which we were born and the one in which we become ourselves. The one, you could say of the latter, that finds us and reminds us of a past—a future—we didn't know we have. That's how Kyoto struck me, especially along its eastern hills: the secret, unofficial home that could be the only place where I might wish to belong.

I left my office in Manhattan and arrived on the backstreets, with a large suitcase, to stay in a room in a temple a little bit like this one. All around me, along the eastern hills, were other temple roofs. If they were not the ones I had imagined, that in itself was a liberation. Nothing went the way I had planned for my “temple year,” which was a daily blessing.

So when I look at this image now, even if I can't make out all its details, it reminds me of the time when I found the land, the lifestyle, and the partner I hope will be mine forever. The year this photograph was born was the year when I, in near-finished form, came to life as well.

PI

Kyoto Possibilities

On my first visit to the lovely city of Kyoto in late September 1987, I recall, with some degree of nostalgia, memories from when everything in Japan was new and exciting to me. I would walk for miles, entranced, observing everything I could, exploring nooks and crannies, and I photographed. I remember wandering along the lanes of Gion, shyly entering dark, exotic Buddhist temples and bright, colorful Shinto shrines. I attended ritualistic tea ceremonies, marveled at beautiful scrolls with inscrutable kanji characters. I discovered the mysteries of hot *ofuro* bathing, and slept on tatami floors in an old riverside ryokan. I dined in convenience stores and attempted my first faltering words of Japanese. Falling in love with Japan, then and there, quickly, quietly, and inexorably, was inevitable.

Pico's wonderful love story, *The Lady and the Monk*, only came into my life some nineteen years later and became my favorite book of all time. His experiences echoed, articulated, and brought into focus so many of my own that had faded over the years. He wrote what I felt, but hadn't the means to express. I had not even heard of Pico Iyer at the time, and the book just fell into my hands on my first day in India. Little did I know that it would be the start of an unexpected extremely rich and greatly appreciated friendship.

Pico lived in Kyoto for some years. He spent his time observing and making notes (as well as falling in love with his wonderful wife Hiroko san). When I first devoured his book, I lived vicariously through his dancing, insightful, and suggestive words. Very surprisingly, it took several readings before I made the elementary deduction that, just like in Oxfordshire and California, we would have been in many of the same locales in Kyoto at the very same time. Perhaps, as I observed and photographed these temple rooftops on a cloudy early morning, Pico might have been walking nearby, busily scribbling his own observations into one of his many notebooks. Whether or not that happened is ultimately immaterial. It is the possibility that makes me chuckle.

MK

 Temple Rooftops, Kyoto, Honshu, Japan, 1987

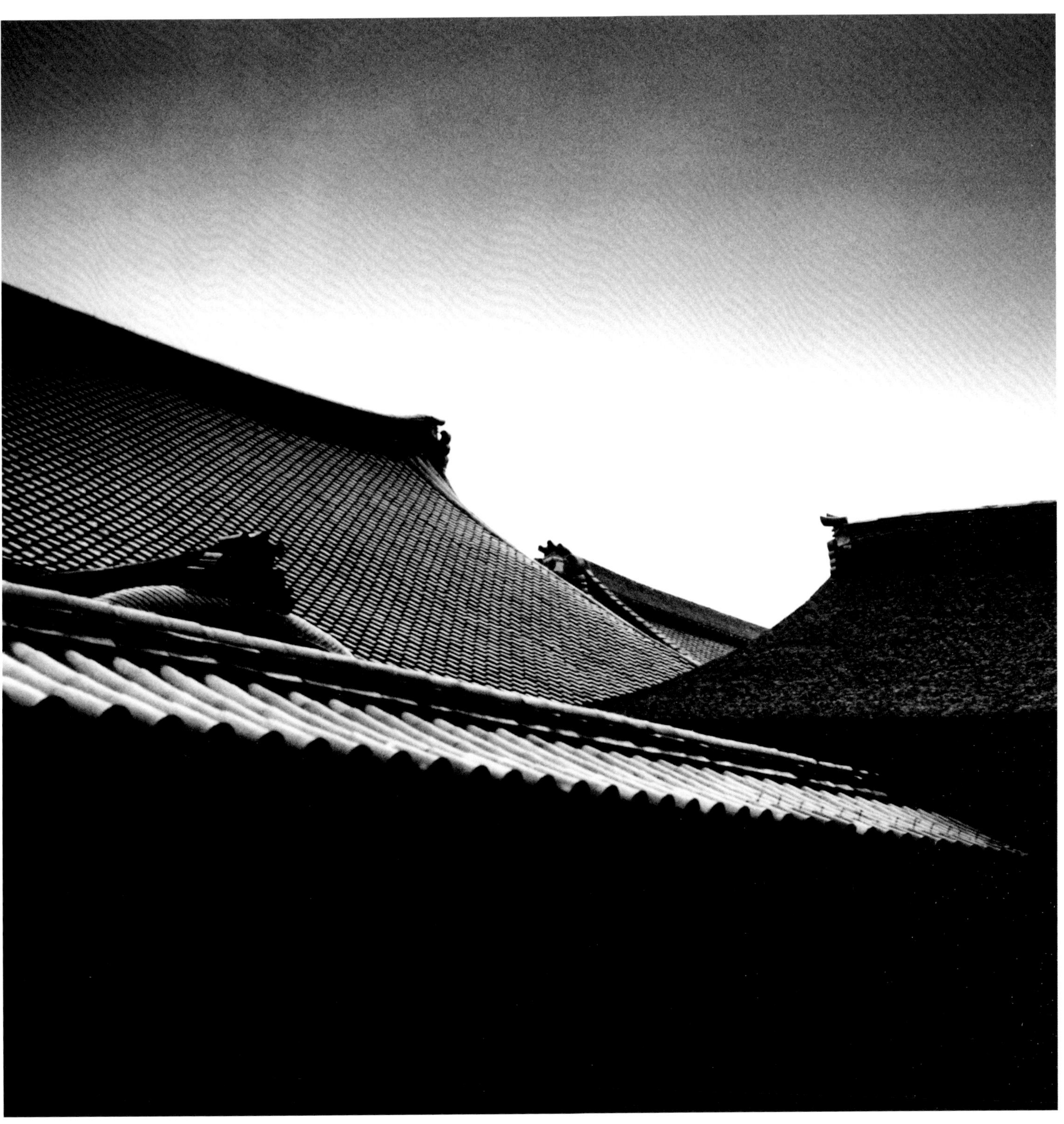

Orpheus with no Eurydice

I turn away from this image and pretend I never saw it. Pyramids fascinate many of my friends as monuments to human devotion, the sites of spiritual ceremonies. From Egypt to Mexico, they represent grand gestures towards the heavens. But for me they represent the underground, something inverted and pointing towards the center of the earth.

At eighteen I was wandering around buildings such as these in Guatemala and I got lost. I was in the middle of the jungle; the darkness was falling and at one point I fell into a ditch.

I have no memory now of how I emerged and made my way back to the simple lodge, but the pyramids seemed to bring me down, to my knees and beyond, towards the land of the dead.

The next year I took my girlfriend of the time to Egypt. In the dark privacy of the pyramids, a wizened old man led her into a corner, and then started pawing her, while I, in a different corner, felt strange hands moving all over me.

Twenty years on, I brought my wife-to-be to the pyramids in Mexico and she clambered up them, delighted by the prospect. I stayed where I was, always wary of heights, and feeling these structures were homes to the dead more than sanctuaries for anyone who lives.

Is this a comforting image? Not for me.

PI

Disconcertingly Beautiful

I had visited Teotihuacan back in the 1970s, in the days when I was an impoverished student living hand to mouth. It was in late August, and I was there along with countless other tourists, under a blazing hot sun. In complete awe of these gigantic constructions, as all the others, I waited in a long line for my turn to climb to the top. None of my photographs from that first visit are memorable, albeit the experience was. Some thirty years later, here I was, with Mamta, my wife-to-be, in total darkness, waiting for the dawn. My guides had driven us from Mexico City and had arranged special permission to photograph before the site opened to tourists. One of the great advantages of commercially assigned work is that sometimes it is possible to access restricted places of beauty and mystery.

The pouring rain stopped just as the first light began to appear on the horizon. Mamta and I had already climbed the Pyramid of the Moon and now we were looking out over the great expanse in front of us. I began a series of long time exposures of some of the smaller pyramids, with the great Pyramid of the Sun looming in the background. Standing there, I felt grateful, fortunate, and blessed. Before us was the presence of a phenomena beyond our comprehension. Visually, I was stunned. Intellectually, I couldn't help but consider how these monumental pyramids were constructed. No doubt thousands of laborers were involved, probably slaves. Many must have experienced their darkest hours here. Nobody truly knows how or why the pyramids were built, although many theories abound. The relationship between what we see, what we know, and what we imagine can be curiously disconcerting, excruciatingly beautiful, and very uncomfortable, all at the same time. A bit like life.

MK

Teotihuacan Pyramids, Study 2, Mexico, 2006

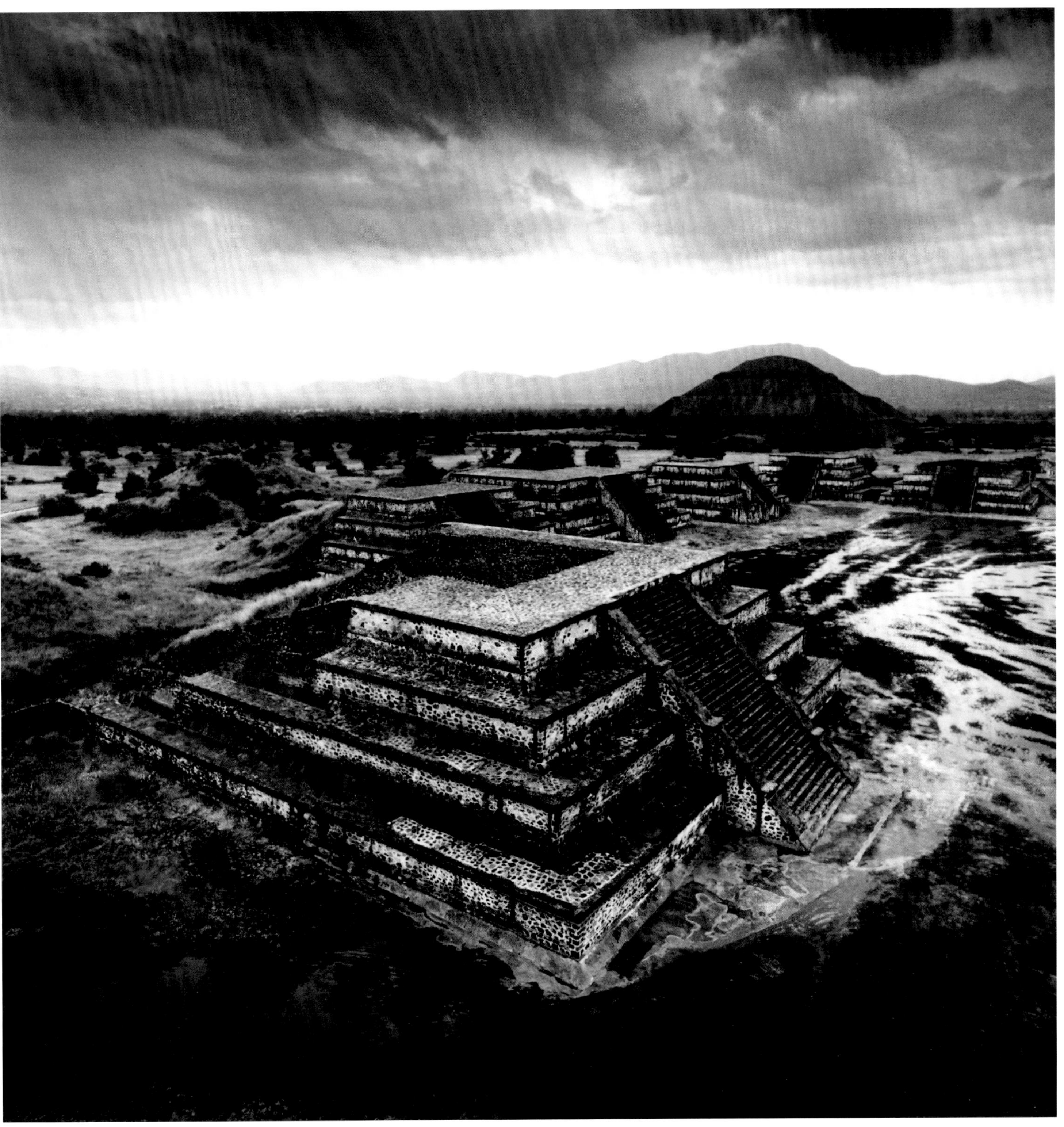

Backstage at Dawn

Every morning I stepped out onto the Bund in Shanghai, to find senior citizens serenely waltzing in the early light. They'd set out boom boxes beside them—this was late in the last century—and they were silently guiding one another around as if in the dancehalls of Vienna a hundred years before.

Around them, other grandparents were practicing tai chi as the light came up above the quiet street. Ghosting their way through wind and water as their ancestors from a thousand years before might have done in perhaps this very space. Some were performing calisthenics, a few bright sparks were even racing past in a morning jog. But still the couples elegantly went about their movements, starting each day with the body's equivalent of a prayer.

Across the street the old guys who'd been playing in the jazz band in the Peace Hotel had all gone home. Shanghai lived still in a kind of time warp, a sleeping beauty that had not been jolted awake in sixty years.

Now I look at this photograph and see how much has changed. The city's stylish kids cannot even remember the twentieth century. But venture out at dawn, when all the lights have dimmed and the streaking city is still abed, and perhaps you'll find those same couples, even now, keeping the ancestral rites alive.

PI

Bar on the Bund

Multitasking is not my thing, So, it is a rare treat to sleep at night, knowing that I am also being productive and creative. Night photography entails setting cameras on tripods, opening their shutters for many hours, and forgetting about them. Whatever happens does so without the photographer needing to predict, control, or otherwise be involved. Sheer luxury. Of course, one shouldn't have high expectations, or any expectations at all. Night photography can be a valuable lesson and practice in the art of letting go, allowing external events and actions to orchestrate their own story. On a practical level, once the shutter is open, it is not even possible to see through the viewfinder, and, sometimes, it is a relief to no longer have that responsibility.

In my limited experience, the Shanghai Bund is a constant hive of activity both during the day and at night. When photographing, it is necessary to be vigilant, to not miss the action that happens in front, to the side, and behind. How convenient it was to stay in a hotel with such a fine perspective on the river. Once the hotel guests left the cozy bar, around midnight, I set up and started with various short exposures, before bidding my camera and tripod goodnight, leaving with the shutter left open. I returned perhaps six hours later, before dawn, to close the shutter, not knowing what, if anything, had recorded on the film.

Shanghai apparently does not sleep, judging by the activity recorded while I was in dreamland. The resulting image shows us the evidence of several ships sailing along the Huangpu River, with some docking for the night. The famous Zhongshan Road, with its crazily fantastic vistas of the Pudong, the other side of the river, had been equally busy, judging by the number of light lines left on the negative. The photograph reveals what the eye cannot see, accumulated time, in a city that apparently never, ever, rests.

MK

The Bund, Study 1, Shanghai, China, 2011

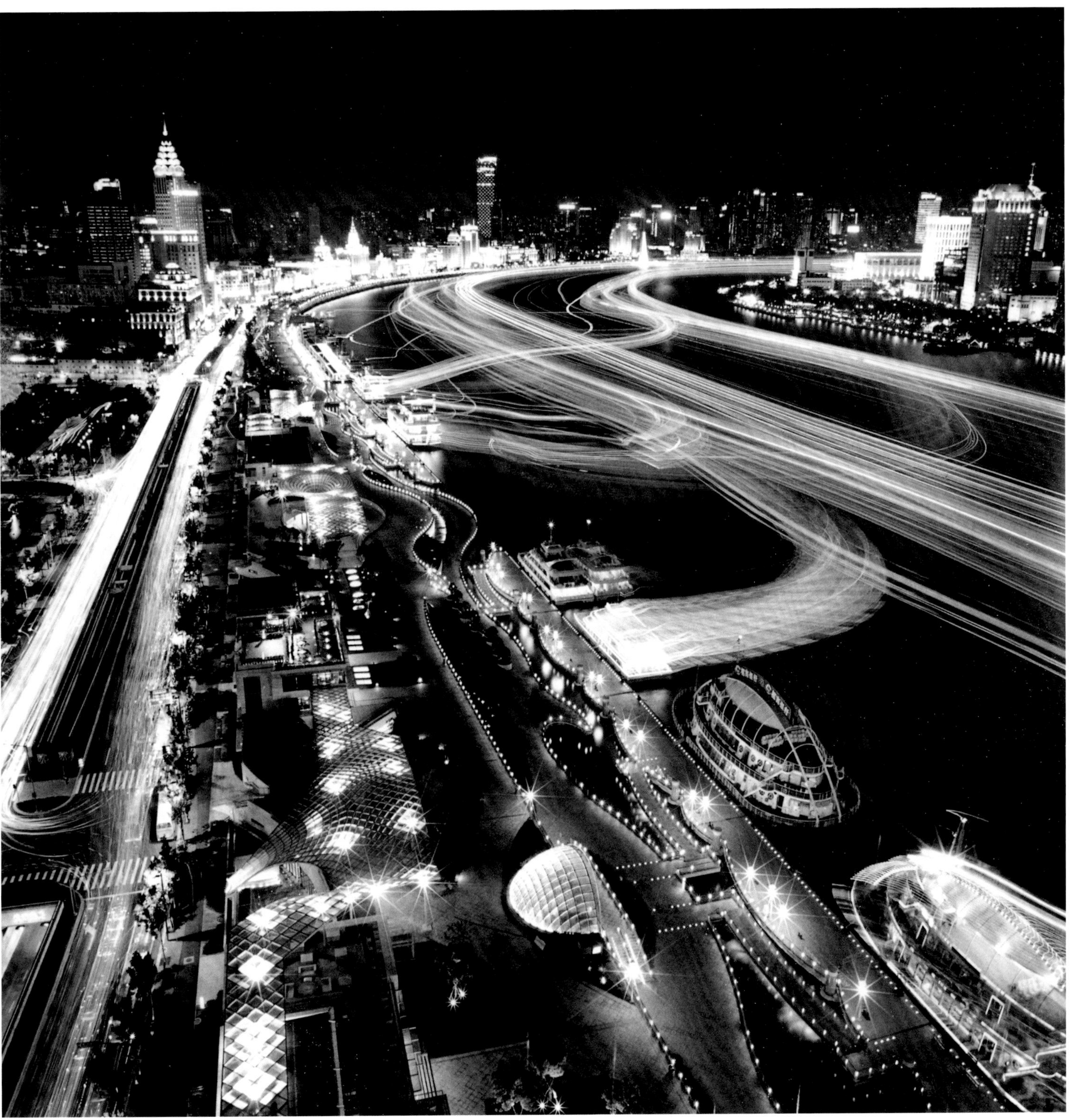

Interdependence

When first I stepped off the plane in Thailand, in 1983, Buddhas were the last thing on my mind: the little van that took me into town from the small and broken airport was bumping through rain-streaked alleyways with neon here and there above the red lanterns. Shops were open to the street; figures were stepping gingerly across back roads that were turning into streams. Bangkok's first few shiny shopping malls were all that suggested I wasn't in a city-sized aquarium.

Today, after more than forty years in Asia, I'm not surprised to find every border between living things and humans dissolved. Interdependence seemed to be what the Buddha was teaching: care for every sentient being. In Kyoto more than two hundred trees are officially designated as guardians of the ancient capital, as essential to its welfare as the wooden temples all around. In all kinds of ways, we've come to see that the environment is as much a part of us, and we of it, as fingers and a hand.

In Bali, when I took my Japanese wife there, she pointed out that it was impossible to tell where the humans ended and the trees began. Or—once the dancing started—where either one gave out and the gods or spirits appeared. I had such a simple idea of this-and-that when I arrived in the East. Now I hardly distinguish between one kind of living creature and another; they all seem to be wound around one another in a tight embrace.

PI

Multidenominational Flora

I first experienced Buddhism in 1987, in Japan, and was mesmerized by the complex and imaginative rituals and iconography. I find much of Buddhist imagery to be powerful and inspiring, as well as being calmly peaceful and serene. Photographing in temples and pagodas is an aspect of my work that runs parallel to and integrates into a whole range of other subject areas. So, having photographed a water lily in Laos in 2015, which I misguidedly thought was a lotus flower, and then dedicating it with the wrong title to my wife, I was very happy to try and make amends by photographing these actual lotus flowers in an Ayutthaya temple in Thailand four years later.

I write these few words while looking at the Andaman Sea in Phuket a few hours before sunset. I feel this country in my skin, having visited most years since 2009. Mamta and I even had a Buddhist Beatles and Bollywood wedding party here with family and friends in 2011. Now we often return, and when possible we like to visit temples, such seductively atmospheric places, fragrant with exotic incense, and replete with offerings of fruit and flowers, where one can hear evocative sounds of bells, ritual chants, and incantations. These spaces hold a fascination and attraction close to how I felt in the Catholic churches of my youth.

Ultimately, in my life, the specificity of religion doesn't matter so much to me anymore. We each have our preferences and persuasions, perhaps based on tradition, or our own life experiences and learning, but I believe these flowers would be as gorgeous in whichever institution of worship they adorned.

MK

Three Lotus Flowers, Ayutthaya, Thailand, 2019

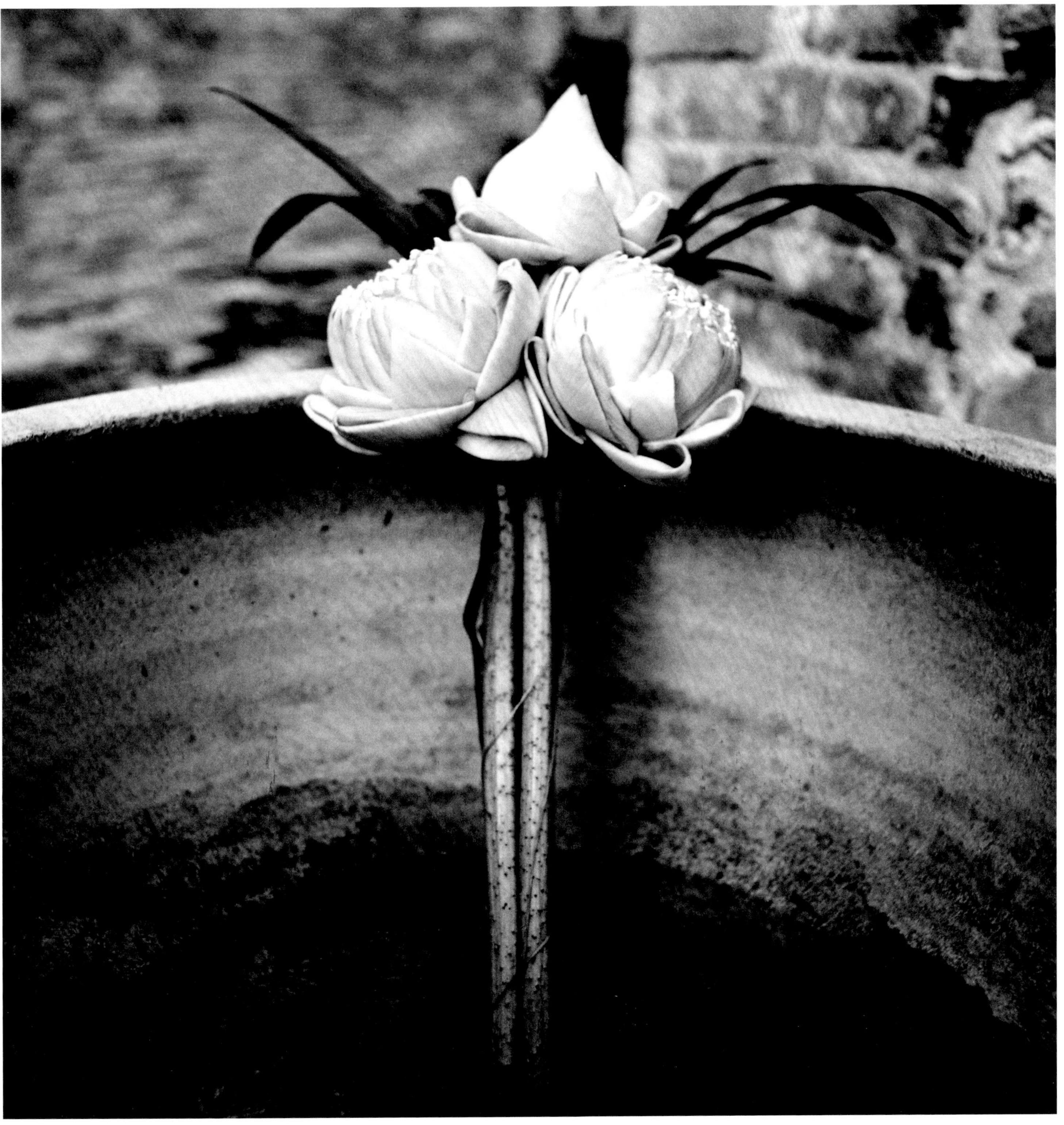

The Domino Effect

As a boy, I kept hearing of the "domino effect." If just one country fell, we were told, again and again, all its neighbors would go too, till the whole world had entirely collapsed. It takes only one tilting pole to crash upon another, and a whole cycle is set into motion from which there can be no recovery.

But what if the dominoes bring delight? What if happiness is infectious and kindness begins to trigger one act of selflessness after another? What if the domino effect is a tipping point, and what these poles promise to bring us is something good?

When I traveled around Cuba, north and south and in every direction, just three years after this image came into the world, I saw old men gathered everywhere, on the broken streets, to play dominoes. They had little food; there was no work that would reward them. I learned to bring bars of soap and tubes of toothpaste and every kind of essential to an island of bare shelves.

But they had the game and the domino effect: one man's joy was giving rise to his neighbor's, till all of them, with nothing else to do, were making merry. One woman gave her neighbor chicken; the neighbor reciprocated with some beer.

Maybe this picture could be an image of delight and even solidarity?

PI

The Teeth Have It

My first student summer job, at age fifteen, was at Bowens Chemicals, Widnes. The factory was old and decrepit, and work involved emptying and sieving large bags of malic acid onto a motorized machine, eight hours a day. The foreman introduced me to the other all male workers, asking them to go easy on me, explaining with a wink that I was a young seminarian, studying to become a priest. This chat took place in the small hut where we gathered for tea breaks and ate our packed lunch sandwiches. It was plastered, wall to wall, with colorful and explicit magazine centerfolds of naked women.

The work was monotonous and tedious, in an environment of rusting pipes and clanking machinery, accompanied by strange and often obnoxious smells. I made up my own crossword puzzles on discarded acid sacks to pass the time. One afternoon, in a remote part of the factory where I wasn't supposed to be, I climbed up a ladder and looked into a gigantic centrifuge that was mixing chemicals. The center of this large vat was visually hypnotic and appeared to recede and almost disappear, sucking me in.

I heard a distant siren getting closer, louder, and more irritating. I couldn't move. My face and head hurt as I woke up, as if from a nightmare. Nothing made sense. I was horizontal, strapped into a bed in the back of an ambulance, speeding towards a hospital. I'll never know exactly what happened, but I had been knocked unconscious and the right side of my jaw was shattered.

Years later, I traded a print of this image with a kindly dentist in San Francisco who told me that he saw the white posts as teeth. Having had my jaw wired together for many months after the accident, I have since had a rich and eventful dental history. Now, whenever I see this image, I also can't help but think of teeth, and then Bowens.

MK

 Tilted Poles, Rhyl, Clwyd, Wales, 1984

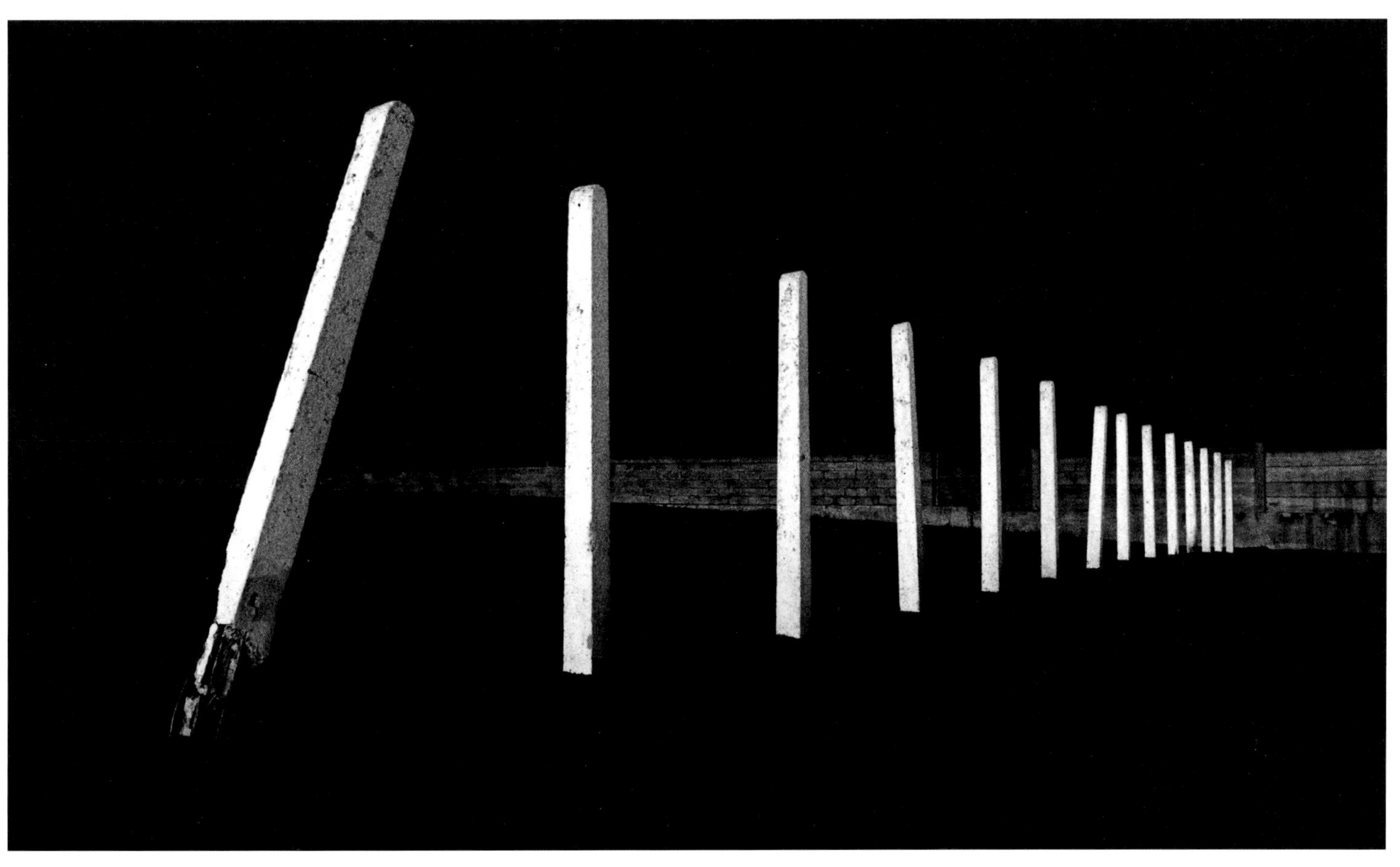

The Bullet Train of History

I arrived in China by train from Hong Kong in 1985. I got out in Guangzhou, and could not read a sign. Nearly everybody was wearing the blue clothes mandated by Mao Zedong. There was no traffic in the streets, almost nobody—except for restless students—spoke English. There were no billboards, no bright lights, and at the center of the broad main drag people were playing leisurely games of badminton while cyclists thundered past.

What could I do? No visitors were expected then, and every office I entered led to another office and then another in a labyrinth of bureaucracy that threatened to leave me stranded at the station for life.

Finally, with the help of a kind student, I boarded a train for the long, long trip to Beijing.

Returning now, I find Chinese trains crisscrossing the land at dizzying speeds; flying across the Pacific to Shanghai, I board a maglev train at the airport that whisks me into the midst of seven hundred many-colored skyscrapers at 225 miles per hour, leaving me as bewildered as a newcomer from the countryside (or from some forgotten century).

No wonder the transformation of China is the most striking historic development of my time, other than the creation of the cyberworld. These trains might almost be waiting for a future that will never come, as much a relic of the past as the terracotta warriors in Xi'an.

PI

Trainspotting

The smell of burning coal, oil, metal, and steam lingered around the Widnes North train station, a ten-minute walk from our house. I spent hours and days there, running up and down the two platforms, writing down numbers located on the side of locomotives and carriages. Whenever possible I picked up discarded passenger tickets to add to my collection. In the early 1960s, steam engines still plied their way between Liverpool and Manchester, passing through Widnes. An advancing white cloud would be seen in the distance, puffing its way towards us. Then a repetitious rhythmic chugging noise could be heard, increasing in intensity as the train approached. Sometimes, I would run up onto the steel bridge that joined the two platforms and thrill in the warm embrace of the damp steam cloud as it passed beneath me.

Car numbers also interested me. When not at the station, I might be found sitting on the steps of our main road front door, collecting and writing down license plate numbers that I would sort and alphabetize. I collected cigarette boxes, matchbox labels, and stamps. I collected rugby league programs and passionately attended all the Widnes matches I could. My first part-time paid job, when I was nine or ten, was selling lottery tickets and programs at these fixtures. Sometimes, my dad would go to away matches and bring back programs from exotic-sounding neighboring towns such as Batley, Bradford, Halifax, Huddersfield, Swinton, and Wigan. Years later, I would photograph these places. I also collected postcards from our summer one-day family coach excursions to seaside destinations such as Blackpool, Llandudno, Rhyl, and Scarborough, places I would also later photograph. I even had a collection of glass bottles, under an old tombstone in the nearby Saint Bede's cemetery, and a collection of beer bottle tops from the adjoining working men's club.

It is said that necessity is the mother of invention. With little pocket money, few possessions, and even fewer distractions, collecting took up much of my boyhood time. I think this early penchant greatly influenced my later life as a photographer. Little has changed, for I now spend most of my time collecting images.

MK

 Train Yard, Beijing, China, 2016

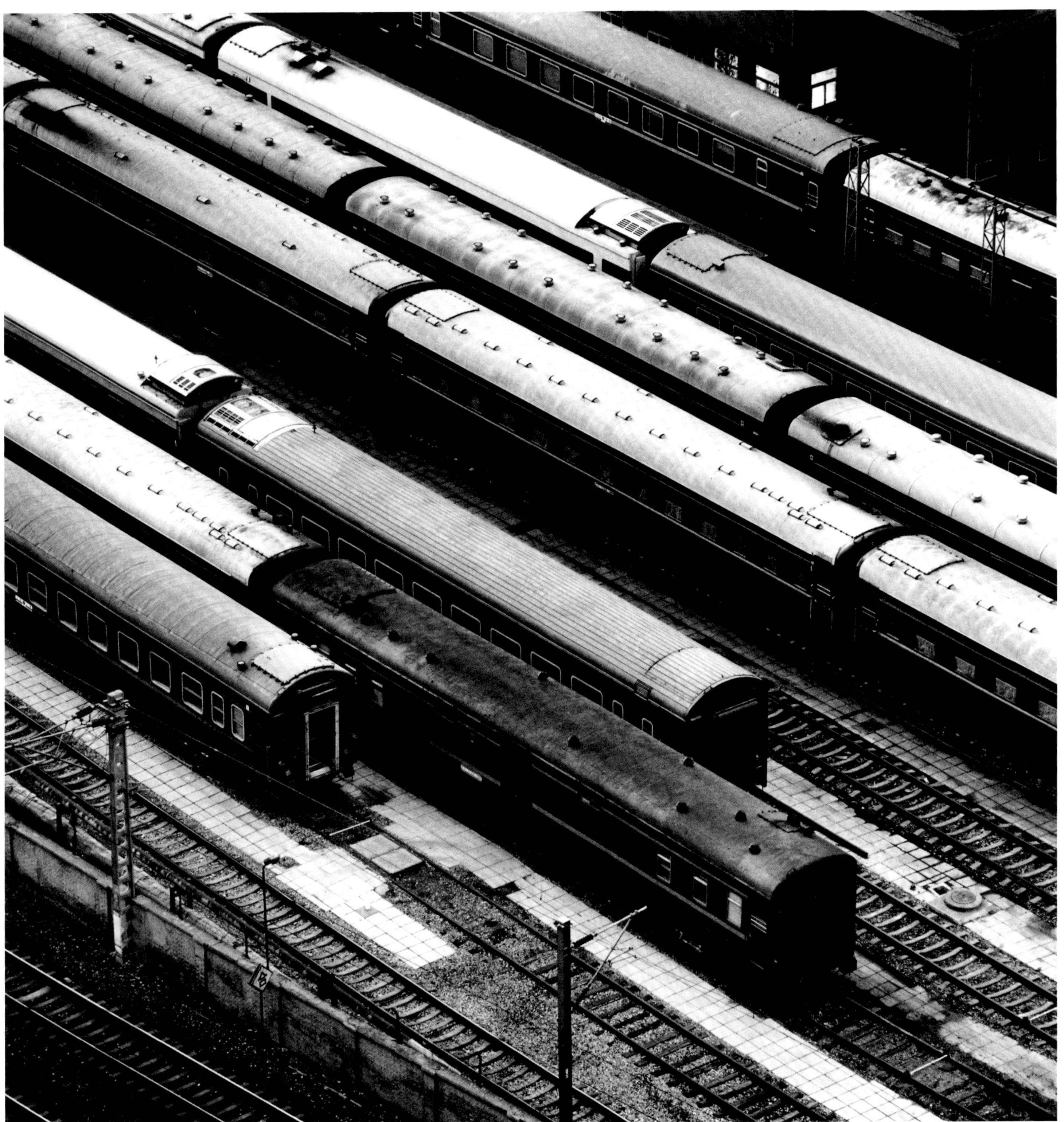

Break Point

It is the special treat of every English midsummer: houses across the land fill with screens showing perfectly trimmed green lawns, and the soundtrack of every home becomes polite applause, an umpire's recitation of mysterious numbers, and (in my day at least) one Dan Maskell, on the BBC, after a dazzling rally, simply murmuring, "Marvelous!"

Wimbledon, the tennis tournament, is too easily the home of a never-never kind of nostalgia for a land that's rarely so decorous or orderly or full of curtsies. But how can I deny that it evokes my sweetest memories from boyhood, a collective calm that now I try to revive by sitting in front of a television, on the far side of the world, and watching the changeless ballet of white-clad competitors and the couples in cool sunglasses who observe them?

The year this image from Wimbledon emerged, I was waking up before dawn in my parent's house in California to gather with my mother in front of the TV: "Breakfast at Wimbledon" with the stylish and marveling Dick Enberg, next to the over-heated dynamo and fountain of enthusiasm known as Bud Collins.

We sat, rapt, as Borg and McEnroe exchanged one long rally after another, and this is what I see now, superimposing my memories upon the bucolic silence: Borg as steady, as invisible, as the trees in the background, always there, while McEnroe bends and twists in front of us.

Would anyone looking at this picture register that it's taken in a busy and not so pastoral suburb of London? Formality and elegance take so many (sometimes more than human) forms.

PI

Prescient Pico Prevails

As with millions of others, Wimbledon means tennis. The annual championships, now televised internationally, have been held there for almost one hundred and fifty years, and as I write these words, the 2025 tournament has just finished. Early on, in the opening rounds, Pico wrote to me with his preference for the Polish Iga Świątek, and the Italian Jannik Sinner. I chose the Belarussian Aryna Sabalenka, and the Spaniard Carlos Alcaraz. Of course, tennis followers will now know the perfectly prescient Pico prevailed on all counts. Writing to congratulate him on his astute choices, I received an automated reply apologizing that he was on retreat for some days. I surmised that he was taking a timeout, in his beloved California hermitage, away from the noise and distractions of daily life, away even from the ongoing England vs. India cricket match, to recharge and just be. Nothing to be sorry about, Pico!

The exposure for this photograph was a fraction of a second, and the image is still here, forty-five years later. Astonishing! Time is such an all-pervading ingredient of life, physically measurable and quantifiable, yet subjectively immeasurable, sometimes seeming to shrink, at others to telescope and stretch. Time heals us and kills us. We count in seconds, days, and years, and time ticks on regardless, not waiting for anybody or anything.

This morning, during Shavasana, at the end of a yoga class, I heard the instructor's gentle words: relax, be still, this is your time. I know what he meant, but couldn't help thinking that everything we claim to own, is borrowed, including time. Acceptance of the past, the present, and the future, with equilibrium and patience, is perhaps the way to go. But, dammit, it's not easy!

MK

 Trees, Wimbledon Park, London, England, 1980

There's Rosemary, That's for Remembrance

When Ophelia starts scattering flowers in *Hamlet*, she begins by assigning a mental activity to each: "There's fennel for you and columbines; there's rue for you, and some for me." I never dreamed I would meet such a grace in life till I stepped into Japan and met my wife-to-be.

Whenever we visited someone's house—that of my boyhood friend Martine, for example—she would choose flowers carefully calibrated to match the person she imagined (or remembered) at the other end. The flowers were as alive to her as the people; in time she would tell me, if I were cursing my computer, to talk to it as a friend and, as soon as I did, sure enough, it would respond better. When we stepped into an elevator, she would say, "This elevator's name is Tom," and suddenly a routine mechanical trip turned into a human and engaging conversation.

Nothing is inanimate in Japan and very little is accidental; the gods live in the details. All of which is one reason why we knew, before we met him, that Michael must be Japanese, within; there's so much human emotion in his canvases, though they contain no humans.

I'm sitting here on a rainy day in Vancouver even as my wife is hoping to greet Michael and Mamta at an exhibition in Kyoto. I can't help wondering which flowers she will choose for them today, to match—or even to anticipate—their beings.

PI

La Vie en Rose

Albert Einstein once remarked, "There are only two ways to live your life. One is as though nothing is a miracle. The other is as though everything is a miracle." Most certainly, Martine Renaudeau d'Arc was a miracle. For well over twenty years, I was blessed to have her as my agent for Europe. She was a supremely powerful advocate. Like her namesake and ancestor, Jeanne d'Arc, Martine was neither afraid nor frightened of anything or anybody. With her passionate spirit and drive, her relentless enthusiasm and energy, her infectious smile and laughter, she was a shining example of how to do good in this world. Her sudden passing was a tragedy when she accidentally reversed her car off a small cliff in her beloved village of Bargème, crashing into an unforgiving road below.

I am trying to remember the occasion for these thirty-four roses. Perhaps it was to celebrate Martine's March 22nd birthday. I know that I made the photograph in her Paris apartment on rue Daniel Stern after she had cooked her specialty dish of salted white fish with buttered new potatoes, followed by her signature quatre-quarts pound cake, the remainder of which I always took with me on my photography adventures.

Martine loved to smoke cigarettes, which is now considered unhealthy and rightly so. None the less, after a delicious dinner with red wine, it was her great joy to light up and savor one or two. Sometimes, she would send me out to buy her a pack from the local *tabac*. For years, she tried to give up the habit. Her family and friends pressured her with many arguments that all made sense then, and still do now. Yet when she died, far too young, and much too early, one of my first thoughts was that I wished she had enjoyed her tobacco, guilt-free. Smoking gave her such pleasure and happiness. I hope you will not judge this strange stream of consciousness too harshly. From flowers to cigarettes then. *Au revoir, ma chérie. Bon voyage et bon courage. Merci bien pour tout. Je t'aime.*

MK

Trente-Quatre Roses, Chez Martine, Paris, France, 2009

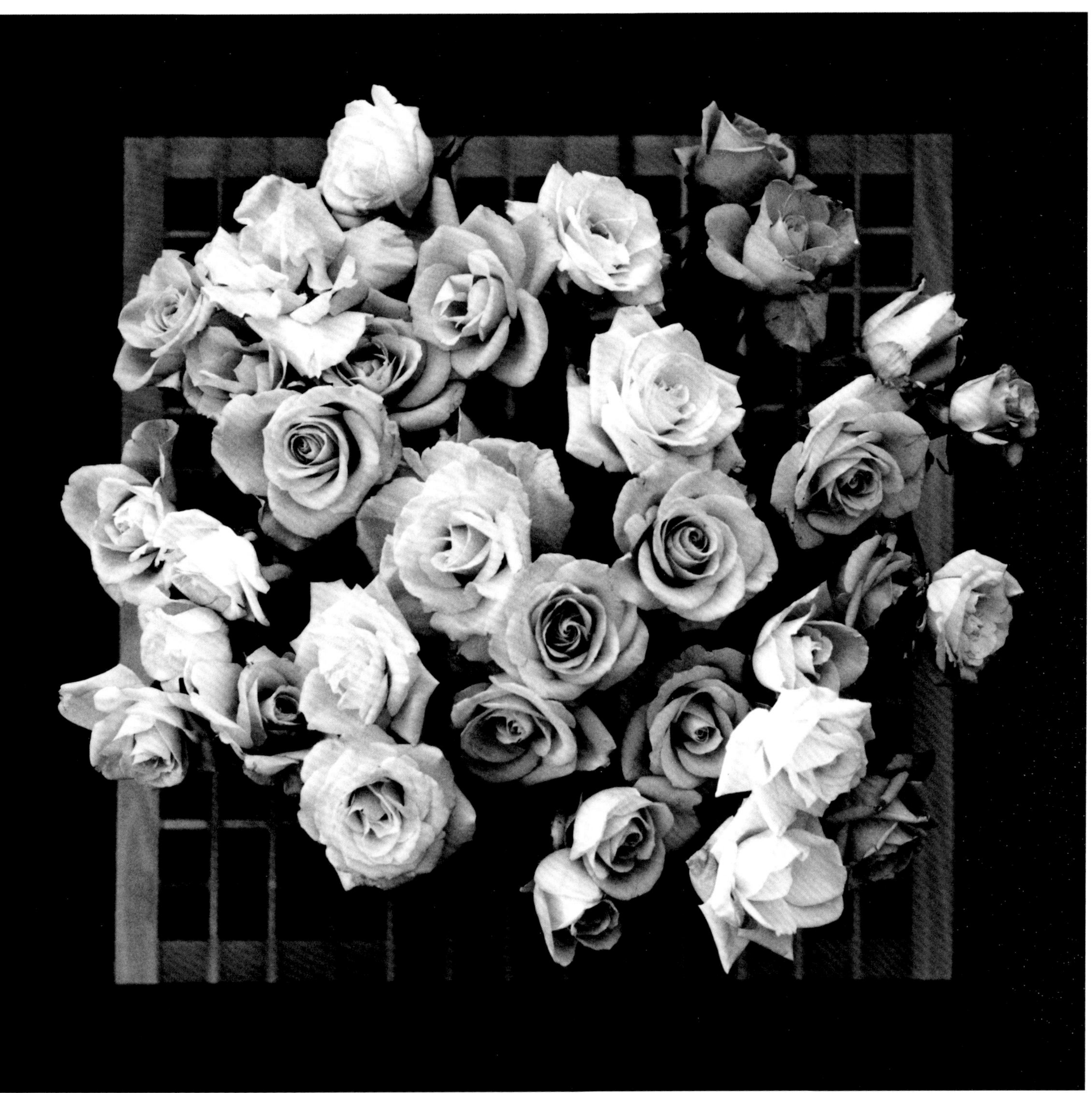

Figures in the Distance

You could say that this image is an exercise in scale: the figures at the top give emphasis, by being almost invisible, to the power and size of the stone in the foreground. They turn the photograph into a kind of allegory: thanks to their presence, it's not a landscape painting, but perhaps an image of a pilgrim's progress. What might such people be talking about when confronted with such an enigmatic site?

Or maybe they're holding their breath. Perhaps words are beside the point in the presence of such mystery. Humans fill the space that surrounds stone circles with theories and speculations, but none of those feels quite so solid as the stones themselves.

Some devotees of the Kenna oeuvre will gleefully note that this is the rare photograph of his in which humans figure. They will debate about his choices, ask why in this one instance he elected to include them (and celebrate them in his title). They may even suggest that the humans are effectively serving as sticks, poles that make the larger geometry more haunting.

I prefer to think that their presence reinforces an absence—and makes this, perhaps, deep down, an image of everything that makes human explanations very small indeed.

PI

Light Bulbs and Ancient Stones

Other than "What sort of film do you use," the second most frequently asked question is "Why don't you include people in your photographs?" Attempting humor, my standard answer is that people will not sit still for the required hour exposure, and that I prefer to make portraits of trees as they seem rarely disappointed with my efforts. More thoughtful responses might include that figures give scale and specificity to an image, they attract attention, and take away from our own imaginative storytelling. I prefer to invite viewers into an empty space where they can wander, away from chatter and distractions, and perhaps enjoy a moment or two of peace, or even recharge, before returning to their everyday lives. I often used a theater analogy. I am more interested to photograph the atmosphere contained in the pregnant pauses before a performance, or the residual thoughts, feelings, words, and actions floating around after the curtain has come down. In short, the presence of absence. The performance itself is a whole different world where we are encouraged to follow the actors' actions and words, their stories.

In this photograph, I was and still am fascinated by the simple connection of foreground and background planes of space. In the camera viewfinder, I often float abstract arrangements of backgrounds and foregrounds around the image rectangle. I love to create patterns, configurations, and contractions, and, occasionally, fascinating juxtapositions happen. Here, figures in the distance, on a hillside, appear to walk on an ancient Avebury standing stone. Perhaps in our day and age of digital manipulation, this is not as astonishing as it was to me back in the day. Nowadays, digital manipulation could easily import and place those figures. Maybe this image hearkens back to a time of photographic innocence when its power was locked more into its connection to reality. Made almost fifty years ago, this simple picture was a light-bulb moment for me, and it remains very dear to my heart.

MK

 Two People, Avebury Stone Circle, Wiltshire, England, 1977

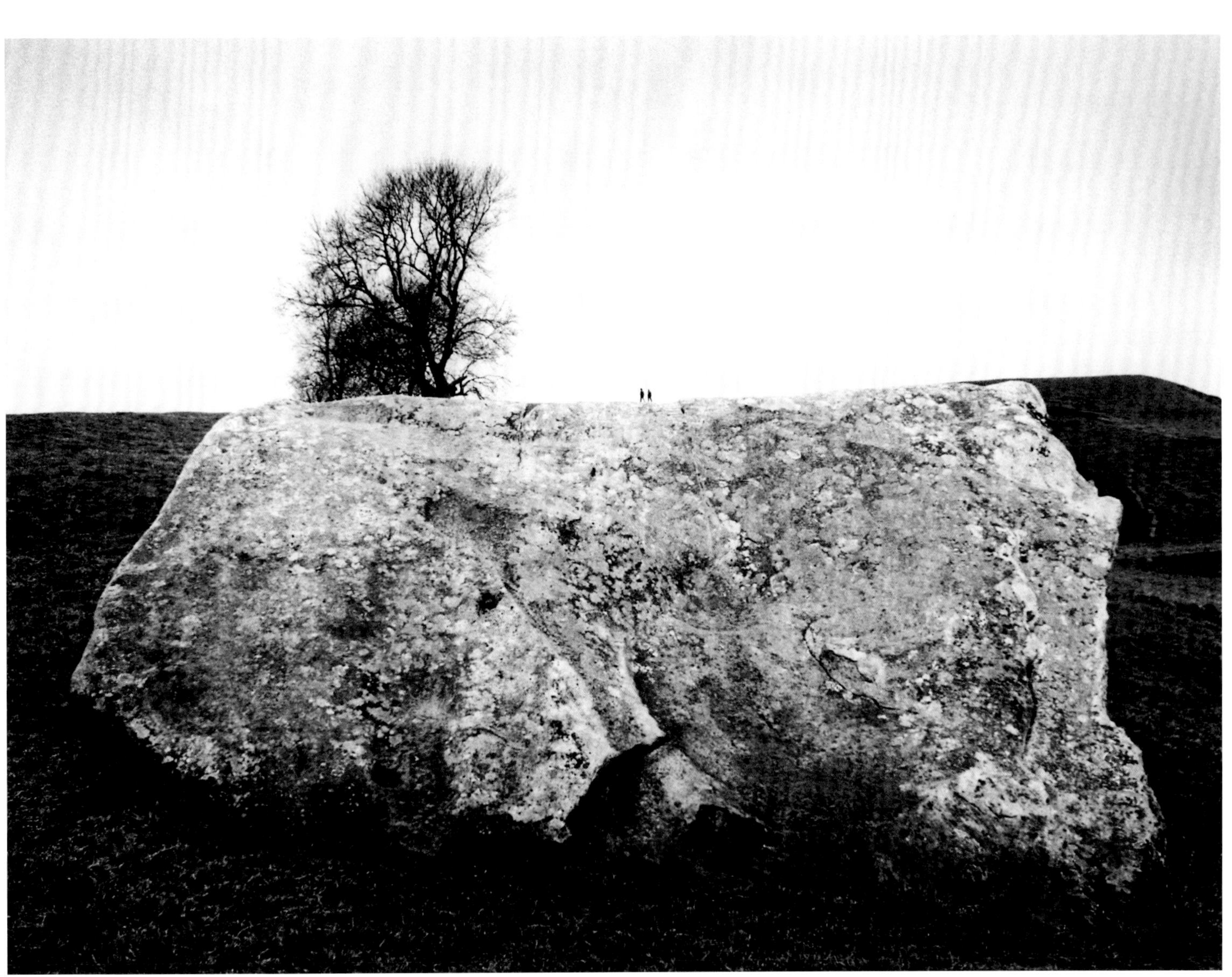

The Flight into the Future

Maybe this stylish image speaks for the reason that both Michael and I ended up moving across the Atlantic and settling in the open spaces of the New World. In England I'd been surrounded by artifacts of the past, growing up in musty cloisters where I could hardly move for the crowds of ghosts. At school we recited speeches in ancient Greek among busts representing poets and prime ministers from ancient history; in the evenings we gathered in the oldest classroom on the planet, constructed in 1441, to recite the Lord's Prayer in Latin.

Inscribed on the benches on which we sat were the names of all the boys who had suffered through such arcane rites in previous centuries; along the walls, as we walked to breakfast, were long, long lists of names of all those lost to one war or the next. We could scarcely breathe for the presence of generation upon generation of those who had knelt and prayed and longed to escape just as we now did.

I arrived in California and stepped into a world as elemental as sun and cloud. An unhistoried land that seemed to exist outside of time. It felt like a parable, or a landscape made for myth; the dominant forces were trees and sky and ocean and sand. Humans could barely be seen in this wilderness.

For one who'd grown up on a tiny island where we could scarcely move for the presence of our predecessors, this was emancipation into a land of allegory.

PI

Puddings and Koans

It is said that every picture tells a story, but I'm not confident that is completely accurate. I think images might suggest stories, but they need viewers with their creative and individual imaginations. I look at this image and imagine a "morning after" scenario. I question what happened on that particular beach, the night before? What conversations occurred, stories related? How did a chair end up upended in the incoming tide? Or is it outgoing, and is that even relevant to the story? What was the photographer thinking? How was this image made? It is up to the viewer to decode, narrate, and extrapolate. At the end of the day, isn't that what it's all about—a conversation between photographer, subject matter, and viewer? Do images exist when nobody is looking at them? Could that be considered a Buddhist koan akin to "What is the sound of one hand clapping?"

Recently it was written by one of my professional associates, "Obviously, Kenna is English so he cannot have a clear opinion." Whereas that is probably true, as my opinions and ideas shift with the wind, I do believe, at least for now, that images are catalysts for storytelling, starting points for our ideas and imaginations to fly. This theory provided the initial seed for this collaborative book. I began to send images to my dear friend Pico, not so that he could write about them, although of course he is a trained professional and would be more than capable of doing a brilliant job. No, I wanted him to let his creative stream of consciousness lead him to whatever destination it might. I was not intending the picture to tell the story; it was most definitely going to be Pico Iyer. Later, Pico ever so kindly suggested that I also scribble down my thoughts and feelings on each image. The eventual juxtapositions of our texts, written independently, unseen and unread by either of us, might make for an interesting dialogue. It was an experiment, a leap of faith, far more from Pico's side than mine.

Well, as it is also said, the proof is in the pudding...

MK

 Upset Chair, Pompano, Florida, USA, 1992

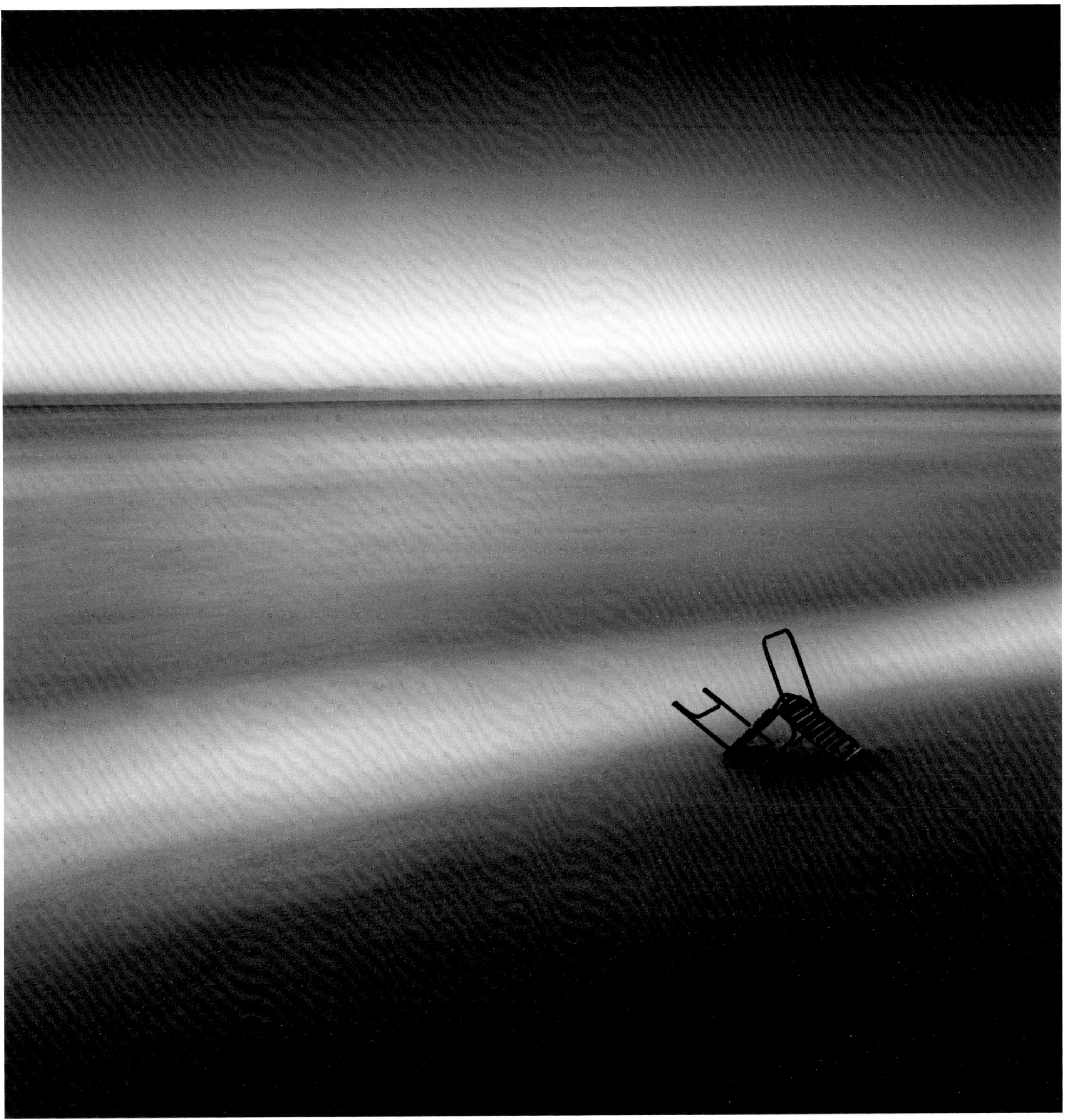

Our Secret Maps

The older I get, the more I come to see life as a simple progression, from romance to realism, and beyond, culminating finally, perhaps, in the awareness that reality itself, if properly viewed, can be the greatest romance of all.

At eighteen, just released from school—and one year before this image was made—I set my sights on the Andes. There were many reasons to head off for South America's highest mountains—Paddington Bear, adventure, romance, an encounter with the indigenous rites of Bolivia and Peru. But one among them was the chance to see the Nazca lines, those geoglyphs that are said to be discernible only from a great height.

To a teenager, they suggested aliens, UFOs, occult astronomical calendars, or just the wide fancies of science fiction.

Only sixteen years on did I learn that ley lines are a property of England, too. That mystical signs might crisscross the plain, unremarkable fields among which I'd grown up. These too seemed to constitute a hidden map of sorts, linking the land's most ancient sites. A proof that one did not have to go far to find mystery.

The shape, the enigma—the existence—of such lines is magical, especially when disclosed by a master photographer. But perhaps the best thing about them is that they can be a feature of our home. Nothing is without wonder if inspected with fresh and open eyes.

PI

Procrastination Makes Perfect

As a student in swinging London during the psychedelic 1970s, my work was predictably more experimental, and even colorful, than it is now. On a London College of Printing class field trip to Wiltshire, we had stopped at the famous White Horse of Westbury, drawn in lime on the hillside. While everybody else was admiring and photographing the magnificent horse, I was looking at the strange patterns on the lower valley floor. I rather think it is the proclivity, if not duty, of those in creative fields to look right when others are looking left.

My penchant for not following trends, fashions, and movements started a long time ago. For example, my dad was an avid Liverpool FC Reds supporter, so I, of course, became a die-hard Everton Blues fan. No need to tell you who won the premiership title last season, but at least my team avoided relegation, once again. My aversion or resistance to following is possibly one reason why I have not yet embraced the digital revolution and still work with an antiquated, archaic, and delightfully analog process. Anyway, shunning Ansel Adams's excellent and very popular practice of pre-visualization, I was much more a follower of Jerry Uelsmann's theory of post-visualization, putting off until later decisions that could be made right away. Some might use the other term—procrastination.

This image literally came together, weeks after the photograph was made. Technically, it is one negative printed twice—a straight print and then flipped and printed in reverse. The two are joined together, rephotographed, and printed again. The result, at least for me, is more than the sum of the two parts. Even back then, I was more interested in photographing what we cannot see, but can perhaps imagine, than making accurate and descriptive records of what was in front of me. I now like to think this was the first of many Buddhas I would photograph, although I had no clue at the time.

MK

 Valley, Westbury, Wiltshire, England, 1976

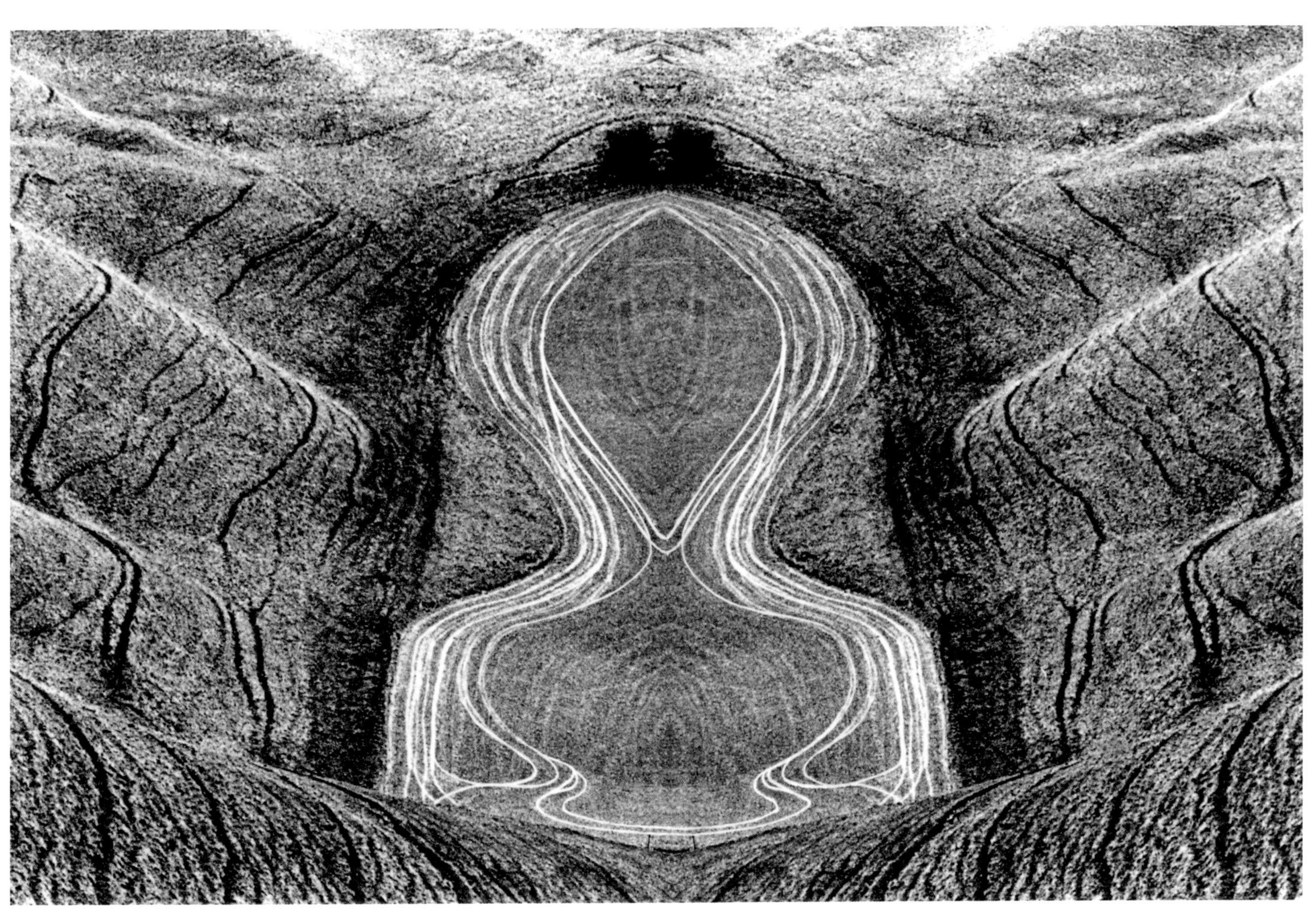

The Light in the Wind

We're all buffeted, more and more, by strong winds. Hurricanes, typhoons, those sundowners that whip fires across the dry hills and rewrite lives and upend telegraph poles in an instant. The world itself seems to be at the mercy of gale-force winds these days: not those gentle breezes that soften the warmth of a summer day, but stormy explosions that overturn every expectation and leave our homes in rubble.

The result is what King Lear calls "the tempest in my mind." We're so storm-tossed within that we're always braced for turbulence: that fresh notification, the beeping phone, this blast of breaking news. That decision from the government, this news of an earthquake claiming hundreds. Strangers work to capture and hold our attention with updates, tweets, and cries of wild emotion that leave us anxious and unsettled even when we never move.

Yet, through it all, the sun continues to shine. Reliably, sometimes daily and even on many of the most thunderous days. The light is unaffected by the wind; they live side by side like our sorrows and our hopes. That's one reason why I wanted to use this image as the cover of a book I wrote; it looks to me like a quiet, and restoring, portrait of real life.

The wind keeps tearing at the curtain, but the light remains unmoved.

PI

Behind the Veil

We all want to discover what is inside the wrapping, around the next corner, on the following page, or over the horizon. The search for what is behind the veil is something of a universal motivator. Buddhism teaches the practice of mindfulness and the need to be in the present. In a recent yoga class, the instructor told us to concentrate on breathing, to stay in the here and now and forget everything else. The future cannot be reached. The past is history, never to return. The present is what we have. All extremely good theories, and very difficult to put into practice.

Photography is an accurate and efficient way to document and record details. Technology has continued to advance since the early days of Daguerre and Fox Talbot, to the point that it is now possible to photograph pretty much anything and everything, from submicroscopic atoms to distant galaxies. We could therefore conclude that seeing and photographing behind the veil has already been achieved. Yet, the mystery of not knowing, of theorizing, guessing, searching, continues, and how could it not? We can at least be sure that we will die, but who knows what happens next, or should we even think about it? Religions, philosophers, soothsayers may have their answers, but they differ so widely that a reasonable conclusion is—nobody knows what lies behind that particular veil.

Back to this image in which a simple veiled curtain hangs in front of a shuttered window. Soft light seeps and flows into a darkened room. For me, a visual haiku poem, with few elements and numerous possible interpretations. What is revealed suggests and asks questions of what is hidden. The photograph is an invitation to dream, and maybe to open the window and look out. A kind gift of the commonplace, as the photographer Ruth Bernhard would eloquently inform us.

MK

Veiled Window, Siena, Italy, 1980

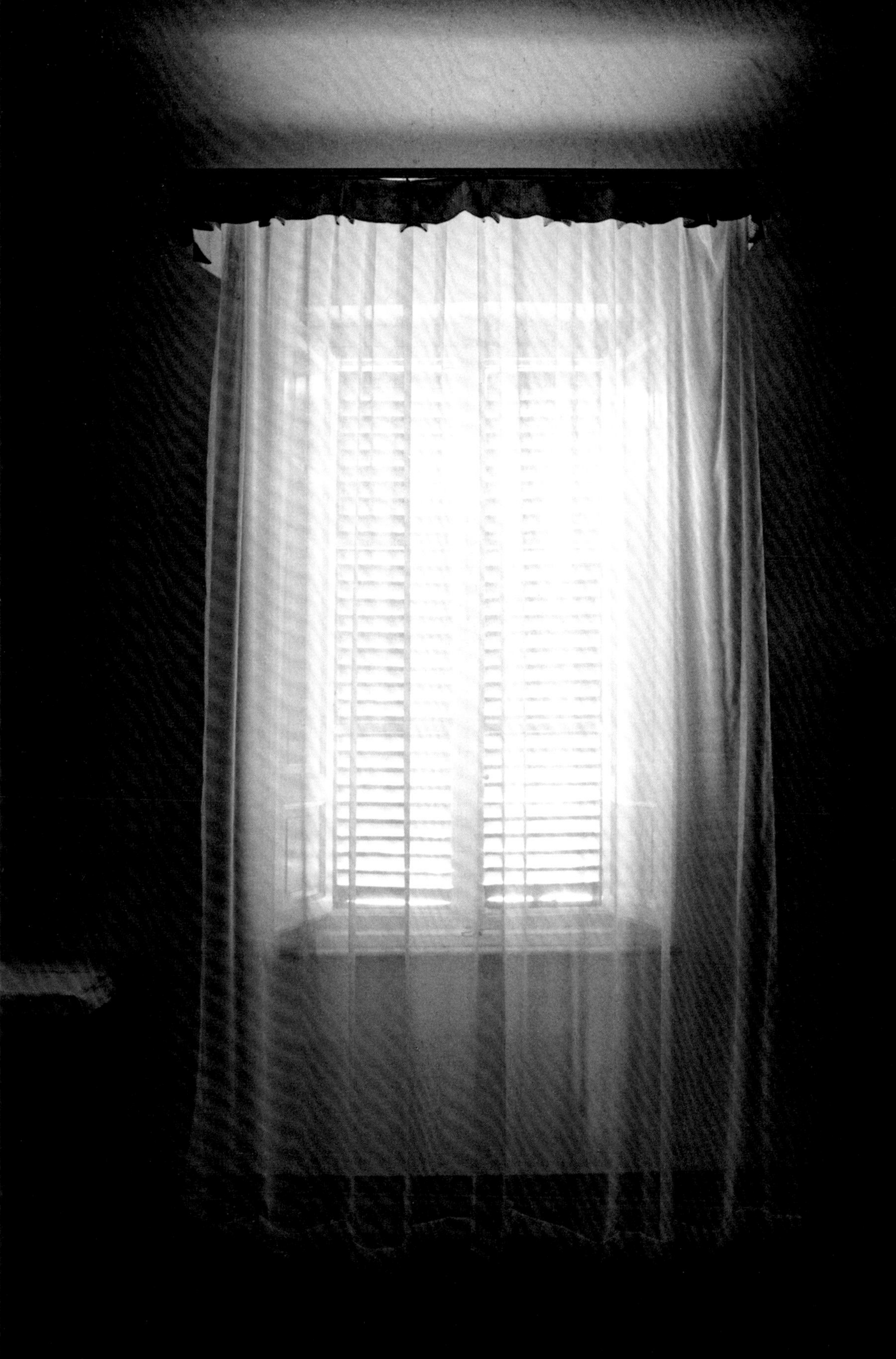

The Rickety Watchtower

A watchtower suggests vigilance, protectiveness, care for and by other humans: a lifeguard on a crowded beach, perhaps, ensuring that no child is left behind. But when I see this sad, jerry-rigged structure, I think of the folly of war and the flimsiness of the divisions we create between one neighbor and another. A relic of a conflict from seventy years ago that never really ended and keeps everyone on permanent alert.

Trip Advisor assures me that Sampo Beach "is a happy rest area for many vacationers, and in spring and fall, it is filled with joy and memories for many guests." The ubiquitous announcements not many miles to the north tell everyone that their country of starvation and shaky stage sets is a joyful earthly paradise. The sands we see around this tower are only twenty miles from the DMZ Museum, commemorating watchtowers on both sides of a ghostly conference room of chairs in which nothing has been agreed upon for three quarters of a century.

I look at this image and think of my trips to the DMZ on both sides of the border. Of wandering around the giant statues and empty streets of North Korea in the twentieth century and again in the twenty-first. Of air-raid drills in the South while I was covering the Summer Olympics there. A brutal division that keeps millions on edge, but revealed in this haunting photograph to be nothing but an emblem of loneliness and dereliction.

PI

Go North Young Man

I first visited South Korea in 2005 for an exhibition at the Whitewall Gallery in Seoul. The gallery kindly arranged for me to spend some days exploring outside of the city, including the Seoraksan National Park area, the Gangwon-do coastline, and the infamous Demilitarized Zone (DMZ). This zone is two hundred and fifty kilometers long, four kilometers wide, and runs across the thirty-eighth parallel, dividing the Korean peninsula into North Korea (Democratic People's Republic of Korea) and South Korea (Republic of Korea). Thousands of troops are stationed on both sides of the DMZ with constant visual and electronic surveillance. Electrified barbed wire fences, armed guard posts, and watchtowers defend the perimeters of the zone. Land mines and heavy weapons are in place, ready to be used.

It is only in Korea that I have seen barbed wire fences protecting coastal beaches. In my imagination, the lifeguard towers there resemble and echo the watchtowers I had earlier photographed in the Nazi concentration camps throughout Europe. I felt the Korean watchtowers became more ominous the closer they were to the DMZ, and Sampo, where this photograph was made, is very close. I began to photograph all the watchtowers I could find and have so far printed sixty studies; the most recent image is from 2024.

Over the two decades since my first visit to South Korea, I have returned many times and explored throughout the country. Subject matter has included industry, trees, seafronts, islands, landscapes, mountains, rocks, urban structures, buildings, temples, and statuary. I have had the good fortune to photograph in the sunshine, rain, snow, fog, and wind, during the day and at night. Despite several attempts, I have not yet been able to visit North Korea, a place Pico knows very well. That ambition remains, so far, an unfulfilled dream.

MK

 Watchtower, Study 1, Sampo, Gangwon-do, South Korea, 2005

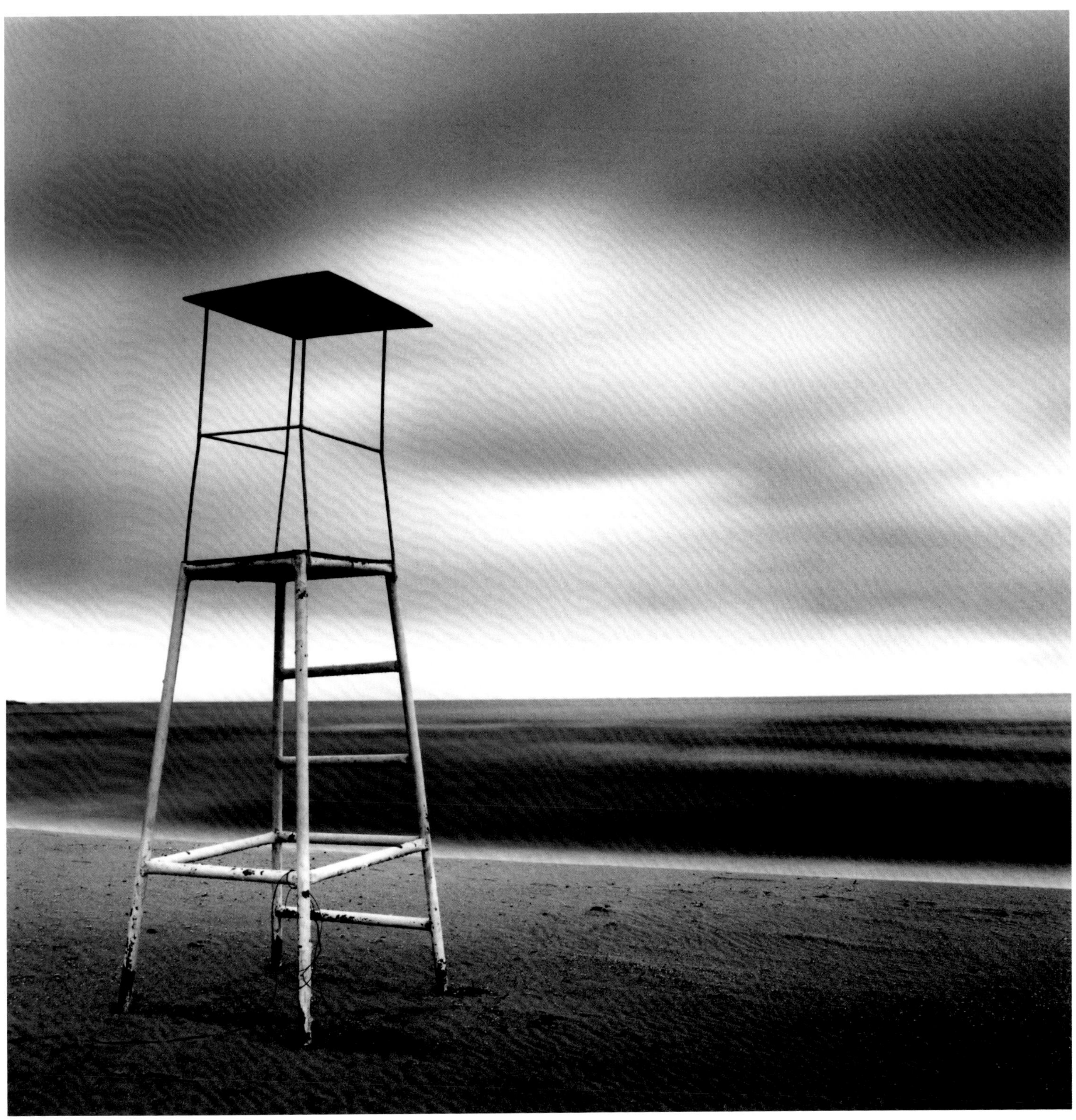

Our Pilgrim Paths

In November 2003, little knowing that Michael was making a pilgrimage around the temples of Shikoku, I met up with my friend of twenty-nine years, the Dalai Lama, at a temple in Nara, two hours away. What followed was a long series of pilgrimages across Japan with His Holiness.

For ten straight Novembers, he arrived in Japan and my wife and I traveled with him for every hour of his working day, taking lunch with him every day, attending all his public events, sitting in on all his private meetings, with scientists, priests, even heavy-metal musicians.

We journeyed from Okinawa to a Fukushima village devastated by the 2011 tsunami, from Kyushu to the Japanese parliamentary building in Tokyo. We went with him to find new eyeglasses in a Yokohama shopping mall; we stopped along quiet roads to sip from cans of tea with him at a convenience store. More than once our travels took us to Shikoku, since the Dalai Lama's Vajrayana Buddhism has one of its closest cousins in the Shingon esoteric Buddhism commemorated on that pilgrimage, all mantras and mandalas and mystical rites.

I could never have guessed as I watched this waterfall of wisdom and kindness enter quiet halls and buildings around Shikoku that Michael and I were walking along the same path yet again. Or that, just three years later, an editor in New York—soon to be a world-famous novelist—would invite Michael and me to collaborate on a piece about the last stop along his pilgrim's path—where sometimes I went to stay with the Dalai Lama and his monks: the temple-filled mountain of Koyasan.

Michael and I may have both thought we were on pilgrimages, but really we were shadowing one another, yet again.

PI

Starting and Stopping

Life is a pilgrimage, to an unknown destination, for unknown reasons, or so I like to think. There is a start, and there will be an end. The distance, the time it takes, the route and stops along the way, and the ultimate destination point, are unknown, to be discovered. The whys and wherefores remain baffling also. Every day, I grow increasingly conscious that I am reaching the final stretch. Every day, I am grateful for the possibility to continue. Every day, I say thank you, to the gods, to the universe, to my family and friends, to my aging body for surviving the journey for over seventy years. Every day, I end with an acceptance that tomorrow might not come.

As part of my fiftieth birthday celebrations in November 2003, I spent a month completing the eighty-eight-temple pilgrimage in Shikoku, Japan, which I had started two years earlier. The original temple pilgrimage was founded in memory of the monk Kukai (aka Kobo Daishi), who, in the ninth century, brought from China the esoteric Shingon Buddhist practices and rites. At each temple, I paid my respects to the deities, recited the Heart Sutra in Japanese, had a book signed and stamped by the monks, and then photographed whatever I found interesting. It was a memorable, insightful, and enriching experience.

In Temple #11, Fujiidera-ji, I found this small waterfall and made several experimental long-exposure photographs. At the time, it felt like a quiet moment of meditation rather than an exciting photo session. The resulting negatives both surprised and intrigued me enough to print. I would later learn that waterfalls in Japan symbolize duality, impermanence, change, and purification. These associations have only added to my great affection for this image, the pilgrimage, and for the many stops along the way.

MK

Waterfall, Fujiidera-ji, Tokushima, Shikoku, Japan, 2003

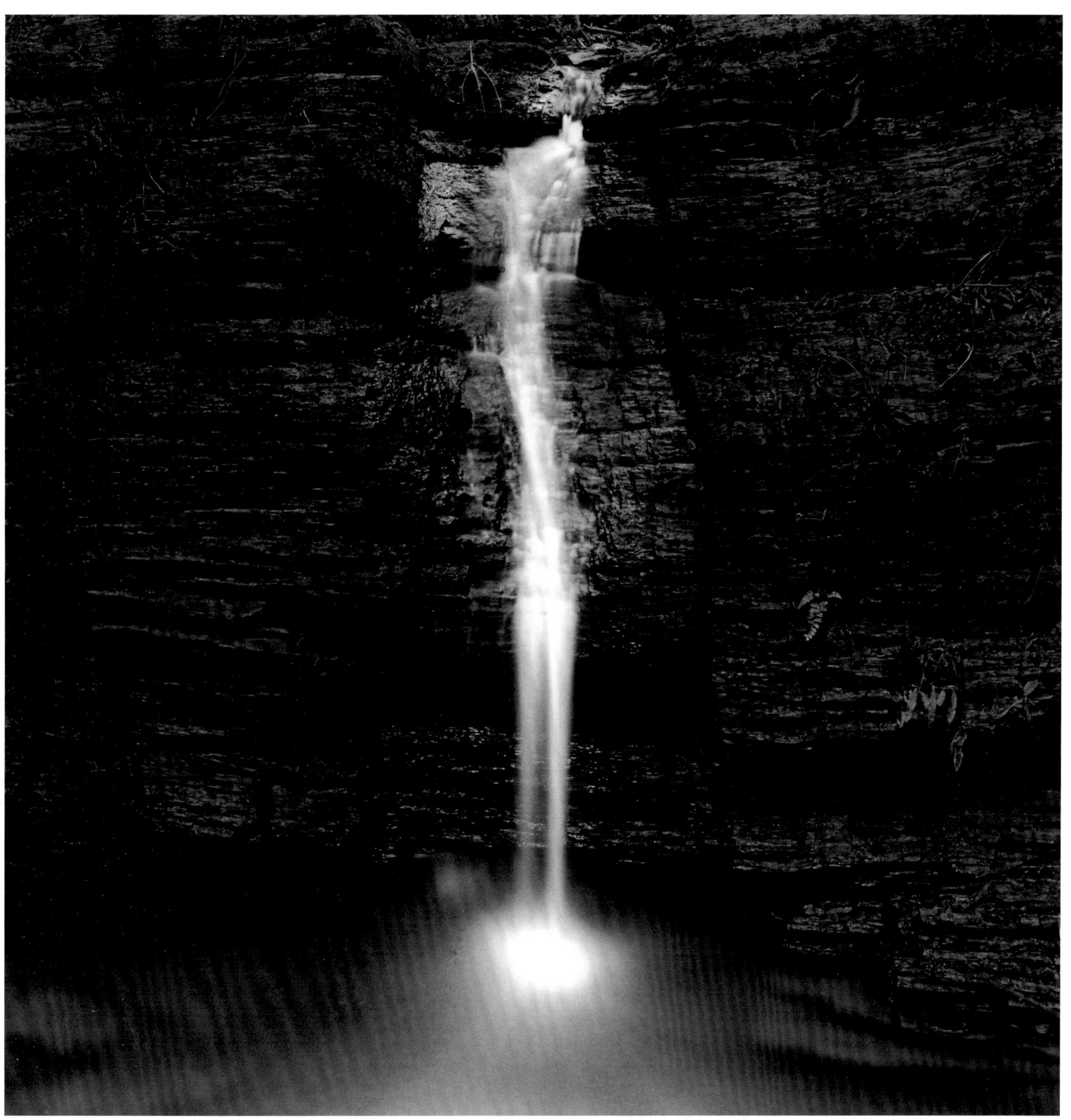

Moved Without Motion

"Why go on retreat?" a friend asks me.

"So you can hear everything that's drowned out in your normal life," I answer. "Everything within you and without." So you can catch the small print of the world and everything that's far richer and more interesting than your thoughts. So you can wake up to whatever is not in your head.

A monk, it is said, can attain so clear and deep a stillness that he can hear the tip of a stick of incense fall to the floor in the next room. He can catch the waves receding in the far distance. He can hear something more secret than the whisper of his best friend: the whisper of the wind—and all his friend is saying when he isn't saying a word.

I'm not a monk and if ever I attain that state of attention, it doesn't last for long. But if I can find the kind of concentration that arises when there's no phone to ring, no traffic to navigate, no screen to watch, and no society to worry about, I'm suddenly encircled by whispers of the wind.

I see a photographer alone in a field, standing so still and waiting so long that at last everything around is whispering inside him.

PI

Life Lesson

I like my solitude, and, generally, when I photograph I prefer to do so alone. I find it is easier to listen, concentrate, and focus. Photographing in China is sometimes a challenge. People there are exceedingly friendly, curious, and often loud. Whenever and wherever I set up my camera on a tripod, groups of onlookers gather behind me, attempting to peer into the viewfinder. I am asked about my photo equipment, the film I use, what I am photographing and why, and what I like best about China. Everybody is exceedingly nice and friendly, but it can be awfully distracting.

While photographing along the banks of Erhai Lake one morning, regrettably, I became impatient. I just couldn't seem to escape from conversations and inquiries. I cannot say that I am proud of my behavior, but in a petty tantrum, and also as an experiment, I set up my camera on the side of the road with absolutely no subject matter in front of me. Within minutes, cars stopped, people got out and made the same photograph—of nothing but grass. I was soon causing a traffic jam and had to move on, probably muttering to myself, which is not an attractive look.

Imagine my surprise then, some months later, after processing the film, to find this beautiful photograph (even though I say so myself). Nothing but a blade of grass, a whisper in the wind. This image is yet another reminder that beauty is ubiquitous, everywhere, in all circumstances. We just have to open our eyes, accept our surroundings, and be grateful. As my mentor Ruth Bernhard would say, "The Gift of the Commonplace is all around us." I am sure she would also add that life is far too short to act like a grumpy foreign tourist.

MK

 Wind Whisper, Dali, Yunnan, China, 2014

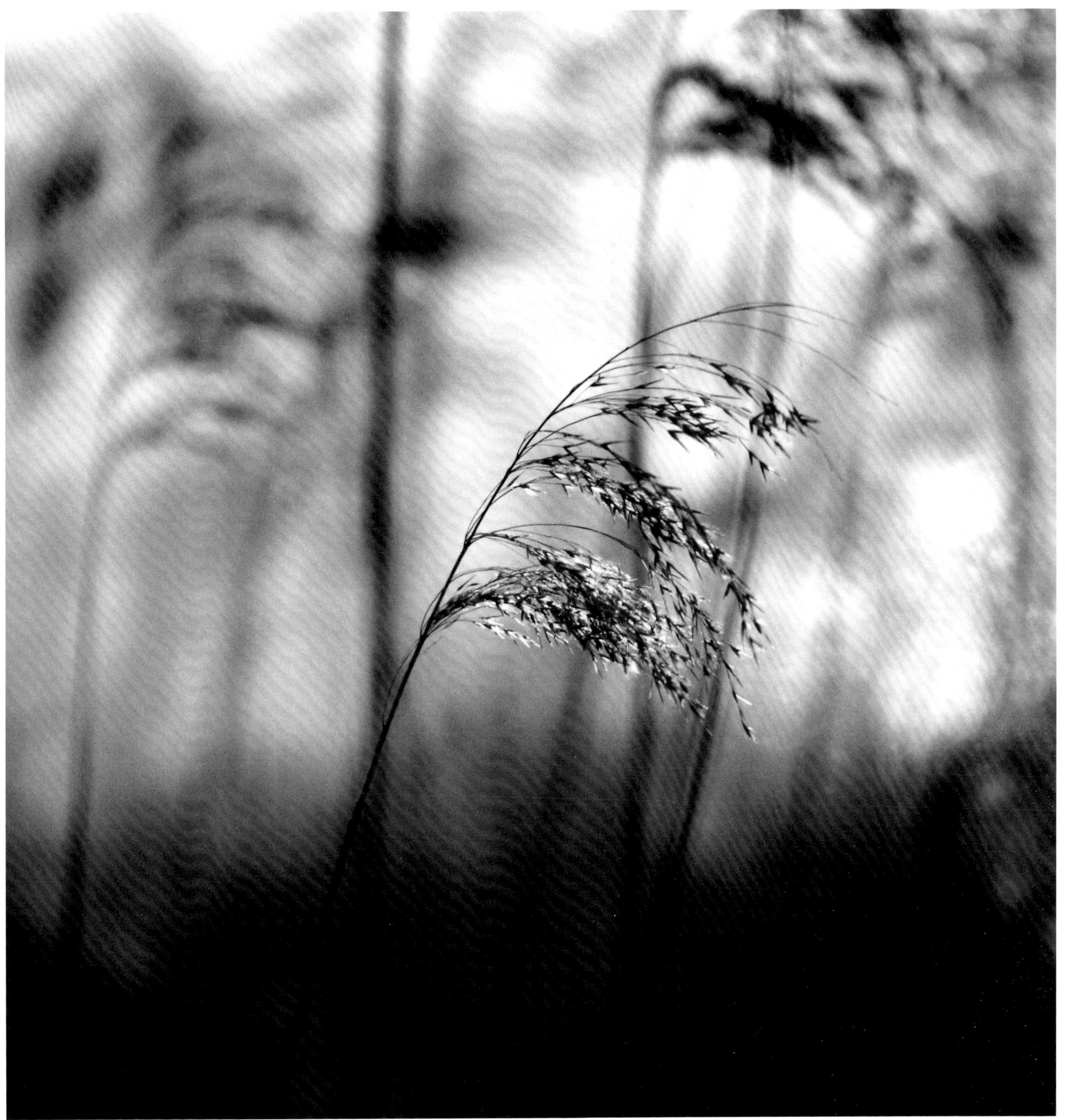

Transit Notes

Stumbling into random airport lounges, pretty much anywhere around the world, day or night, my first thoughts, other than the time of my next departure, and perhaps what to eat or drink, usually wander off to that well-known, jolly, roving, ping-pong playing, writer chap named Pico Iyer. In life, we gravitate towards certain people and places, often for reasons beyond our understanding. There is even the East Asian philosophy of the invisible Red Thread believed to connect those destined to meet. Well, Pico and I almost met on so many occasions, unknown to either of us until much later. We could easily have bumped into each other in Oxford, California, Kyoto, Easter Island, Koyasan, Rio, Paris, and a whole host of other places we mutually visited or lived in, at roughly the same time. Yet, it seems that we were destined to finally meet, with our respective wives, on rue Dauphine in the sixth arrondissement of Paris at approximately 4 p.m., on July 12, 2022.

Recently listening to a podcast, while wandering along empty early morning streets of Vancouver, Canada, I heard that Pico routinely likes to travel in a window seat on the right side of the plane, and his preferred drink is tea. Weirdly, I write this while traveling to South Korea, sitting in a window seat, on the right, drinking tea. OK—just another coincidence, but they do add up. After several serendipitous meetings in Kyoto, Nara, Paris, and Seattle, conjecture led me to the grand theory that Pico is a man always punctual, even early. This conclusion, recently confirmed by the international man of mystery himself, derived partly from the basis that we have exchanged more emails while waiting in airport lounges than from anywhere else (albeit not yet scientifically proven). I strongly suspect this aspect of his character—to be punctual and considerate of others' time—derives from the years he spent in strict boarding schools where consequences for tardiness were severe. It takes one to know one.

I too have a tendency to turn up at airports at least three hours early, and have spent many a cold hour waiting on empty train station platforms (much to the bemusement of my wife), based on a belief that it is better to be an hour early than a minute late. Perhaps this procliv-ity is a built-in counterweight to life's unpredictable and uncontrollable nature. For example,

I recently walked for well over an hour from a Paris hotel to Gare d'Austerlitz, only to find that my train to Strasbourg would leave from a completely different station, Gare de l'Est, in forty-five minutes' time. I was still able to take a metro, purchase my customary *sandwich mixte* and *grand crème*, and board the train in good time. When I considered the catastrophic inconvenience I would have caused others if I'd missed it, I inwardly shuddered and renewed my vows to turn up even earlier for the next journey. My apologies. I digress, although I am confident that Pico would understand.

When it comes down to it, and as you may have read and noticed in this book, Pico and I have similar jobs, albeit he uses a pen or pencil, and I prefer cameras. I like to think of Pico as a scribe, me a snapper. The way I see it, our fundamental missions are basically the same, simply to notice and record the phenomenal creations and quirks of the universe, and share these observations with others. This takes time, commitment, training, hard work, discipline, etcetera, of course, and, let's face it, most of us are so busy living, we don't have or take that time to notice a lot of life's idiosyncrasies. Sharing some similar backgrounds, my point of view often converges and coalesces with Pico's. Fortunately, our different genealogies guarantee that many other perspectives shift and slant in unfamiliar and compelling directions. I suspect our mutual terror would be to be boring.

There are no sufficient or adequate thanks that I can offer Pico for his willingness and enthusiasm to enter into this whimsical and experimental collaboration. Somehow, he has retained his optimism and good humor throughout our project together. I am thinking, with all due respect and deference to the mysteries of synchronicity, that one day I might surprise him by having a few orders of his beloved Lawsons convenience store spicy chicken delivered to him. But, knowing the forever humble Pico, he'd probably consider that extravagance to be one compliment too far. Maybe just one order then.

Michael Kenna
July 27, 2025
Seattle, Seoul, and Phuket

Acknowledgments

I would like to thank my heroic and open-hearted new friend Michael Kenna; my wonderfully kind and inspiring editor on my own books, Jynne Dilling, for allowing me to play truant for the duration of this work; Jonathan Fox, for a thoughtful and diligent copyedit; and the editor of this book, Curt Holtz, for taking a chance on this improbable conspiracy.

Pico Iyer

I thank everybody that has played a part in this project: my family and friends, without whom none of this would be possible; my wife Mamta, for providing a consistent bedrock of love and support necessary for my creative endeavors to flourish and fly; Curt Holtz, for his confidence in this rather unusual project; Jonathan Fox, who has copyedited the texts; Hannah Feldmeier, the designer of the book; Mark Silva, my assistant for over two decades; and, of course, Pico Iyer, for his steadfast friendship over the recent years and his immense leap of faith in this delightfully curious collaboration. I thank you the reader and viewer, for your patience and imagination—you crucially complete the circle of creativity and bring this publication to life.

Michael Kenna

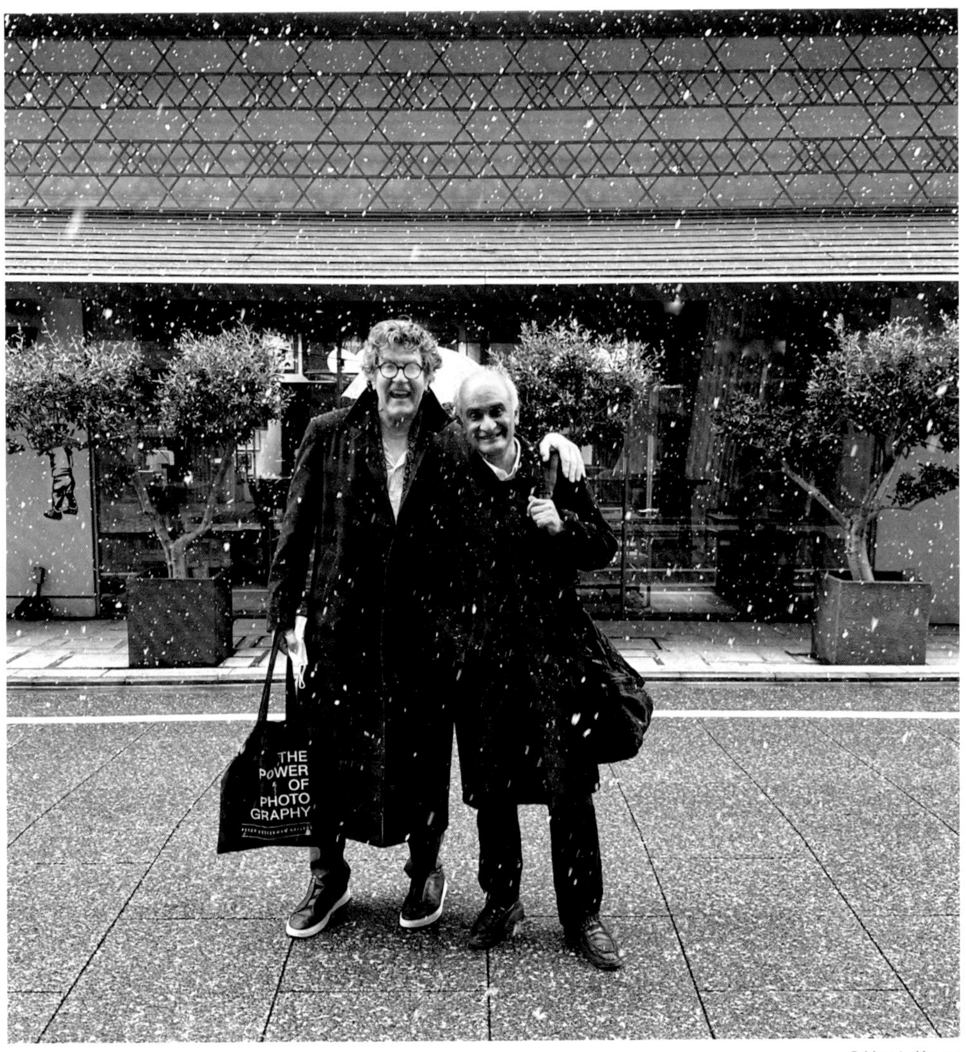

© Mamta Kenna

Michael Kenna and Pico Iyer, Kyoto, Honshu, Japan, 2023

Pico Iyer is the author of seventeen books, translated into twenty-three languages, among them *The Open Road*, *The Art of Stillness*, *The Half Known Life*, and *Aflame*, all of which were bestsellers.

Michael Kenna has published more than one hundred photography books, including the bestselling *Forms of Japan*. He recently became an Officier des Arts et des Lettres.

© Prestel Verlag, Munich · London · New York, 2026,
a Member of Penguin Random House Verlagsgruppe GmbH
Neumarkter Strasse 28 · 81673 Munich
produktsicherheit@penguinrandomhouse.de
(The above information is mandatory according to GPSR)

© texts by Pico Iyer, 2026
© images & texts by Michael Kenna, 2026

Front cover:
Huangshan Mountains, Study 6, Anhui, China, 2008. See p. 61
Back cover:
Kussharo Lake Tree, Study 17, Kotan, Hokkaido, Japan, 2007. See p. 69

First edition

A Library of Congress Control Number is available. A CIP catalogue record for this book is available from the British Library.

The publisher expressly reserves the right to exploit the copyrighted content of this work for the purposes of text and data mining in accordance with Section 44b of the German Copyright Act (UrhG), based on the European Digital Single Market Directive. Any unauthorized use is an infringement of copyright and is hereby prohibited.

Editorial direction: Curt Holtz
Copyediting: Jonathan Fox
Design and typesetting: Hannah Feldmeier, Leipzig
Production management: Corinna Pickart
Origination: Longo AG, Bolzano
Printing and binding: Longo AG, Bolzano
Paper: Arctic Volume White

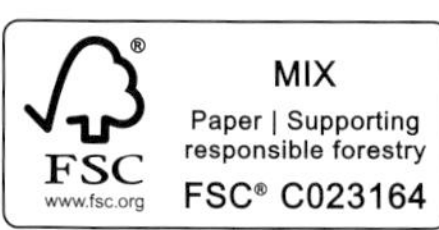

Penguin Random House Verlagsgruppe FSC® N001967

Printed in Italy
ISBN 978-3-7913-9405-3

www.prestel.com